The American Civil War

American History in Depth

General Editor: A. J. Badger
Advisory Editor: Howell Harris

The New Deal
A. J. Badger

The American Revolution (2nd edn)
Collin Bonwick

American Foreign Policy: Carter to Clinton
John Dumbrell

Colonial America: From Jamestown to Yorktown
Mary K. Geiter and W. A. Speck

McCarthy's Americans
M. J. Heale

Women in the United States, 1830–1945
S. J. Kleinberg

The American Civil War
Adam I. P. Smith

The American Civil War

Adam I. P. Smith

First published 2007 by
PALGRAVE MACMILLAN
Houndmills, Basingstoke, Hampshire RG21 6XS and
175 Fifth Avenue, New York, N.Y. 10010
Companies and representatives throughout the world

PALGRAVE MACMILLAN is the global academic imprint of the Palgrave Macmillan division of St. Martin's Press, LLC and of Palgrave Macmillan Ltd. Macmillan® is a registered trademark in the United States, United Kingdom and other countries. Palgrave is a registered trademark in the European Union and other countries.

ISBN-13: 978–0–333–79053–3 hardback
ISBN-10: 0–333–79053–7 hardback
ISBN-13: 978–0–333–79054–0 paperback
ISBN-10: 0–333–79054–5 paperback

This book is printed on paper suitable for recycling and made from fully managed and sustained forest sources.

A catalogue record for this book is available from the British Library.

A catalog record for this book is available from the Library of Congress.

10   9   8   7   6   5   4   3   2   1
16   15   14   13   12   11   10   09   08   07

Printed in China

For Caroline

As a nation of freemen, we must live through all time, or die by suicide.

Abraham Lincoln (1838)

We are sometimes asked in the name of patriotism to forget the merits of this fearful struggle, and to remember with equal admiration those who struck at the nation's life, and those who struck to save it—those who fought for slavery and those who fought for liberty and justice . . . may my tongue cleave to the roof of my mouth if I forget the difference between the parties to that bloody conflict . . . I may say that if this war is to be forgotten, I ask in the name of all things sacred what shall men remember?

Frederick Douglass (1871)

Contents

List of Maps

Preface

The Civil War haunts and inspires the American imagination in equal measure. The bloody conflict of 1861–1865 that cost over six hundred thousand lives—more than in all of America's other wars put together—has been described as the "American Iliad," the "Second American Revolution" and the "Rebirth of the Nation." The epic qualities of the American Civil War lie not only in the tales of individual bravery and the great heroes it produced but also in the profound issues at stake. In the twenty-first century, when the United States of America bestrides the world as a military and economic colossus, it is not surprising that many find it compelling that a hundred and fifty years ago the republic experienced a terrible civil war that could have left it divided and weakened. If one categorical result of the war was that the unity of the American republic was established, the other was the end of slavery. As Abraham Lincoln insisted, the nation was given a "new birth of freedom." When Lincoln spoke those words he had in mind the renewed republican freedom of white Americans at least as much as the freedom of black slaves, yet emancipation appears to bestow on this war to save the Union a nobility not accorded to the other nationalist wars of the nineteenth century.

Nineteenth-century America was a society convulsed with rapid change. The boundaries of the nation were continually expanding, the population—both free and slave—was growing at an exponential rate, and its economy was undergoing a series of interconnected revolutions that created, in often unpredictable ways, winners and losers. All this happened in the context of a de-centralized political system, in which the world's first mass political parties contested for power in robust, colorful elections and in which print culture connected Americans who had never met each other with shared ideas. At the center of the unfolding crisis that engulfed the American republic was slavery. White southerners struggled hard to maintain the unimpeded right to slaveholding within the Union, giving up on that crusade only when confronted with what seemed to them to be incontrovertible evidence of northern opposition. Thereafter they attempted to create a slaveholding republic in the South, enduring remarkable sacrifices in pursuit of that goal. In the final analysis, slavery caused the Civil War. But the relationship between slavery and the outbreak of war was not straight-forward. The Civil War did not come because slavery was an intolerable violation of the nation's dedication to freedom. The vast majority of northerners did not go to war in 1861 to abolish slavery and the vast majority of Confederate soldiers had never owned a slave. To say that slavery was fundamental to the causes and course of the war is, there-fore, not to say that a moral contest over the rights and wrongs of slavery led in some ineluctable way to conflict, although in one sense the war certainly represented a moral crisis. The precise political meaning of slavery and its salience in the public consciousness was continually re-framed by unpredictable events, just as it interacted in a dynamic way with fundamental structures and processes. The irony is that slavery would probably have survived long after 1865 had slaveholders not brought about a war. Secession turned out to be a catastrophic miscal-culation. But it was an understandable one, a gamble that could have paid off. Had the South won decisive victories early in the war, when Confederate morale was highest, or had the Union been less effective at holding together its diverse society with its conflicting conceptions of the war, then southern independence is perfectly conceivable.

If the American Civil War has to be understood in relation to the particular characteristics of this Anglo slaveholding republic, the great crisis was also, of course, configured by the moment in world history in which it took place. North America was far from unique in the nine-teenth century in experiencing violence and bloodshed over basic ques-tions of national identity and state formation. The processes of economic development, as well as ideas of nationhood, state-building, progress and "modernity" transcended the borders of the United States. In these middle decades of the nineteenth century it gradually became clear that nation-states, rather than empires or confederations, would dominate and define the political organization of the world. The liberal nation-alism which had animated the European revolutions of 1848 found its echo in Lincoln's faith that what was at stake in the preservation of the Union was no less than the future of democracy and liberty around the world. Northern politicians made a natural connection between their war to defeat the rebellion and a worldwide battle between liberal constitutionalism and autocracy in its many forms. When the British liberal politician Richard Cobden told an American friend that "you are fighting the battle of liberalism in Europe as well as the battle of freedom in America" or when the Italian nationalist Giuseppe Mazzini wrote that the war in America was a part of "the great battle—to which all local battles are episodes—fought on both continents . . . between liberty and tyranny, equality and privilege, . . . justice and arbitrary rule," their comments evoked the wider context in which the great Civil War in America took place.[1] Lincoln was a spokesman for many of his fellow countrymen when he insisted that the war affected not just the future of the Union, but the "whole family of man."[2] It was fitting, then, that Lincoln offered Garibaldi, the great military hero of the Italian struggle for unification, a commission in the Union army.

As historians are increasingly recognizing, military history written in a political, social and cultural vacuum explains very little. It is equally true that historians whose interests take them behind the lines are sometimes vulnerable to the criticism once leveled at Republican Senator Charles Sumner that he regarded the war itself as an "unfortunate and most annoying, though trifling, disturbance, as if a fire-engine had passed by."[3] Communication between soldiers and civilians in this highly literate society was continuous and intense. This study therefore seeks to integrate military events into a wider political and social analysis of the impact of the war. Battlefield successes and failures were the dominant influence on such matters as homefront morale, electoral politics, international diplomacy and economic confidence. Equally, the shape and conduct of the war reflected the values and tensions of the societies of which the soldiers were a part. Two fundamental features of mid-nineteenth-century American society—both North and South—were especially important in this regard. First, this was a deeply religious society. Both sides were steeped in Protestant values, and evangelical revivals had profoundly re-shaped American culture since the Revolution. Second, this was also a world in which politics mattered in a way that we can barely comprehend today. The republican political culture of each section generated a heightened sense of the conflict between liberty and power, of the need for vigilance against the ever-present danger of tyranny. To the modern reader, one of the most extraordinary themes of soldiers' letters is the strong emotional identification with their governments expressed by northerners and southerners alike. White men in Civil War America thought the political system belonged to them. The massive voluntary mobilization of the civilian populations on both sides was testimony to the close identification of the vast majority of ordinary people with their cause, and their hands-on experience of democratic government and "free institutions," and a sense of their rights as republican citizens, profoundly shaped the culture and conduct of Civil War armies.

The war was fought almost entirely on southern soil, and consequently southern civilians were often drawn into the conflict in a very direct way as advancing Union armies confiscated goods and property, freed slaves and sometimes left a trail of burned property and scorched farmland in their wake. But even in the North, far from the battlefield, people back home were connected on an almost hourly basis to the fortunes of Union arms. Nineteenth-century America was a newspaper-reading society, and cheap and readily available print had done more than any other technological development to shape a national culture before the war. Between 1861 and 1865, newspapers' ability to bring news—albeit often no more than unreliable gossip—to the home front within hours of a battle taking place struck people at the time as marking a dramatic shift in the nature of the war experience, bringing civilians even closer to the action and even shaping the ways in which soldiers themselves understood the meaning of what they were doing. The war as experienced on the home front—"the war of the public imagination" as it might be termed—was closely related to the "real war" but it was viewed through a distorting lens that magnified some events at the expense of others. There was no co-ordinated system of monitoring and censoring newspaper reports about the movement of armies or the morale of troops. In addition to the war reporters who followed both armies, soldiers of all ranks could earn some extra money by writing dispatches for their local newspapers. On several occasions, the enemy learned valuable intelligence by the simple expedient of obtaining newspapers from the other side. Newspaper reporters had rarely had any previous experience of war, and so were not usually in a position to offer the kind of expert overview that the uninitiated American public badly needed. Newspapers reinforced the general assumption that big battles determined the war, and that the side who held the field and refused to retreat was the winner. Generals were turned into celebrities, and their personalities and political preferences given huge weight in the perceived outcome of battles. The giddy surges of optimism experienced successively by each side, fuelled by press reports, were inevitably followed time and again by bitter disappointment. Even by the end of 1864, press reporting and commentary on military matters was strikingly simplistic.

The tone and content of newspaper coverage reminds us that this was a war fought before the battlefields of the Somme seeped in irony notions of the glory of war—at least for western Europeans. No one in 1861, not even the saintly Robert E. Lee or the sage Lincoln had any conception of the nature of the conflict that lay ahead. Even West Point–trained officers had almost no actual battle experience—other than in the Mexican War, which was a lopsided contest that offered few useable lessons for the Civil War. By the end of 1862, if not earlier, northern military leaders had recognized the necessity of waging war on those southern institutions that supported the Confederate military effort—including slavery. The characterization of the Civil War as the world's "first modern war" captures an important truth. The role of the press and public opinion, the extent to which mobilization required an expanded state to direct the economy, the use of railroads to move reinforcements from one battlefront to another, the revolution in communication represented by the electric telegraph, and the centrality of ideological and nationalist appeals to the mobilization strategies of both sides all anticipated the characteristics of modern war that in Europe are associated with the First World War. Yet the notion of a "modern war" is also misleading. Military historians endeavoring to make sense of campaigns can sometimes impose a patina of order and deliberation that belied the limited grasp of tactics, poor communication and sheer luck that characterized most Civil War battles. The Civil War resembled a twentieth century war more than a Napoleonic-era conflict insofar as battles were generally indecisive and the war dragged on, yet in tactical, technological and psychological terms, and even the scale of battlefield casualties, it was strikingly pre-modern. To a remarkable extent Civil War Americans clung to antebellum notions of heroism and valor. Newspaper men reported battles using the latest telegraphic technology but often failed to understand what they saw, interpreting battles as antebellum Americans had imagined battles, as a test of masculine virtue.

The Lincolnian notion of the war as national redemption still colors the image of the Civil War today. Visitors to Civil War battlefields find that these great stage sets for the imagination are also shrines to the "sacrifice" of the men who died there to bring about the apparently intertwined goals of freedom and nationhood. Professional historians, film-makers, re-enactors, novelists, even the National Park Service all have succumbed at times to the temptation to "make sense" of the war by lauding the good that came out of the tragedy. All too easily the survival of the Union and the eradication of the great moral and political problem of black slavery can come to seem inevitable, the war the apotheosis of American ideals, the "sacrifice" somehow necessary and noble.

The American Civil War was, like every war, more terrible than anyone expected. Like every war, it involved chaos and brutality as well as strategy and honor. And like every war, its participants had mixed and sometimes impenetrable motives, and its results were ambiguous and in some ways paradoxical. Slavery was eradicated, and the post-war constitutional amendments ratified the principle of equality before the law, but a new dawn of racial equality did not ensue. Northerners who went to war to preserve a republican society of small-scale property-owners ended up living amid the destabilizing mass industrial capitalism of the Gilded Age. In countless ways, the transformations the war wrought were reversed or nullified in the years that followed. Even fighting one of the world's first industrial wars with a mass citizen army did not lead to the permanent expansion of the national government, although in important ways it did re-forge the basis of American nationalism. The Civil War exposed profound institutional disorganization, incompetent leadership and deep social divisions, as well as innovation, inspiring rhetoric and surprising resilience in the face of extraordinary pressure. The challenge for historians is to peel back the layers of rhetoric, to see beyond the heroism, to listen for more than patriotic airs and the sound of gunfire.

This book is written in the spirit of an interpretative essay rather than with any ambition to be comprehensive. It seeks, first and foremost, to offer a guide to one of the most enduringly fascinating and significant events in modern history. In offering my own overarching interpretation of the great crisis of 1861–1865, I have tried to draw on the most recent scholarship on every facet of the war. In the last twenty or thirty years historians have shown a renewed interest in the relationship between the home front and the battlefield, and in the ideological, religious and cultural dimensions and implications of the great struggle; my analysis reflects those trends. I also pay particular attention to dimensions of the Civil War experience which I think have been underplayed or misunderstood in the existing literature, such as the importance of northern public opinion. Finally, I try to set the war in the wider context of the nineteenth-century world, a broader global perspective that is still surprisingly absent from almost all writing on the war.

Like any work that attempts to survey such a huge subject in so (relatively) few words this book is heavily dependent on the work of others. The Guide to Further Reading indicates some of the work that has had the most impact on scholarship generally as well on my own thinking about the war, but it cannot fully convey the debt I owe to the regiment of scholars—including some of the most gifted and insightful of all historians—who have trampled over this bloody ground before me. In particular I owe thanks to Robert Cook, David Brown and Martin Crawford, and an anonymous reader for the press, all of whom have kindly read all or some of my first draft and offered wise suggestions for improvement which I have attempted to implement. I am indebted to Tony Badger for inviting me to contribute this book in the Palgrave *American History in Depth* series, and to Terka Acton, Beverley Tarquini, Felicity Noble and Sonya Barker at the press for their professionalism and patience. I am grateful to the History Department at University College London for giving me research leave in 2005–2006, and to the Gilder Lehrman Institute for a fellowship which enabled me to spend time in New York thinking about this project even while I was working on another one as well. I would also like to thank the following people for their friendship, hospitality and encouragement while I was writing this book: Mike Ebied, Kira Gould, Simon Kennedy, Larisa Mendez-Penâte, Will Niblett, Sanjay Ruparelia, and my friends in the History Department at UCL. Finally, Caroline Brooke has read and re-read every word of my prose and walked the battlefields of the Civil War with me, and the book is dedicated to her, with love.

List of Abbreviations

ALP	Abraham Lincoln Papers, Manuscripts Division, Library of Congress
CWAL	Roy P. Basler, ed., *Collected Works of Abraham Lincoln* (9 vols, New Brunswick, NJ: Rutgers University Press, 1953–1955)
GLC	Gilder Lehrman Collection, on deposit at the New York Historical Society
LoC	Manuscripts Division, Library of Congress
OR	*The War of the Rebellion: A Compilation of the Official Records of the Union and Confederate Armies* (Washington DC: Government Printing Office, 1880–1901)
RWAL	Don E. Fehrenbacher and Virginia Fehrenbacher, eds, *Recollected Words of Abraham Lincoln* (Stanford, Cal.: Stanford University Press, 1996)

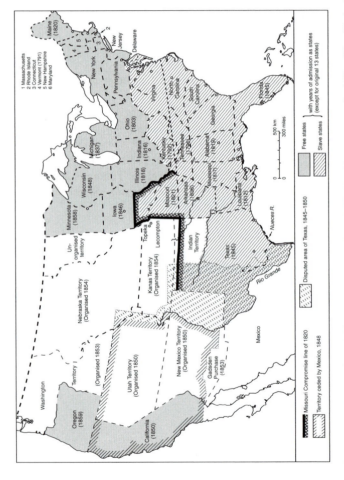

Map 1 **The United States on the eve of Civil War.** Adapted from Peter J. Parish, *The American Civil War* (New York: Holmes and Meier, 1975), pp. 18–19. This map shows the division between slave states and free states, the expansion of the nation through the Louisiana Purchase and the Mexican War, and the Missouri Compromise Line which was repealed in 1854 when the Kansas and Nebraska territories were organized.

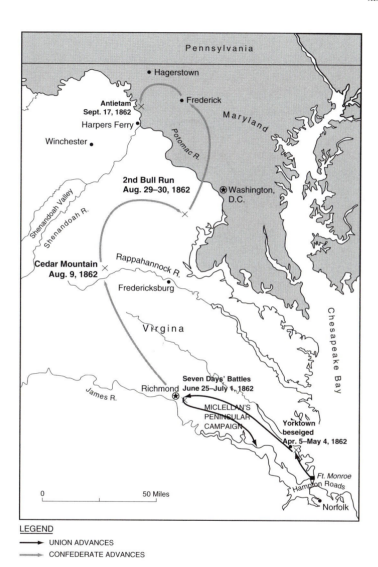

Map 2 **The eastern theater, 1861–1862.** Adapted from Michael Fellman, Lesley J. Gordon and Daniel E. Sutherland, *This Terrible War: The Civil War and its Aftermath* (New York: Pearson Education, 2003), p. 128. This map shows the sites of the main battles in the eastern theater in 1861 and 1862 and the routes of the two big movements – McClellan's failed Peninsular Campaign and Lee's audacious invasion of Maryland, which ended at the battle of Antietam. Note the rivers running west–east which formed a series of natural barriers between Washington and Richmond.

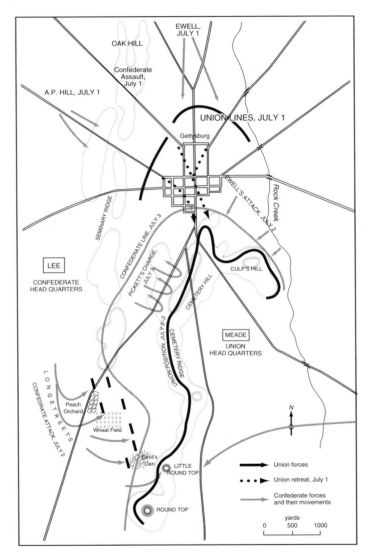

Map 3 **The battle of Gettysburg, July 1–3, 1863.** Adapted from James M. McPherson, *Ordeal By Fire: The Civil War and Reconstruction* (Boston: McGraw-Hill, 2001), p. 326. The map shows the major movements of the three-day battle. On the first day, Union forces were forced back from their positions north of the town, through the streets of the town itself and onto high ground to the south, forming a distinctive "fish hook" shape along the top of Cemetery hill and Cemetery ridge and down to Little Round Top. On the second and the third day, Confederates made repeated assaults on the Union lines, but were driven back.

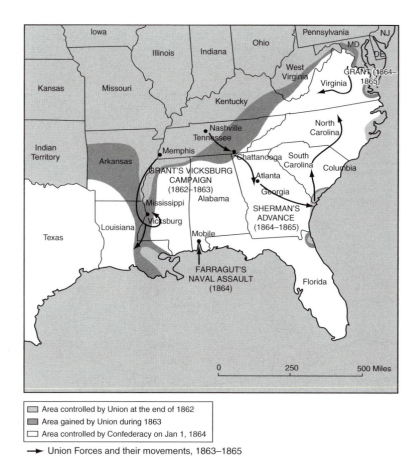

Area controlled by Union at the end of 1862
Area gained by Union during 1863
Area controlled by Confederacy on Jan 1, 1864

→ Union Forces and their movements, 1863–1865

Map 4 **Overview of main campaigns, 1864–1865.** Adapted from Michael Fellman, Lesley J. Gordon and Daniel E. Sutherland, *This Terrible War: The Civil War and its Aftermath* (New York: Pearson Education, 2003), p. 249. This map shows the territory still in Confederate hands at the start of 1864 and the main lines of Union attack. In September, Atlanta fell to Sherman and he then led the famous march to the sea and then on through the Carolinas.

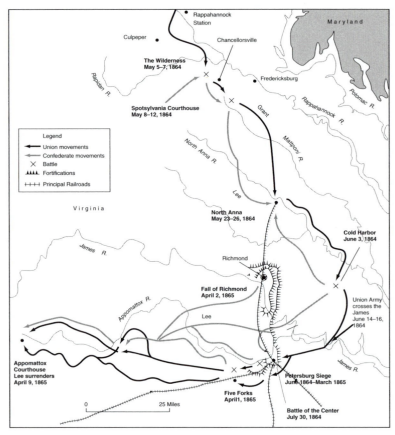

Grant's Virginia campaign 1864–1865

Map 5 **Grant's Virginia campaign, 1864–1865.** Adapted from Michael Fellman, Lesley J. Gordon and Daniel E. Sutherland, *This Terrible War: The Civil War and its Aftermath* (New York: Pearson Education, 2003), p. 265. This map shows in more detail Grant's advance through Virginia in 1864–1865. Between April and July the two armies clashed repeatedly as the Army of the Potomac tried and failed to flank Lee's Confederates until they reached stalemate outside Petersburg. When the Union army finally broke through in March 1865 it was only a matter of weeks before Richmond fell, and Lee's men, in a vain attempt to escape into North Carolina, were cornered and forced to surrender at Appomattox Court House.

1 Slavery and the American Republic

In the first decade of the nineteenth century, when the American Union was still in its infancy and the blood sacrifice of the revolutionary war patriots still a fresh memory, Kentucky was frontier country. Every spring brought thousands of migrants westward, along turnpikes, trails and roads through mountain passes, or on flatboats on the Ohio River. Land could be bought from the government for two dollars an acre, but many settlers "squatted," at least at first. Braving epidemics of cholera and typhoid, they cleared trees and undergrowth, walked miles to fetch freshwater, ploughed the soil and built simple one-room cabins, and only if they could scratch a living did they try to buy the title to their plot. A few pioneers, migrating from Virginia or perhaps the Carolinas, brought with them their black slaves. It was here, only eight months apart, that Abraham Lincoln and Jefferson Davis were born.

The future president of the Confederacy and the sixteenth president of the Union both had fathers who struggled as farmers, and both were poor, although Samuel Davis owned not only the land he farmed, but also a few slaves. Lincoln was reputedly named for his grandfather who had been shot by Indians, Davis, in honor of President Thomas Jefferson. After only a few years, the Davises and the Lincolns moved on in search of better land, one family south into Louisiana and then Mississippi, the other north into Indiana. Davis became a West Point—educated soldier—and the owner of slaves. After spending his boyhood in Indiana, Lincoln became a lawyer on the Illinois prairie, making his way in what he called the "race of life" in a lily-white state where slavery was illegal but black people were barred from entering. For all that one grew up in a society where there were slaves and the other where there were none, and despite the fact that they became active in opposing political parties, Lincoln and Davis shared not only the same native state but also basic values and assumptions about their nation and its world-historical significance. What they had in common tells

1

us as much about the coming of the Civil War as do the differences between them. Lincoln and Davis shared the nationalism of their age. As young men, both spoke of the value of free institutions, and expressed their faith in progress. Both were drawn into politics by their concern with economic development in an age of bewildering technological and social change. It is true that in innumerable large and small ways, Lincoln and Davis, like millions of other Americans, did not always mean the same things when they spoke of their American identity. But in the final analysis, the story of how Lincoln and Davis ended up as opposing leaders in one of the most savage wars in modern history is not the story of two men from different cultures coming into irrepressible conflict but that of how the issue of slavery came to overshadow what they shared.

NATIONALISM, DEMOCRACY AND REPUBLICANISM

Hindsight is the stock in trade of the historian, but it is a tool which has to be used with great caution. The knowledge that, in 1861, North and South went to war has tended to color the way in which historians have viewed the first half of the nineteenth century. Even the term scholars give to this period, "the antebellum era," defines it in terms of what came next. This is especially true of discussions of state-building and nationalism in the early republic. Not surprisingly, perhaps, given the collapse of the Union in the 1860s, historians have dwelt on the de-centralized and limited government, the strength of regional and local identities, and the centrifugal forces built into American institutions.

It is certainly true that secession was often mooted and long predicted. Never before had a republican form of government been tried on so extensive a scale—Washington called the new United States the "grand experiment." If Americans of the generation of the founding fathers had looked into a crystal ball and seen fratricidal warfare, they would have been dismayed but not entirely surprised. It was a risk inherent in a polity founded on the principle of de-centralization. After all, if there was one political impulse that united the colonists in the struggle against the British government, it was a dread of concentrated power. For Revolutionary-era Americans, the best government was assumed to be the most minimal that good order and freedom required. Liberty and power, argued the founding fathers of the American republic, were opposing forces that it was the purpose of constitutions to balance.

Getting the balance right was the aim of enlightened statesmanship. On the one hand, excessive liberty could undermine the sanctity of property, as the Jacobinical excesses of the French Revolution were to illustrate; on the other, the tendency of all government was to encroach on the liberty of the people. Classical republicanism had relied on civic virtue to counterbalance the tendency toward corruption and tyranny, although experience showed that it could do so for only so long. With Gibbon's example of the Roman Republic resonant in the mind of every educated man, the result was a rather pessimistic, cyclical view of the rise and fall of freedom. For many Americans in the revolutionary era, Great Britain had exemplified this trend. Once the freest constitution on earth, it had—in the view of the colonials—become stagnant, complacent, decadent and corrupt under the Hanoverians. What would prevent the new American republic succumbing eventually to the same fate? In the early decades of the nineteenth century, post-revolutionary France was held up by conservative Americans as an even more frightening example of the fate that could befall republican experiments. In his first extant public lecture, delivered to the Young Men's Lyceum of Springfield, Illinois, in 1838, Abraham Lincoln argued that the danger to the American republic lay only from within. "All the armies of Europe, Asia and Africa combined, with all the treasure of the earth (our own excepted) in their military chest, with a Buonaparte for a commander, could not by force take a drink from the Ohio, or make a track on the Blue Ridge, in a trial of a thousand years," Lincoln proclaimed. "If destruction be our lot, we must ourselves be its author and finisher. As a nation of freemen, we must live through all time, or die by suicide."[1]

The instability—or to give it a more positive term, "dynamism"—of American society in the first half of the nineteenth century is its defining feature. In the years between the birth of Lincoln and Davis and the firing of the first shots of the Civil War, the population of the United States grew from under six million to over forty million. In the same period, the United States was transformed from a cluster of Atlantic ex-colonies still heavily dependant on trade with the former colonial power into a largely self-sufficient exporter of agricultural and industrial products which already, by the 1850s, was in some respects exceeding British productivity rates. The "American System" of manufactures, whereby component parts of articles like clocks, guns, boots and clothing were produced at standard sizes so that they were interchangeable, enabled mass production of goods. By 1860, the United States boasted vastly more railroad mileage than any other country in the world. This did not mean that the United States had fully industrialized. By the time of the Civil War, less than a quarter of the working population was engaged in industrial activity of any kind. The vast majority still worked the land, and almost all American politicians assumed that industrial and commercial activity would only ever be supplementary to agriculture. Nevertheless, the basis for future industrial expansion was firmly in place in the northeast by the time of the Civil War. By 1860 New York City had become a teeming, bawdy, multi-ethnic city of over a million people. Immigration from Europe accounted for some of this growth. In the immediate antebellum decades, the most visible immigrants were Irish Catholics. Wherever there was industrial activity there were immigrants—not only in the urban metropolises of New York, Philadelphia and Boston but also in the mining areas of Pennsylvania and wherever railroads were being built. The presence of an alien Catholic population seemed threatening in a Protestant nation that thought of itself as having a divinely ordained place in human history. Moreover, this new urban proletariat seemed a harbinger of Old World class conflict. But though poor Irish immigrants worried wealthy established elites, they also provided the labor that was essential for industrial development. Eighteenth-century republicans had assumed that responsible citizens had to be self-reliant farmers or artisans, the owners of productive property. As immigration stepped up a pace in the 1850s, the proportion of Americans who were wage earners increased dramatically; a threat, or so it seemed to some, to the republican spirit of the nation.

The sense of boundless and uncontrolled growth was most visible in the territorial expansion of the nation and the gradual westward migration of the population. In 1804, President Thomas Jefferson had exploited the preoccupation of European powers with fighting each other in the Napoleonic wars to negotiate what has been called the "greatest real estate deal in history," the purchase of the vast Louisiana territory, which at a stroke doubled the size of the American republic. In the 1820s, hopeful southern farmers struck by "Alabama fever" moved west to plant cotton, a crop that seemingly guaranteed ever-greater profits. At the same time, new canals, improved roads, and eventually railroads began to connect farmers in New England and the "West" (the area now known as the Midwest) to growing urban markets in the eastern cities. In recent years, historians have followed Charles Sellers in grouping the multiple technological, economic and social changes of the early nineteenth century under the heading "the Market Revolution."[2]

The spread of capitalist relations altered the way in which localities and regions interacted with one another, as independent regional economies were integrated into a truly national market. The South became largely devoted to, and defined by, its output of staple crops, the Northeast by its greater industrial growth, and the West by its production of food.

As print became cheaper and more widely disseminated, early-nineteenth-century Americans became ever more closely interconnected by common reading habits. A shared sense of themselves as a distinctive nation and a characteristic Victorian faith in progress and destiny was inculcated by such literary hits as Mason Locke Weems's life of Washington, which, like millions of other Americans, the young Lincoln and Davis both devoured. Weems's *Washington* was a patriotic morality tale for children in which readers learned that Washington "could not tell a lie" and were encouraged to emulate his selfless virtues in order to preserve the blessings of free government. Tellingly, Abraham Lincoln used his very first public address, when he was a candidate for the Illinois state legislature in 1832, to make an argument for the importance of public education on the grounds that everyone should be "enabled to read the histories of his own and other countries, by which he may duly appreciate the value of our free institutions."[3] Such sentiments could be found everywhere in the antebellum era. Americans were not shy about trumpeting the genius of their republic, as countless foreign visitors attested. In comparison to Europe, Americans of the early nineteenth century may have had an absurdly brief national history, but they more than made the most of what they had. The founding fathers, and especially Washington, were revered as demigods, and tales told of their Christian and republican virtue.

The fact that the federal government was small by European standards was a source of pride for Americans; it certainly did not in itself diminish the loyalty that Americans felt toward it. In fact, the locally constituted nature of nineteenth-century government gave American nationality an anchor in the real lives of its citizens. To a truly remarkable degree, Americans felt ownership of their government because their government meant their community, leaders they knew, had voted for, could speak or write to, heckle and jostle if they wished. The Post Office was the federal institution that most antebellum citizens were most likely to encounter in their daily lives. The US Post Office, often with the stars and stripes flying from the roof, was a proud, tangible and highly useful indication of the beneficent power of republican government. Antebellum citizens might also encounter the federal government if they wanted to buy land in the West at bargain-basement prices. In the 1850s, the amount of land sold in the west by the federal government was equivalent to the acerage of the entire state of New York. Religion was an important component of national identity. In the first decades of the nineteenth century, an evangelical Protestant movement known as the "Second Great Awakening" took hold, especially in the West. Charismatic Methodist preachers carried an Arminian message of personal salvation to farmers who had often previously been exposed only to the threats of hellfire and a religion of chastisement. The growing strength of evangelical Protestantism was fueled by a number of factors, among them the laissez-faire attitude of government toward the regulation of religion which created a free market among competing religious groups and the psychological needs of a society undergoing tremendous change. Evangelicalism also thrived because it re-configured secular republican values to suit the more individualistic demands of an expanding capitalist society. The values of hard work, self-discipline and personal salvation were fused into an American creed that was simultaneously religious and nationalistic.

Race was also a common foundation of American nationhood that transcended class, gender and region. Antebellum Americans boasted of their free institutions, their common inheritance from the Revolution and of the blessings of liberty, but this "civic" component to their national identity was limited by racial (and also gendered) assumptions about who was eligible to enjoy the benefits of American freedom. Black people accounted for 15 percent of the population by the time of the Civil War, but only a minority of them—around 450,000—were free, concentrated in the Upper South with a smattering in northern cities. Almost without thinking about it, the vast majority of white Americans assumed that theirs was, and would remain, a white man's republic. They believed that one of the things that set the United States apart from the other republics of the New World was the superiority of the Anglo-Saxon race over the "mongrel" peoples of Mexico and South America. The 1790 naturalization law excluded only two groups of people from the possibility of US citizenship—aristocrats who refused to renounce their title, and nonwhite people. Both groups were assumed not to have the capacity for self-government necessary for republican citizenship. Catholic Irish and other non-Anglo immigrants were legally entitled to citizenship, but for much of the nineteenth century they existed in a shifting middle ground between "whiteness" and something else. National identity—like other forms of identity, including race—is malleable and historically contingent. Antebellum American nationalism usually reinforced, rather than undermined local, state and regional identities. "The South" certainly conceived of itself as a separate entity long before the Civil War, and slavery was evidently crucial to that process of self-definition. In truth, there were many Souths, not one. The Appalachian region which straddled western North Carolina, northeastern Alabama, east Tennessee and western Virginia was a distinctive geographical region, as was the swampy coastal region of the Florida panhandle, or the Mississippi River Valley, or the plains of Texas. The upcountry and mountainous parts of the South had a very distinctive culture and social structure—a land with comparatively few slaves, less productive land, and fiercely independent and self-sufficient farmers who regarded with suspicion and even hostility the more hierarchical lowland and piedmont regions of their states where the slave-owning planter class built their elegant mansions. Even so, the legal status of slavery, and a shared suspicion of the Yankee North, gave this region a sense of commonality, and from that developed ever more elaborate ideas about a distinctive southern "civilization."

In retrospect it is easy to identify the ways in which the antebellum political system made war possible. De-centralized government interwove free institutions into the fabric of local communities, making an abstract entity like the nation not only tangible, but also subject to multiple local and regional interpretations. In constitutional terms, the power of state governments created an inbuilt source of potential opposition to the federal government. But in the final analysis, Americans did not go to war between 1861 and 1865 because they lacked national institutions or a fervent sense of nationhood. Instead, it was the corrosive impact of the slavery issue which led to secession and Civil War. It was slavery, for example, that split apart the churches in the late 1840s, creating a schism in national bodies that anticipated the larger split to come. In the end it was Northern and Southern identities—rather than ethnic conflict, or competition between the frontier West and the urbanizing East, or the tensions between nonslaveholding whites and the rich planters in the South—that turned out be the subnational line of division that mattered. And although many factors were involved in the articulation of sectional identities in the decades preceding war, all were subsidiary to the one compelling problem of slavery.

THE SLAVERY ISSUE

For centuries after the fall of the Roman Empire, slavery in Europe had been a matter of degrees. In place of a clear-cut division between the free and the unfree, complicated and mutable layers of power and obligation connected kings, lords, freemen and peasants. As the European colonization of the Americas began in earnest in the seventeenth century, chattel slavery—the doctrine that men, women and children could be owned, bought and sold just like any other type of property—was reinvented in its modern form. Unlike slavery in the Roman world, it was race-based. In theory, and almost invariably in practice, only people of sub-Saharan African descent could be enslaved. Black slavery was a hard-headed answer to a very practical problem: for western Europeans in the early modern age, the challenge of the New World was largely a problem of labor supply. An Eden of immeasurable vastness and tantalizing natural wealth was there to be exploited, but as the germs from European settlers spread, the native population appeared to be in rapid terminal decline. Neither immigration from the Old World, the indentured servitude of poor European immigrants, nor the impressments—by threats or by promises—of the local population offered a sufficient labor supply to provide a large enough return for investors. The solution was found in the use of African slaves.

In the eighteenth century it was Britain that harnessed slavery most effectively to the engine of its commercial economy. The wealth "piled by the bond-man's two-hundred and fifty years of unrequited toil," to use Abraham Lincoln's phrase, was mainly used to supply addictive drugs.[4] Economic growth was fueled by the dependence of increasing numbers of Europeans—but especially the British—on coffee, tobacco, and, above all, sugar. Later, cotton cultivation in the new world provided the raw material for the textile mills that symbolized and catalyzed the fundamental shift in the organization of work and the scale of production that we know as the Industrial Revolution. Yet the culture that grew fat on the use of slave labor contained within it the seeds of its own destruction. Abolitionism developed hand in hand with the humanist doctrines of the enlightenment but most powerfully with the evangelical Protestantism and the sentimental, Romantic Tory sensibility of men like William Wilberforce or Samuel Taylor Coleridge.

The stirrings of the first great assault on slavery coincided almost exactly with the American Revolution. In 1770 about 460,000 slaves were held in the North American colonies, concentrated in Virginia and South Carolina. The British antislavery movement that developed in the late eighteenth and early nineteenth century made the growth of antislavery feeling in the newly independent United States unremarkable. In New England and the mid-Atlantic states, where slaves were few, and of limited economic importance, newly independent legislatures enacted emancipation laws with relatively little fuss. In the South, where slavery was concentrated, immediate emancipation was debated but came up against implacable opposition from planters who feared economic ruin if they were deprived of their forced labor, and from many other people who worried that a large population of free blacks would be an incendiary force. Yet even in the South, the idea that slavery was an outmoded and unfortunate institution had some purchase. Slaveowners' anxieties about the security of their institution were stoked by the apparent willingness of the British to use slave insurrections as a weapon against the rebellious colonists in the Revolutionary war. The Royal Governor of Virginia, Lord Dunmore, became notorious for his proclamation offering to free any slave who would take up arms on behalf of the king. When the British were defeated, thousands of American slaves fled to the Bahamas or Canada. An even more nightmarish vision of the violent overthrow of slavery was the revolt in St Domingo (present-day Haiti) led by Toussaint L'Ouverture during the 1790s, which retained a powerful grip on the imaginations of white southerners for decades to come. In 1800, an abortive slave uprising in Virginia led by the black preacher Gabriel Prosser confirmed southerners' worst fears that the doctrine of bloody revolution against oppression was about to be used against them.

The Virginian Thomas Jefferson embodied the slaveowners' dilemma. Jefferson was the author of the Northwest Ordinance of 1787 which prohibited slavery from the large swathes of US territory not yet incorporated as states. He also established the mechanism for admitting new states on the basis of equality with the original thirteen after a territory had acquired a sufficiently large population, a constitutional principle that was to shape the course of American history in profound ways. The Northwest Ordinance was an expression of the generally held view of the founding generation that slavery was an institution that was to be tolerated, but which was held to be ultimately incompatible with free institutions. Later generations of northerners exaggerated only a little, when, like Lincoln, they expressed confidence that the founders, while tolerating slavery where it currently existed but prohibiting its spread into new, as yet unsettled territories, had placed it "where the public mind shall rest in the belief that it is in course of ultimate extinction."[5] Certainly, Jefferson at times made clear his own pious hope that public opinion would eventually turn against slavery. In his 1783 "Notes on the State of Virginia" he wrote that "there must doubtless be an unhappy influence on the manners of our people produced by the existence of slavery among us." In 1808, President Jefferson encouraged Congress to follow the example set by the British parliament and ban the Atlantic slave trade. After he left the White House, Jefferson continued to write about his fears that slavery corroded the white man's republic. In the midst of the War of 1812—the so-called "second war of independence" in which the British had once again threatened to use slaves against their enemies—he expressed his conviction that "the hour of emancipation is advancing, in the march of time." The manner of its coming, though, was yet to be decided:

> It will come; and whether brought on by the generous energy of our own minds; or by the bloody process of St. Domingo, excited and conducted by the power of our present enemy, if once stationed permanently within our Country, and offering asylum & arms to the oppressed, is a leaf of our history not yet turned over.[6]

Contrary to the hopes of some and the fears of others, slavery did not die without the lifeline of new legal imports from Africa. On the contrary, it flourished. Prices rose, and, unlike in male-dominated Latin American slave communities, the slave population expanded naturally at the same healthy rate as the white population. Slavery, Jefferson ruefully concluded in 1820, was not only a highly dangerous but an intrinsically insoluble dilemma: "We have the wolf by the ears, and we can neither hold him, nor safely let him go."[7]

Up until the late 1820s, political antislavery movements in the United States had been relatively genteel. Southerners could engage in discussions about emancipation because no one important in public life was suggesting anything so radical as forcible, immediate abolition. Searching for a way to cut the Gordian knot of Jefferson's dilemma, some southern slaveowners found an individual solution in the widespread practice of providing for the manumission of their slaves in their wills. George Washington's will, for example, declared that his slave property would be free after the death of his surviving wife Martha. One can imagine the nervousness this must have caused the widowed Mrs Washington as she dealt on a daily basis with men and women each of whom had a very personal stake in hastening her end. By deferring emancipation until after the slaveowner's death, this practice was a manifestation on a personal level of the response of southern white society as a whole: to wish the problem away, and in effect to bequeath it to succeeding generations. For most antislavery Americans—northerners as well as southerners—between the Revolution and into the Civil War, the best solution to the problem of the wolf held by the ears was to expel the wolf. Colonization of black slaves either in Africa or in some other tropical place outside the territory of the United States was widely seen as the only sensible solution to the problem. The American Colonization Society, or the American Society for the Colonization of Free People of Color, to give it its full title, was founded in 1816 to promote the idea of emancipation conditional on removal. Arguing that freed black people would always be impoverished and unequal if they remained in the United States, the society raised funds to found Liberia, a colony for freed American slaves on the west coast of Africa. Only a tiny numbers of free blacks ever went to Liberia, and the fact that this pathetic scheme was taken seriously by so many intelligent men in antebellum America is an extraordinary testament to the power of self-delusion where matters of race and status are involved. It had the support of numerous leading politicians as well as the young Illinois state legislator Abraham Lincoln. The ideas the society espoused retained a powerful grip on the imagination of some northern politicians well into the Civil War.

The early 1830s were a watershed in the history of modern slavery. In 1833, after a long struggle, abolitionists finally succeeded in passing an emancipation measure through the parliament at Westminster. Henceforth successive British governments took the moral high ground over slavery, just as the Royal Navy had done over the slave trade in the preceding two decades. The South was becoming isolated. The abolitionist movement that developed in the northern states in the early 1830s had markedly different aims and assumptions from those of the Colonization Society. Calling for immediate, rather than gradual emancipation, the new abolitionists introduced a tone of moral outrage into public discourse. Whereas colonization supporters, some of whom owned slaves themselves, tended to see masters as well-meaning and benevolent, abolitionists saw them as sinners. While colonization supporters for the most part saw the slavery question in practical, pragmatic terms, abolitionists saw it as a violation either of the religious idea that all men had a spark of divinity, or of the enlightenment idea that all men were created equal, or both. The first shot in this new high-stakes battle over the right and wrong of slavery in the nation which contained the world's most powerful slaveowners, was fired by David Walker, a free black born in North Carolina and now living in Boston. In 1829, Walker published *An Appeal to the Colored Citizens of the World*, which called on black people to unite in opposition to slavery, by force if necessary. But he also challenged white antislavery moderates by bluntly stating that "America is as much our country as it is yours." For Walker, as for many subsequent radicals, Jefferson's apparently unequivocal statement of the "unalienable truth" that "all men are created equal" was both inspirational and sickeningly hypocritical. "See your Declaration Americans!!!!" he thundered. "Do you understand your own language? . . . I ask you candidly, was your suffering under Great Britain, one hundredth part as cruel and tyrannical as you have rendered ours under you?"

As he must have expected, Walker's pamphlet made him a marked man. Several southern states placed a price on his head. In 1830, he died in mysterious circumstances. A year later, however, the first edition of *The Liberator*, the newspaper of William Lloyd Garrison's new abolitionist society, was published in Boston. This was to be the leading voice of the abolitionist movement. Garrison promised to be as "harsh as truth and as uncompromising as justice." He was proud not to "think, or speak, or write with moderation." He delivered on that promise, condemning slaveowners as "an adulterous and perverse generation, a brood of vipers" and reveling in the notoriety that followed. "I will not equivocate", he declared, "I will not retreat a single inch—and I will be heard." Garrison vociferously argued that freed slaves must become a part of American society. Abolitionists spread their message using the latest technology. Steam presses pounded out millions of pamphlets, newspapers and broadsides. Antislavery lecturers traveled the country by rail, speaking in public meetings and using the organizational tactics as well as the rhetorical style of evangelical revivalists. This was an age when, as foreign observers often commented, Americans were enthusiastically joining voluntary organizations. The American Anti-Slavery Society was created in 1833 to campaign for immediate abolition. By the end of the decade, 100,000 northerners had joined this and similar groups. That was a terrifying number to slaveowners who had never before been subjected to such vitriolic attacks, but it was a tiny proportion of northern whites.

To the vast majority of northern whites, immediate abolitionism was dangerously extremist. Violent antiabolition mobs attacked prominent abolitionists, destroyed presses that printed abolitionist literature and disrupted antislavery meetings. Accusing abolitionist speakers of inciting black men to rape white women, antiabolitionists revealed that to many northerners, abolitionism was a serious threat to the racial and social order. In the 1830s, local communities across the northern states used violence and intimidation to try to silence antislavery activism. When, in 1833, a Quaker teacher, Prudence Crandell, tried to open a boarding school for black children in Canterbury, Connecticut, incensed locals responded by terrorizing the children and poisoning the school well. The state legislature promptly passed a law banning schools for black children. The most notorious incident was the murder of Reverend Elijah P. Lovejoy, the editor of an abolitionist newspaper in Alton, Illinois, in 1836. By attacking the Constitution as a sordid "covenant with death," Garrison placed himself outside the boundaries of mainstream politics. His language was deliberately extreme, but the point he was making was an important one. The debate about slavery was indeed constrained by the Constitution: unless slave states voluntarily chose to pass laws of emancipation, there was no possibility of immediately abolishing slavery in any constitutional way. Instead of celebrating July 4, black abolitionists provocatively celebrated August 1, the date of emancipation in the British West Indies. Ties to the British antislavery movement heightened fears that abolitionists were being controlled by foreign agitators.

Along with its humanitarian appeal to natural justice, the *Liberator* made at least one argument that echoed the "Jeffersonian" antislavery arguments of the Revolutionary period. That was the idea that slavery poisoned white man's democracy. For all his concern for universal equal rights, Garrison also pointed to the corrosive effect of slavery on all those who were complicit in it, and in particular on the illegitimate power of slaveowners. Abolitionists laid the foundations of the concept of the "Slave Power"—the idea that there was an oligarchic, anti-democratic, unrepublican class of slave owners who had perverted southern politics and were trying to control the nation as a whole. It was this line of argument that was eventually to carry antislavery ideas from the periphery to the mainstream of northern politics. Although only a minority of northerners ever signed up to all the tenets of immediate abolitionism, the effect of abolitionism far outweighed their relatively small numbers. By provoking a defensive reaction among slaveowners, abolitionists exposed different views about whether owning slaves was compatible in the long run with the dynamic small-scale capitalist society that nineteenth-century America was becoming. As Frederick Douglass, a charismatic former slave said in 1847, "I am delighted to see any efforts to prop up the system on the part of slaveholders. It serves to bring up the subject before the people and hasten the day of deliverance."[8]

The last occasion before the Civil War when real debate over the future of slavery could take place anywhere in the South other than in the northernmost 'border' slave states was the year 1831. In that year, the Virginia legislature defeated a proposal to abolish slavery in the state. The governor who proposed this radical move was no less a figure than Thomas Jefferson's grandson. The advocates of Virginia abolition like the proponents of abolition in Pennsylvania and New York thirty years earlier were happy for slaveowners to sell their slaves "down the river" to the Deep South. Like many "antislavery" people who followed them, their self-interested wish was that the entire "Negro question" would simply disappear. Their opponents, though, were aghast at the thought that Virginia could even consider removing almost her entire labor force at a stroke. And the state did not have the financial resources to adequately compensate masters for the loss of their property. The property-owning classes united to defeat the measure. The emancipation measure received enthusiastic backing from the western counties of Virginia where the slave population was small or nonexistent, but was defeated by the eastern slaveholding counties, which were overrepresented in the legislature. The price of emancipation seemed greater than the price of building up the defenses of slavery ever higher.

The Virginia emancipation debate was prompted in part by the most famous slave rebellion in US history. It was led by Nat Turner, a slave preacher from Southampton County, Virginia, who believed that God was calling him to lead a rebellion. Telling his followers of visions in which black and white angels fought in the sky until the heavens ran red with blood, Turner gathered a small band of supporters, and on August 22, 1831, he attacked farms, indiscriminately killing about sixty white people, many of whom were women and children. The militia was called out and Turner's band captured and sentenced to death. As he was led to the scaffold, Turner was said to have cried out, "was not Christ crucified?" On one level, Turner's example revealed the futility of direct violent confrontation between slaves and a white majority who were united and heavily armed—unlike in the Caribbean, where blacks were heavily in the majority and the chances of a successful uprising consequently greater. In the American South only an external force could tip the balance of power away from the slaveowners. Even so, the psychological impact of Turner's rebellion on white society was profound. Like the ghost of Toussaint L'Ouverture, the leader of the successful Haitian slave rebellion, Turner challenged the illusion that slaves were content with their bondage.

Nat Turner and William Garrison prompted a pro-slavery backlash. After their appearance, the space for discussing antislavery ideas in the South closed down. For the first time, southerners began to argue that slavery was not just a necessary evil but a positive good. After about 1830, slavery was no longer a problem that could be discussed openly in half the nation. Slaveowners' fears were ultimately a product of the weakness of their institution. A system that depended on the brutal exercise of physical force could not bear critical scrutiny. Slaveowners responded by tightening slave codes and increasing the level of visible violence meted out to the enslaved population. Lynching increased. New laws were passed across the South making it a criminal offense for a white person to teach a slave to read or write. The voluntary manumission of slaves was prohibited. No longer could southern gentlemen ease their consciences as Washington had done by freeing their slaves in their wills. All this was designed to prevent subversive ideas spreading among the slave population. Fearing that abolitionist ideas would be spread by northern free blacks, South Carolina passed a law which meant that black sailors on northern ships that docked in Charleston harbor overnight would be imprisoned until their vessel was ready to sail. At the same time as slaveowners tightened the security around their peculiar institution at home, they sought to stifle subversive ideas at their source. Southern congressmen succeeded in introducing "gag rules" lasting from 1836 to 1844 preventing Congress from debating emancipation petitions.

What most observers in the eighteenth century had assumed was an institution of limited economic value was transformed by technological advances which made the large-scale production of cotton possible and by the soaring demand for raw cotton from Britain and the northeastern United States. Slave prices were based on demand and on confidence in the system. By these measures slavery was flourishing at the time of the Civil War. Between the Revolution and 1860 the slave population had increased by a factor of ten to nearly four and a half million. The center of gravity of the slave economy had shifted south and west from

Virginia. By the time of the Civil War, it was concentrated in the lower south states of South Carolina, the hotbed of secessionist "fire-eaters"; Georgia, originally founded as a free colony but now with an expanding slave population; Florida, barely populated in the swampy south, but with thriving cotton growing areas in the panhandle; Louisiana and Mississippi, the new heartland of the big cotton and sugar plantations; and, to the west, the slave frontier in Texas. Slavery was also firmly established in the upper south states of Virginia, Tennessee, Arkansas and North Carolina, although in each of those states there was an upland area of small-scale white farmers with few slaves and only a tenuous connection to the market economy. Such areas were to be fertile ground for southern Unionism during the war. In the 15 states of the Union where it was legal to hold human property, slaves accounted for 32 percent of the total population by 1860. In the 11 states that seceded to form the Confederacy, the ratio was even higher: five and a half million whites lived alongside three and a half million blacks, almost all of whom were slaves. To foreign travelers slavery was the most obvious defining feature of the South. Northerners who went south were also struck by the large plantations with what appeared to be a feudal social structure. Only 3 percent of southern families owned plantations, defined as holdings with over 20 slaves, but this small elite owned more than half of all the slaves in the United States. Especially in these large plantations, slavery—southerners evasively called it their "peculiar institution"—was domesticated and mythologized by analogy with the patriarchal family.

Slavery by its very nature was an economic as well as a human institution. Mythologizers of the "lost cause" in the late nineteenth and early twentieth centuries would later fit slavery into the paradigm of the "white man's burden," arguing that slaveowners willingly perpetuated an economically inefficient labor system in order to maintain social stability and racial harmony. From a very different perspective, Marxist historians like Eugene Genovese and John Ashworth have also come to the conclusion that the slave South was not fully capitalist since brutal coercion and neofeudal ties of mutual obligation rather than wage labor formed the basis of social relations.[9] The problem here is one of definition. If the "cash nexus" is the arbiter of whether a society is considered capitalist, then the antebellum South clearly fails the test. But large-scale slaveowners were fully integrated into the international market economy, and, despite their rhetoric, they acted like good capitalists when they made decisions about buying and selling land

and slaves. Their aim was to maximize returns on their investment, and slavery was a matter of huge-scale investment. Despite the paternalist myth, profit was the bottom line.

The southern defense of slavery was certainly motivated by unquestioned assumptions of racial superiority (which were shared by most northerners) and by a certainty that only slavery could maintain racial order, but it was also a hardheaded defense of a mammoth financial investment. Antislavery campaigners rarely seemed to recognize the brute economic forces that sustained and stimulated the defense of slavery. The wealth per head of the southern white population on the eve of the Civil War, if one includes wealth held in the form of slave property, was, according to the economic historian James Huston, far in excess of that in the northern states.[10] One measure of the impact of the Civil War on the economic and political geography of the United States is that on the basis of wealth per white household Mississippi was the richest state in the Union in 1860; ever since the Civil War it has been one of the poorest. Unlike other moral issues which enter politics, abolitionism threatened millions of dollars of investments. In many ways, including a strict financial reckoning, southerners had much more at stake than northerners. The increasing economic value of slavery augmented the deep-seated attachment of the vast majority of white southerners to an institution that they thought underpinned the status of poor whites, provided the only conceivable means of maintaining economic output and guaranteed the stability of their social order.

THE POWER OF SLAVEOWNERS

The American Civil War arose from a fatal irony: slavery was a highly vulnerable institution but slaveowners were politically powerful. Like stand-up comedians or operatic prima donnas—but with far more serious consequences—the defining characteristic of the southern slaveowner in the three decades preceding the Civil War was a combination of insecurity combined with an inflated sense of their own importance. Only in the republic that was dedicated in its founding document to the principle that "all men are created equal," and which was a synonym for the great experiment in democratic government, did slaveholders resort not to delaying tactics but to a full-scale defense of their right to keep slaves, indeed to the argument that slavery was both divinely ordained and modern. Defying what in retrospect appears to be the irresistible trend of the nineteenth century, slaveowners in the southern United States confidently set out to do what their British West Indian counterparts would not have dreamed of doing: founding a slave-based republic in the second half of the nineteenth century. The "corner-stone" of the Confederate States of America, according to its Vice President Alexander H. Stephens, was laid "upon the great truth that the Negro is not equal to the white man; that slavery, subordination to the superior race, is his natural and moral condition."[11] Southern slave-owners wielded much greater political power than their counterparts in Latin America, or the British, French or Spanish Empires, yet could not escape the paranoia that was the fate of slaveholders in a world in which slavery was contested. The increasing assertiveness of slave-owners who demanded more and more evidence that the free states were willing to recognize the legitimacy of slavery was the principal driver of sectional conflict. Slavery required not just the absence of opposition but positive support in order for it to survive. Slaveowners were caught in a vicious cycle whereby as more and more people loudly denounced slavery they needed ever-greater reassurance. Not only their honor and self esteem, their sense of social order and their conception of right and justice, but also an immense amount of capital was at stake in their fight to preserve their world. Slavery involved such fundamental issues of honor, identity, security and economic interest that it drove otherwise loyal Americans to secede from the Union; and only secession could have prompted Civil War.

Abraham Lincoln's confidence that the founders had placed slavery "on the course of ultimate extinction" suggests that the republicanism of the revolution with its egalitarian and democratic impulses must have been inimical to slavery. But the reality was more complex. If the resort to mass violence was demonstrably a catastrophic failure of the democratic process, by the same token it can also be argued that the democratic republic created circumstances in which war could happen, even which—given the economic imperatives of the age and the cultural framework through which nineteenth-century Americans viewed the world—made war likely.

The interrelationship between republicanism and slavery had a long pedigree. Dr Samuel Johnson, the author of the first English dictionary and one of a breed of Tory antislavery Englishmen, famously and dryly asked of the revolutionary American colonists, "Why is it that we hear the loudest yelps for freedom from the drivers of Negroes?" What he imagined to be evidence of hypocrisy was in fact easily explained: the colonists were in revolt about many issues but at the core of the conflict was the issue of property rights. Colonial leaders denied that parliament in London had the authority to tax (i.e. to deprive a person of some of his property) without due consent. Since for so many revolutionary leaders property included slave property it followed that they were equally exercised about any interference, from government or from other private citizens, with their absolute right to hold and dispose of that particular form of property as well. Indeed it was for that reason that the Declaration of Independence included—in several long paragraphs that have been eclipsed by the familiar ringing opening phrases—a long list of specific grievances against the King, including against his alleged attempts to stir up "servile insurrection."

Some historians have labeled the antebellum South a *herrenvolk* democracy, invoking a parallel with the Boers in South Africa, in which a doctrine of equality for white men is predicated on the existence of a servile race. Much as they may have resented having to do it, even the grandest southern slaveowning "aristocrat" had to court the votes of poor whites if he aspired to political office. And although blacks were not so visible in the North, the concept of *herrenvolk* democracy could be applied more broadly to the antebellum republic. This was a republic in which the gradations of freedom and unfreedom which continued to characterize European society were collapsed into a much sharper distinction between white Protestant men—among whom there was indeed a remarkable degree of political and economic equality—and the rest. Far from being polar opposites, slavery and freedom were mutually dependent in antebellum America. The culture of equal rights for white men implicitly—and at times explicitly—sanctioned and explained the continuation of slavery. It is revealing in this context that slavery continued to be a concept much used by antebellum politicians—just as it had been for the revolutionary generation—to describe perceived slights. Another answer to Dr Johnson's presumed paradox was that it was precisely because the "drivers of Negroes" knew perfectly well what slavery meant that they "yelped" for freedom and continually saw the struggle for power through the dichotomy of slavery and freedom.

If American national ideology was a double-edged sword which could be used to defend as well as attack slavery, antislavery politics was also blunted by nineteenth-century Americans' shared racial ideology. In the United States (and also, earlier, in the British West Indian colonies) the African slave population had maintained a healthy rate of natural increase. A gender and age balance in the slave population meant that the black community was self-sustaining. In much of the rest of the new world, imported slaves were almost entirely men, and inevitably racial intermingling with the Creole community took place on a much larger scale. To a much greater extent than was ever true in Latin America, Anglo Americans saw themselves as a community set apart by God for some divine purpose and they had much less interaction with native peoples and more rigid systems of racial separation between themselves and their African slaves. Historians are becoming increasingly aware of the comparative fluidity of racial identities in the eighteenth century, but the intensified pro-slavery stance of southern slaveowners in the three decades before the Civil War reflected a wider shift within European society toward a markedly more rigid and hierarchical conception of race.[12]

In theory, the presence of a large class of nonslaveholding whites should have been a major threat to the slave system. A large literature has developed over the last 20 years or so exploring the class tensions within white southern society.[13] But real as these divisions were, the critical fact was that the vast majority of nonslaveholding southern whites, unlike increasing numbers of white northerners, accepted the legitimacy of property in slaves. The bottom line was that antebellum southern elites were wealthy only so long as their right to slave property was recognized. So long as everyone accepted slaves as property, class tensions could be managed. So long as nonslaveholders aspired to become slaveowners, or at least did not challenge the right of their richer neighbors to invest their money in human beings, the internal stability of southern white society could be maintained. For increasing numbers of northerners, slavery epitomized opposing values. Ordinary white southerners saw no contradiction in signing up to the same proscription for a fair society as their northern cousins. North and South were both free labor societies for whites. Most Americans in both sections shared an optimistic and egalitarian outlook on life. Whatever their starting point in life, northerners and southerners shared the common aspiration of property ownership, and they believed that they lived in an open, free society where hard work was rewarded. The difference was that most southerners were comfortable with the idea that black people were just another type of property. So where many northerners understandably saw slavery as reminiscent of medieval serfdom, an alien, unrepublican transplant on free American soil, white southerners simply saw another type of property. "You speak of African slavery as if it were the slavery of the Anglo-Saxon or Celt," protested James Henry Hammond to an

English antislavery editor, "But it is not." White southerners affected bewilderment at the line of attack from northerners. "What is there in the character of that property [slavery] which excludes it from the general benefit of the principles applied to all other property?" asked Jefferson Davis in the senate in 1850. He meant it as a rhetorical question, but of course to his opponents the answer was screamingly obvious: "because they're human beings!"

The most basic factor that gave US slaveholders the ability to buck the trend of nineteenth-century antislavery reform was the federal structure of the American Constitution combined with the fact that slavery was geographically concentrated. The idea that groups have been powerfully committed to the principle of "states' rights" has been invoked as an explanation for many things in American history, especially the Civil War. There is no doubt that many people genuinely believed in local autonomy, a principle that flowed naturally enough from the antigovernment rhetoric of the revolution. But "states' rights" should not be reified into an independent force, certainly not one with the power to cause a war. Northerners were as apt to claim states' rights principles as southerners when it suited them—as it did in the 1850s when they passed "personal liberty laws" that were deliberately designed to undermine the federal fugitive slave legislation. Antebellum southerners were in important respects far more keen on an activist federal government than northerners. By pushing through more stringent fugitive slave laws and even, by the late 1850s, demanding federal protection for slavery in all US territories under the control of Congress, they were in effect calling for a huge expansion of the federal government's responsibilities. Yet federalism was still the basic political fact that made secession politically possible and states' rights offered a convenient vocabulary with which to cloak the revolutionary aims of southern leaders. Federalism also gave southerners a platform in the Senate—in which states were represented equally without regard to the size of their populations— much greater than their strength in the census would indicate.

The Federal Constitution of 1787 recognized the legitimacy of slave property even without using the word "slavery." The federal fugitive slave clause by which the authorities in the free states would be bound to return runaway slaves to their masters in the slave states was a nonnegotiable precondition without which the slave states would not have agreed to the Constitution; slavery, after all, was only as secure as its borders. Even more reassuring to slaveowners was the "three-fifths clause" in the Constitution which apportioned representation in

Congress and in the vitally important presidential Electoral College on the basis of the free *population* (emphatically not three-fifths of *voters*) "plus three-fifths of all other persons, excluding Indians not taxed." In other words, slaveowners—astonishing as it seems in retrospect—were allowed to have it both ways. Slaves should be treated as *property* if they absconded and claimed freedom, but as *persons*—or at least as three-fifths of a person—from the point of view of representation. This critical clause gave slaveowners an undue political influence at the national level which endured even in the face of the relative decline of the white southern population. On several occasions the South got its way in a presidential election or in a close vote in the House of Representatives only because of the three-fifths clause.

The basic advantage of the Constitution for slaveowners was that it provided protection to a minority—and as southerners were only too aware, they were becoming an ever-smaller minority, in terms of population, economic output and number of states. The founders fully recognized the philosophical and practical problems posed by slavery but in the interests of national harmony they dodged the question, passing it down to their descendents. Rather than providing a means of resolving differences, the institutional edifice they created polarized northerners and southerners. The Constitution protected slavery and precluded a national response to the problem, and the privileges it gave to southerners were increasingly resented by northerners. Only when their privileged position in the Union was apparently threatened by a northern antislavery majority did southerners give up on the Union.

But the Constitution, useful as it was, was in itself an insufficient means of protecting southern rights. There were too many circumstances in which the South could be outvoted in the House, and even in the Senate. The presidential Electoral College, although weighted to the South by the three-fifths clause and by the overrepresentation of small states, nevertheless responded to the population increases in the North. Furthermore, as we have already seen, the slave interest, for all their states' rights rhetoric, had a vital interest in controlling the national government since only that way could they ensure the protection of their property and the social order that was bound up in it. John C. Calhoun, the leading South Carolinian spokesman for southern rights, proposed that the Constitution be rewritten to give the slave states a formal, permanent veto over anything the North wanted to do. His solution to the shrinking minority status of the South, in other words, was to institutionalize its power irrespective of relative population size.

A more viable political survival strategy for the minority South was to build alliances in the North. This is why the party system became so important. One strategy for slaveowners might have been to make common cause with northern conservatives. Some did this through the agency of the Whig party, which tended to promote economic development in the context of social order. Southern conservatives were attracted by the Whigs' determination to maintain sectional harmony and social order. The evangelical revival created a cultural politics which could unite people in all sections on issues like defense of the Sabbath and the promotion of temperance. Unfortunately for southern Whigs, however, the northerners who worried for the moral health of society were often also those who were most disturbed by slavery. The most promising strategy for protecting southern rights within the Union, therefore, lay in the world's first mass political party—"the Democracy"—which coalesced in the late 1820s and early 1830s in support of President Andrew Jackson. The Democratic Party allied southerners with farmers and urban laborers in the North, tying them together with a shared political vocabulary, campaign songs and slogans. Jackson was the great egalitarian leveler of antebellum America. This reputation propelled him into the rough, whiskey-soaked world of frontier democratic politics and to two terms as president from 1829 to 1837. In complete contrast to his silk-stockinged predecessor John Quincy Adams, Jackson embodied the idea that the people ruled. His log-cabin-to-White-House biography led him from a childhood skirmishing with British soldiers, to fame as the victor of the battle of New Orleans against the British in the War of 1812 and a subsequent career as a fearless Indian killer, to a respectable existence as the owner of a plantation outside Nashville which known as the Hermitage and—naturally enough—the ownership of a hundred or so slaves. The Jacksonian Democratic Party was held together by a commitment to white racial solidarity and—to a greater extent than any other mass movement in American history—to equality of outcome as well as of opportunity. Their vision was an evolution of the Jeffersonian dream of an agrarian republic, an "empire of liberty" in which every white man would have the opportunity to own productive property. The enemy of this smallholders', white man's republic was concentrations of wealth, exemplified by bankers and speculators, who, according to Jacksonian rhetoric, made their money from the sweat of other men's labor. The free labor ideology that was used by Republicans in the late 1850s to condemn slavery gained its power from this rich Jacksonian tradition.

To some Jacksonians it was obvious that slavery violated these ideals, not so much because slaves themselves were being denied the fruits of their labor, but because slaveowners formed exactly the kind of privileged class who undermined the egalitarianism of the republic.

The overwhelming majority of Democrats remained hostile to anti-slavery politics. One of the weak points of recent scholarship on the coming of the war has been that it ignores the fierce resistance by a huge number of loyal northern Democrats to an antislavery interpretation of the nation. The founders had forged a pragmatic compromise that tolerated slavery. On the eve of the Civil War, large numbers of north-erners were more than just tolerant; they accepted black enslavement as a permanent condition. Irish immigrants and southern-born migrants to the North were two groups especially susceptible to this complacent view of slavery, and, disproportionately represented in the northern Democratic Party, these groups formed a buffer against the growing antislavery culture that was gripping many other elements of antebellum northern society. As late as 1858, when Jefferson Davis visited New England for health reasons, his warm reception there convinced him that there were still many northern Democrats committed to protecting the South within the Union.

THE CRISIS OVER THE EXTENSION OF SLAVERY

The great fear of the South in the antebellum period was a united North. The South could not have exercised political power at a national level without the support of northern Democrats at critical junctures. The cause that unified northern and southern Democrats was western expansion. A nationwide depression in the 1840s made the promise of boundless, free land especially appealing. Cheap farms in the west would compensate the indebted farmers of states like Illinois, Ohio and Pennsylvania, who had suffered most from the economic downturn. It promised to unite northern and southern Democrats on a common platform. Yet, inevitably, expansionism undermined the effort to keep slavery out of national politics. Democrats unwittingly let the genie of antislavery politics out of the bottle by creating a new context in which the underlying tensions between slave and free societies could be fought out. In these circumstances, northern Democrats were compelled to support the South, in the tradition of tolerating slavery, and convinced that any other approach would drive southern states out of the Union.

Throughout the 1840s, white Americans moved west. Searching for new opportunities and beguiled by stories of the fertile valleys of Oregon, pioneers made the perilous trek across the Great Plains through Indian country and across the Rocky mountains beyond the boundaries of the United States. Until 1846 Oregon was jointly administered by the United States and Britain, but international boundaries were of little concern to settlers. The westward migration rekindled the old idea that it was the "manifest destiny" of the United States to spread across the continent. From the outset, expansion and conquest had been wired into the DNA of the nation. In the middle decades of the nineteenth century this process sped up. John O'Sullivan, the Democratic publicist who is credited with coining the phrase "manifest destiny," made three basic points in support of territorial expansion: first, population growth required it; second, the United States was, in Jefferson's phrase, an "Empire of Liberty" whose expansion equated with the growth of freedom in the world; and, finally, it was God's will. The first of these arguments—population expansion—was closely related to the other two because most antebellum Americans, especially Democrats in both North and South, believed that American freedom was only possible because of the unique abundance of the new world. Unlike in Europe, landless eastern country dwellers or unemployed urban workers could escape their condition by going west. Although historians have shown that the very poorest section of eastern society were unlikely to travel west (because one needed a certain amount of capital to do so), this "safety valve" theory was an inspiring idea that structured Americans' image of their own society for the rest of the nineteenth century and beyond. In testimony to Congress in 1846, William Gilpin, a Quaker, set out the case for expansion as a righteous crusade:

> The untransacted destiny of the American field is to subdue the continent—to rush over the vast field to the Pacific Ocean . . . to set the principle of self-government at work . . . to establish a new order in human affairs—to set free the enslaved . . . to change darkness into light—to stir up the sleep of a hundred centuries . . . to confirm the destiny of the human race—to carry the career of mankind to its culminating point—to cause stagnant people to be reborn—to perfect science—to emblazon history with the conquest of peace—to shed a new and resplendent glory upon mankind . . . to dissolve the spell of tyranny and exalt charity. . . . Divine task! immortal mission! Let us tread fast and

joyfully the open trail before us. Let every American heart open
wide for patriotism to glow undimmed, and confide with religious faith in the sublime and prodigious destiny of his well-loved
country![14]

Needless to say, manifest destiny was an explicitly racial idea.
"Race," declared John O'Sullivan, "is the key to the history of nations"
and the rise and fall of empires. The superiority of the "Anglo-Saxon
race" justified the expansion of Anglo-America at the expense of
"lesser" peoples, whether they were Native Americans or Hispanics.
Ideas about race hardened in this period, as pseudoscientific theories
of racial difference appeared to provide an explanation as well as a
justification for the domination of one people over another. The "Anglo-
Saxon" race was a nineteenth-century coinage that brought to the fore
the racial basis of American political culture. The Anglo-Saxons were
a "liberty-loving" people. They were defined by their Protestantism,
by their independence, their rejection of tyranny, whether in the form
of aristocrats or the Catholic Church. The racial arguments in favor
of expansion united most southerners and northerners. They justified
the expropriation of Indian lands, and the waging of war against a
"mongrel" Catholic "race" like the Mexicans. The great value of the
West was that in the imagination of most Americans, it was still a virgin
land. The Indians were destined to die out naturally, and the Hispanic
population, small in numbers and easily overwhelmed by Anglo settlers,
could be ignored. But the same racial logic limited the "natural limits"
of the United States: for example, even so passionate a defender of
slavery as John C. Calhoun opposed the annexation of the whole of
Mexico on the grounds that so many Catholic "mongrels" could not be
assimilated.

Southerners did not always take slaves with them when they traveled
west, but many did, and many others were inspired by the thought of
being able to acquire cheap and fertile land with enough capital left
over to buy or hire a slave or two to work it. The profits to be made
from cotton cultivation pushed entrepreneurial southern farmers ever
further westward in search of new lands. When they reached the western
border of the United States, in Louisiana, some kept on going—into the
Mexican border province of Texas. Slavery was technically illegal in
the republic of Mexico, but the writ of Mexico City did not extend to
a troublesome province being rapidly settled by Anglos. When in 1836
a group of American settlers led by Stephen Austin and Sam Houston

led a rebellion against the Mexican government and established an independent slaveholding republic, it was not a great surprise. No sooner had the independence of Texas been proclaimed than southerners were plotting to annex it to the United States.

In the early 1840s, the question of Texas annexation divided Americans. This was one of the first of a series of issues during the 20 years leading up to the Civil War in which the Democratic Party became the vehicle for expressing southern slaveowners' interests. The election of 1844 pitted Democrat James K. Polk, a vigorous supporter of Texas annexation, against the Whig standard bearer Henry Clay who opposed it. Polk was a little-known former Tennessee governor and slaveholder who received the nomination only because the favorite, former President Martin Van Buren of New York had publicly opposed annexation in order to avoid stirring up controversy over slavery. Frustratingly for the Whigs, Polk's narrow victory, one of the closest in any presidential election in American history, was probably due to James G. Birney, the candidate of the antislavery Liberty Party who took votes away from Clay in crucial northern states, especially New York. Both Clay and Polk were slaveowners, and the parties they represented had strength in both sections, but the choice between them was fateful for the nation. Had Clay become president in March 1845, it is unlikely that there would have been war with Mexico. Clay and most of his fellow Whigs worried that acquiring new territories with alien, Catholic populations would undermine republican values and distract attention from the need for economic development. Polk was an instinctive expansionist. Everyone knew that annexing Texas would provoke war with Mexico, and for many of Polk's southern supporters, that was the whole point. Texas was only to be the beginning. Calhoun and Jefferson Davis, now a Mississippi senator, were among those for whom expansion into the southwest was essential for the protection of slavery. Several new slave states could be created, helping to maintain southern power in the senate and the presidential Electoral College. Many southerners argued that the opening up of new cotton fields in the southwest would create more social mobility within southern white society. A few other slavery defenders in both North and South adopted a slightly different approach, arguing that more land open to slavery would spread slavery more thinly, making it a less dangerous and in some senses less visible institution.

The prospect of the annexation of Mexican territory was at least as appealing to many northerners. The motivation for nonslaveholders can be summed up in one seductive word: California. The abundance and fertility of California was mythical, and the temptation to oust the creaking authority of Mexico overwhelming. Not long after assuming office, Polk dispatched an emissary to Mexico offering to purchase California but the Mexican government refused to negotiate. Polk ordered US troops into the vast region between the Nueces River and the Rio Grande (now the western half of the state of Texas), land claimed by both nations. When fighting broke out, Polk claimed that blood had been shed on American soil and called for a declaration of war. War was supported by a majority of Americans, but it also stimulated passionate opposition. The fig leaf of self-defense was utterly unconvincing: in reality this was a straightforward war of aggression. Abraham Lincoln, then a one-term representative from Illinois, made a name for himself by introducing a series of resolutions in the House designed to expose the way in which the country had been misled into war by calling on the president to name the spot on American soil where Mexicans had allegedly attacked. Lincoln, like many other Whigs, was horrified by a war that seemed to undermine the republican experiment and threaten "Caesarism." Abolitionists were even more aghast. Garrison attacked the "cowardly pro-slavery war" as a naked bid for power by the Slave Power.

The Mexican War was probably the most successful war of imperial expansion in modern history. In the summer of 1846, a band of American insurrectionists proclaimed California as liberated from Mexican control and declared John C. Frémont, a dashing western explorer and adventurer, the de facto governor. In February 1847, General Zachary Taylor of Louisiana, a Whig and a slaveowner, defeated the Mexican forces under the control of Santa Anna in the battle of Buena Vista. In September, American forces commanded by General Winfield Scott occupied the Mexican capital city. Jefferson Davis served in the war with distinction alongside other West Point–trained officers whose names would later become famous, including George B. McClellan, Joseph Hooker, James Longstreet, Henry Halleck, George G. Meade, Joseph E. Johnston, Ulysses S. Grant, and Robert E. Lee. (William Tecumseh Sherman was also a junior officer, but missed the fighting, largely because he was sent to California by sea via Cape Horn.)

The fruits of the war were ratified in the Treaty of Guadaloupe Hidalgo. Mexico ceded a half a million square miles, or a third of its territorial area. All of present-day California, New Mexico, Arizona, Nevada, Utah and half of present-day Texas came into the Union under the treaty together with a non-Anglo population of about 75,000 Spanish-speaking Mexicans and over 150,000 Indians. In compensation the Americans paid 15 million dollars, a bargain which looked even more one-sided when, only a year later, gold was discovered in the Sierra Nevada Mountains in California. This was the treaty which established the familiar territorial shape of the United States. The only subsequent territorial gains in North America were a small strip of additional land purchased from Mexico in 1853 (the "Gadsden purchase") and Alaska, purchased from Russia in 1867 and for long afterwards not considered to be of any economic importance.

Victory in the Mexican War was not especially costly in military terms (some 13,000 American soldiers died, mostly from disease), but it set in train events that in the space of just 12 years were to rend the Union apart. The issue it created was whether to allow slavery into this vast new territory. Before the Mexican cession, there was no possibility of any extension of slavery. The last time that the Union had faced the issue of whether to extend slavery into newly acquired territories—after the Louisiana Purchase—a settlement had been reached with the Missouri Compromise of 1820, which created a permanent dividing line between slave and free territory. By the late 1840s, the southern portion of the Louisiana Purchase territory had already been organized into the states of Louisiana, Alabama and Mississippi. The remaining unorganized territory—in present-day Kansas, Nebraska, Wyoming and the Dakotas—was north of the compromise line and would therefore eventually have to come into the Union as free states. Due largely to high rates of immigration into the northeastern cities from Europe, the population of the free states was increasing more rapidly than that of the South, so the slave states were already becoming an ever-smaller minority in the House of Representatives. In the Senate, where the states were equally represented irrespective of population size, the South retained much greater strength, but even here the parity of the early years of the republic was threatened unless new slave state territory could be found. Hence the importance of the Mexican cession to southerners.

Whigs who had opposed the war in the first place had long predicted the confrontation over slavery that would result. Before the war, the party had agreed on a policy of "no territory" in order to keep the northern and southern wings of the party together. Congressman Waddy Thompson, a rare South Carolina Whig, made the case to his fellow southerners that annexation of a vast new territory would benefit northern free laborers more than it would benefit slaveowners because of the practical problems and capital costs of setting up a slave system. His northern colleagues made the same case against territorial expansion for opposite reasons: that new lands would give a new lease of life to slavery and increase the political power of slaveowners within the Union. But it was not a Whig but a northern Democrat, David Wilmot of Pennsylvania, who introduced the resolution that polarized sectional opinion. The "Wilmot Proviso" moved that slavery be banned in any territory gained from Mexico. Under Mexican law, slavery was outlawed. Wilmot argued that he simply wanted to maintain the status quo. Wilmot may have been the man who placed slavery at the heart of national politics, but he was no Garrison. He was motivated, he explained, not by any "squeamish sensitiveness upon the subject of slavery, nor morbid sympathy with the slave." Instead his concern was that if slavery were legal the opportunities for free white laborers to settle and prosper in the new territories would be reduced. His aim, he declared, was to "preserve for free white labor a fair country, a rich inheritance, where the sons of toil, of my own race and own color, can live without the disgrace which association with negro slavery brings upon free labor."[15] With complete plausibility, Wilmot insisted that he was indifferent to slavery where it already existed. In any case, by the late 1840s, slavery was legal only in states, not in territories, and Congress had no constitutional authority to interfere with slavery in a state. Territories were a different matter; no one up until now had disputed the right of Congress to settle the issue one way or another in areas that had not yet been granted full statehood.

The Wilmot Proviso was a grenade lobbed into the delicate balance of the national two-party system. The potential for sectional breakdown was immediately apparent. Northern congressmen voted 83—12 in favor of the Proviso, and southerners 67—2 against. Party lines mattered not at all in the face of an issue that raised in stark form the fundamental question of the status of slavery as either an institution "on the course of ultimate extinction" or one that was fully accepted as legitimate. The Proviso passed the House on three occasions, but each time it was blocked in the Senate, where the South still had the votes to wield a veto. The Wilmot Proviso polarized opinion on both sides. Most northern newspapers enthusiastically backed it, in the South, there was near-universal condemnation. In the senate John C. Calhoun argued that since the territories were the common property of all the states and were merely held in trust by Congress, southerners had an equal claim to the land and could not be discriminated against by being told that they could not take their peculiar species of property there.

Why did southerners push to extend slavery? One reason was rooted in the vulnerability of slavery to being challenged. Even while pro-slavery defenders in the Indian summer of American slavery asserted that slaves were happy with their lot, their words were belied by the concerted efforts of slaveowners to shore up their legal rights and the security cordon around their ever-vulnerable institution. The more northerners attacked the legitimacy of slavery, the more southerners demanded assurances that it would be respected. From the point of view of southern political leaders, the issue was one of equal rights within the Union. All they wanted, they repeated tirelessly, was for their right to take property into the territories to be respected. The Georgia Whig Alexander H. Stephens insisted that the territorial issue was important not so much because he expected slavery to expand into all the areas under discussion, but because it involved the important principle of "constitutional right and equality . . . A people who would maintain their rights must look to principles much more than to practical results. . . . If the slightest encroachments of power are permitted or submitted to in the Territories they may reach the states ultimately."[16] A second, related, motivation was the fear that southerners were losing ground in national politics and that more free states would forever prevent southerners from wielding effective national power. Since slave-owners needed to control the federal government in order to protect slavery, this was a frightening prospect. Calhoun's protégé, the South Carolina planter James Henry Hammond, warned that adoption of the Wilmot Proviso would ensure ten new free states west of the Missis-sippi, and was frank about the implications: "Long before the North gets this vast accession of strength she will ride over us rough shod, proclaim freedom to our slaves and reduce us to the condition of Haiti . . . If we do not act now, we deliberately consign our children, not our posterity, but our children, to the flames."

Just as Whigs had predicted, the slavery extension issue was insep-arable from the deeper issue of the future of slavery. If southerners felt that their honor was at stake, northerners were increasingly concerned that slavery expansion was threatening the nation as they understood it. For many northerners, the question of the expansion of slavery into the territories was not an abstract issue, but a question of individual opportunity. A Kentucky-born Whig, Richard Oglesby, made this point effectively:

> I came myself from a slave state. Poor white girls washed there all
> day long over a hot and steaming tub, and under a blazing sun, for

ten cents a day. And why was this? Simply because a negro wench, equally strong, could be hired for that price. In Kentucky I was a laboring man. I hired out for six dollars a month. Why couldn't I get more? Because a negro man, of equal physical strength, could be hired for $75 per year. He could be fed on coarser food than I, and would be submissive ... Do you want such an institution in your territories?[17]

The migration of free laborers into the western territories would enable the United States to escape from the classic Malthusian dilemma: the population could expand, and wages would remain high and the possibility of economic advancement through hard work would remain undiminished. In the battle over the Wilmot Proviso, northern newspapers began to portray the South as an alien power, a cuckoo in the nest. Horace Greeley's popular *New York Tribune* argued that for years "a spirit has been rampant in our public affairs, styling itself 'the South,' and demanding that the whole nation should fall down and worship whatever graven images it chooses to set up."[18] Increasing numbers of northerners—not just abolitionists—believed that if the new territories were allowed to become a "vast slave empire", the character of the nation would be changed forever and the "right to rise" for the honest white workingman would be sacrificed in the interest of a slaveholding class. No matter that most of the new territory was almost certainly unsuitable for cotton cultivation. Perhaps only southern California offered the right climactic conditions for slavery expansion on a serious scale. The fight over slavery in the territories was not, as one historian once claimed, a fight over an "imaginary negro in an impossible place."[19] Each side saw the question not only as a point of deep principle, but also as an issue of great practical political significance. Ominously, Horace Greeley's irritation at the presumption of power-hungry southerners captured a broader public mood in the North. Increasingly, northerners began to define the American republic exclusively in terms of the virtues of northern free labor society and in opposition to the South.

One group of northern antislavery politicians saw an opportunity in the crisis over slavery extension. For several years, antislavery reformers like Salmon P. Chase of Ohio, a former Democrat, and the Whiggish Bostonian lawyer Charles Sumner, had wanted to cut loose from the compromises intrinsic to the two national parties and create a new "fusion" movement that would unite in one party those who opposed the extension of slavery. With what in retrospect appear to be unrealistically high hopes of breaking the mold of the two-party system, delegates gathered in Buffalo, New York, in August 1848 to found the Free Soil Party. The nominee was none other than former Democratic President Martin Van Buren of New York, who brought with him a faction of northern Democrats (known as "Barnburners") who supported the Wilmot Proviso. Evangelical Protestant Whigs also participated in large numbers. Despite the relative conservatism of the Free Soil platform, some abolitionists, including Frederick Douglass, gave a cautious endorsement to this new departure.

If the national two-party system was to be preserved, and the sectional chasm that Wilmot had opened to be bridged, a new approach was needed, one which adroitly circumvented the Wilmot Proviso without endorsing Calhoun-style slave expansionism. A number of politicians in both parties alighted on the idea of resolving the impasse by passing the buck. Rather than take a decision then and there on the status of slavery in the new territories, Congress would devolve the matter to the territories themselves. This scheme had its origins in the desperate attempts by both political parties to find a way of bridging the sectional chasm that Wilmot had opened up. Lewis Cass, a Michigan Democrat who was his party's candidate in the 1848 presidential election, demonstrated a masterful rhetorical flourish when he called this solution "popular sovereignty," a term which seemed to identify the devolution of the decision about slavery to the territories with the unassailable democratic principles of the republic and the Jacksonian tradition of westward expansion and popular self-government.

Much to almost everyone's surprise, Cass was narrowly defeated in the 1848 election by the Whigs' nominee General Zachary Taylor, the Mexican War hero and a Louisiana slave holder who reveled in the nickname "Old Rough and Ready." Essentially, the Whigs had decided that the only way to avoid further loss of support was to find an attractive candidate and leave the squabbling about policy until after the election. The Free Soil Party polled far more votes than the more radical Liberty Party had in 1844, but arguably had less impact on the final result since they took votes in roughly equal numbers from Democrats and Whigs. The Free Soil Party may have failed, but it was a movement of huge significance for the relationship between the slavery issue and the party system. What Free Soilers had realized was that the free states now had a sufficiently large population that if they could be united, they would produce sufficient Electoral College votes to elect a president even if the South voted as a block for someone else. For the first time in the short history of the American republic, a political party was making a serious bid for national power by appealing to only one section.

COMPROMISE AND ITS CONSEQUENCES

The conflict over slavery extension dominated national politics for two years. The political momentum for compromise was especially strong in the South. To the despair of southern radicals like Calhoun who wanted to create a united southern block, a majority of southern Democratic congressmen remained convinced that only the national Democratic Party could protect southern interests. The loyalty of southern Whigs like Alexander H. Stephens of Georgia to their party was shored up by the presence of a Whig slaveholder in the White House. Although some radical southern politicians threatened secession and even discussed privately plans for the war that might follow, a southern convention that met in Nashville, Tennessee, in June 1850 rejected secession out of hand and reaffirmed the commitment of the South to the Union. John C. Calhoun died in 1850 a frustrated man. Before he did so, the grand old man of Whiggery, Henry Clay of Kentucky, strode onto the national stage to offer a set of compromise proposals. Appealing to patriotism and pragmatism, he urged northerners to recognize that since the Mexican cession was unsuitable for plantation agriculture, their insistence on the Wilmot Proviso was needlessly provocative. "Act as lovers of liberty," he told the antislavery forces, "and lovers, above all, of this Union."[20]

Eventually, a series of measures, collectively known as the Compromise of 1850, were passed by both houses of Congress. Iced milk and pickled cucumbers may have played a role in this legislative breakthrough since President Taylor's Independence Day snack in the broiling heat is alleged to have been the cause of his sudden death from gastroenteritis. The slaveowner president had been pushing his own alternative scheme and his sudden demise opened the way for the up and coming young Democratic senator from Illinois, Stephen A. Douglas, to steer the measures through the Senate. California, deluged with gold-diggers, was fast-tracked into admission as a free state without having to formally pass through territorial status. In a victory for antislavery campaigners, the slave trade was abolished in the District of Columbia, the tiny administrative area containing the national capital carved out of swampy land on the banks of the Potomac River and administered directly by a congressional committee. But these advances for the antislavery cause were counterbalanced by a stringent new Fugitive Slave Act, which provided for a massive extension of federal authority, making it a crime to hide a runaway slave from the authorities. The veteran Massachusetts Whig senator Daniel Webster, who had close ties to the antislavery community in Boston, reluctantly supported the new Fugitive Slave Act in the interests of national harmony, and for the remaining two years of his life he suffered the obloquy of his constituents who saw him as a traitor. On the critical issue of the status of slavery in the non-Californian part of the Mexican cession, Congress endorsed the "popular sovereignty" solution. There was a critical ambiguity to popular sovereignty over the precise point at which a territory was allowed to ban slavery, which enabled it to be supported by southern Whigs like Alexander Stephens as well as moderate northerners like the new president, New Yorker Millard Fillmore. If a territory could delay a ban until it applied for statehood, slaveowners would have at least a theoretical chance of populating the territory and determining the outcome in their favor. This, at least, was the argument that southern supporters of the Compromise measures used to their constituents.

As many historians have pointed out, a closer look at the way in which congressmen voted revealed that this was no true compromise. Douglas' main contribution to the passage of the measures was to break up Clay's omnibus bill into its individual components and to construct separate coalitions to support each one. Southerners broke party lines to vote against any restriction on slavery, and a substantial number of northern Democrats joined northern Whigs in opposing them. Only a minority of congressmen—mostly southern Whigs, some northern Democrats and minority of conservative northern Whigs—formed a genuine compromise block, supporting all the measures. In retrospect we know that the resolution of the slavery question hammered out with such effort in 1850 did not last. But at the time it was widely hailed for its statesmanlike resolution of a seemingly intractable problem. The Compromise removed the sting of slavery from national politics, at least for a short time. Southern radicals and northern Free Soilers had been marginalized.

In 1854 Ulysses S. Grant had resigned from the army after distinguished service in the Mexican War with the permanent rank of captain, only to try his hand and fail successively as a farmer, debt collector, engineer and clerk. Much later, in his memoirs, he (or his ghost writer, rumored to be Mark Twain) offered a perceptive retrospective analysis of the causes of the sectional crisis. "Slavery was an institution that required unusual guarantees for its security wherever it existed," he observed. Since the people of the free states were in the majority, and since they "would naturally have but little sympathy" with demands upon them for the protection of the peculiar institution, "the people of the South were dependent upon keeping control of the general government to secure the perpetuation of" slavery. It was this determination to, in effect, nationalize slavery which the North could not permit. "Prior to the time of these encroachments," Grant wrote, "the great majority of the people of the North had no particular quarrel with slavery, so long as they were not forced to have it themselves. But they were not willing to play the role of police for the South in the protection of this particular institution."[21]

It was this last point—the requirement to be active agents in the protection of slavery not merely acquiesce from the sidelines—that began to erode the sense of the northern public that the Compromise of 1850 was a fair and viable settlement of the slavery problem. One of the purposes of the Fugitive Slave Act in the eyes of its southern supporters was to test the North's commitment to respect southern whites. Runaway slaves undoubtedly posed an economic problem for individual slaveowners, but overall the numbers involved were too small to seriously threaten an institution with over three and a half million slaves. The new Fugitive Slave Law mattered as a symbol of the political power of slaveowners—a political power that was vital for the protection of slavery in the long run. "Respect and enforce the Fugitive Slave Law as it stands," one pro-slavery editor warned the North. "If not, WE WILL LEAVE YOU!"[22] And southern Unionists also set great store by the attitude of the North to the Act. Henry Clay complained of obstruction to the act that "except for the whiskey rebellion, there has been no instance in which there was so violent and forcible obstruction to the laws of the United States."[23]

By demanding that free men be shackled and returned to slavery against the wishes of the local community, the Fugitive Slave Act made the formerly abstract issue of the corrosive impact of slavery on republican government frighteningly concrete. In the years after the passage of the Act, a number of high-profile cases of runaway slaves—or allegedly runaway slaves—being returned to bondage electrified the North. The most famous was the case of Anthony Burns, a black man who had been living as a free man in Boston for several decades. In 1854, when, after a protracted legal battle, Massachusetts state authorities refused to arrest him, the agents of the slaveowner, determined to press the case on a point of principle, demanded, under the terms of the Fugitive Slave Act, that the federal government intervene. An estimated 50,000 Bostonians shouting "shame!" and "kidnappers!" watched in horror and outrage as the manacled Burns was marched by federal troops to the wharfside to be taken back South into slavery. Buildings were draped in funereal crepe; church bells tolled. Even conservative Bostonians were aroused by the appalling scene. "When it was all over, and I was left alone in my office," wrote one old Whig, "I put my hands in my face and wept. I could do nothing less."[24]

Such emotionally charged scenes generated a greater consciousness of the human horror of slavery on the part of northerners, just as they bound together the image of the degraded and humiliated slave with the degradation of the republic and the humiliation of the free white people of Massachusetts who had had to stand by impotently watching tyranny in action. A large section of northern society, perhaps even a small majority, came to see not only the Fugitive Slave Act, but the institution it supported and the politics it created, as a moral outrage. "The Fugitive Slave Bill has especially been of positive service to the anti-slavery movement," argued Frederick Douglass. "It at once dramatized the "horrible character of slavery toward the slave," exposed "the arrogant and over-bearing spirit of the slave States toward the free States" and aroused a "spirit of manly resistance" among northern blacks."[25] For many Americans, the images of grief and outrage that surrounded the Anthony Burns case must have reminded them of the emotions stirred up by the publishing sensation of the decade, *Uncle Tom's Cabin*, by Harriet Beecher Stowe, which first appeared in book form in 1852 (it had been serialized the previous year as in the anti-slavery journal *The National Era*). *Uncle Tom's Cabin* played on the anxieties of middle-class Victorian America about the continued existence of slavery. Stowe, a member of a distinguished family of abolitionists and Congregationalist ministers (her brother, Henry Ward Beecher, was the most famous preacher of his age), saw slavery as an affront to civilized values, an anomaly in a society that believed in scientific, technological and social progress, and which valued hard work, thrift, self-control and individual responsibility.

Stowe captured a growing northern sensibility that slavery was something truly horrible. A large number of northerners, influenced by a powerful evangelical subculture, saw their republic as a righteous crusade against sin. In the autumn of 1854, Caroline Seabury, a young New England woman, journeyed South to take up a position as a teacher at an expensive girls' school in Columbus, Mississippi. Initially unconcerned about slavery—her first impressions of blacks were that they were a "happy, careless, thoughtless race"—she was profoundly upset when she witnessed a slave hiring, in which slaves who were surplus to requirement on a plantation were hired out for a year to the highest bidder. When a woman whose slave husband had been recently killed by their master realized that she was to be separated from her children, Seabury said, I "could not keep back my own tears, though they were unobserved by others."[26] But Seabury could not take refuge in the notion that such abuses were a problem only for the South. The Fugitive Slave law had destroyed once and for all the fiction that slavery was a purely sectional institution. Slavery was a national sin. The most hateful villain in *Uncle Tom's Cabin*, the tyrannical slave driver Simon Legree, is a displaced Yankee while one of the most sympathetic characters is the Harriet Shelby, the deeply religious plantation mistress.

The sentiments and sentimentality revealed by the immense popularity of *Uncle Tom's Cabin* were, in effect, a challenge to the nationalism of men like Henry Clay and Daniel Webster. The two Whig patriarchs represented a grand tradition of compromise that went back to the founding fathers. They believed that capitalist development combined with an earnest nationalism should trump sectionalism and slavery. In 1852, within a few months of one another, both men died. With them, James H. Hammond noted wryly in his diary, died "the last links of the chain of the Union."[27] Within two years, events were to make that remark seem prophetic.

2 Political Crisis and the Resort to War

The road to war is one that has been charted many times since 1861. But however familiar the landmarks might be, their significance in relation to one another continues to be hotly disputed. The story is often told with a pleasing symmetry: the middle ground was eroded from both sides, as North and South became ever more unwilling to compromise. It is certainly true that issues that could be finessed in 1850 could not even be civilly discussed ten years later. But the 12-year crisis that led to war was messier than some of the more teleological accounts might suggest. In his second inaugural address in 1865, Abraham Lincoln looked back to the origins of the conflict that had consumed so many lives. Slavery, he argued, "constituted a peculiar and a powerful interest. All knew that this interest was somehow the cause of the war."[1] That "somehow" is the crux of the analytical problem. If Americans had rubbed along together half slave and half free for seventy-odd years without serious bloodshed, why all of a sudden was slavery a problem insoluble short of war? Sectional conflict need not necessarily have led to war, at least not the war that actually happened. Simply identifying the existence of slavery in the southern states and the reliance on free labor in the North is not a sufficient explanation, even if it is a necessary one. Even granted that slavery could not coexist easily within the same polity as free labor, there are surely other imaginable outcomes short of a destructive four-year war—as the other slaveowning parts of the New World, all of whom avoided such a confrontation, demonstrate. The actions and the assumptions made by particular politicians at particular moments decisively shaped the coming of the war, its timing and its nature.

THE KANSAS NEBRASKA ACT

The revival of the Democratic Party in both North and South after the Compromise of 1850 seemed to convince Stephen A. Douglas that slavery was an issue that could be marginalized by the expedient of not talking about it. The popular sovereignty solution for the Mexican cession was not especially popular with anyone, but it had worked in the sense of kicking the issue into touch. The relative success of the 1850 Compromise induced Douglas to introduce into the senate in 1854 one of the most ill-judged pieces of legislation in the history of the republic. In the course of his meteoric rise to the top of his party, the rotund but diminutive "little Giant" had enthusiastically championed economic development and territorial expansion, two aims that, unlike many Whigs, he believed were entirely compatible. It was natural, then, that the Illinois senator should champion the creation of a great new transcontinental railroad that would connect the settled east and the newly acquired lands on the Pacific coast. In between lay the "great American desert"—arid land occupied by Indians and a few white traders—that had previously been regarded as so unsuitable for agriculture that the land had not yet attracted enough settlers to have been granted official territorial status. Douglas feared that no one would invest in a railroad or land until some form of government was organized. As a major railroad investor and land speculator himself, Douglas also had a financial stake in the outcome. Unlike the Mexican cession, the status of slavery in this region was supposedly a settled question: the Missouri Compromise of 1820 had banned it. But southern Democrats made clear that they would block any measure that would lead eventually to the admission of one or more new free states. Choosing to elide the very different circumstances of land that had already been declared free three decades previously, Douglas reached for the same solution that had appeared to work in 1850. His bill proposed to divide the region into two territories—Kansas and Nebraska—in both of which, the status of slavery would be determined by "popular sovereignty." To clarify the implications of this for his southern allies, the final version of the bill included an explicit repeal of the Missouri Compromise.

For Douglas, popular sovereignty was the perfect solution. It derived from the principles of self-government on which the republic was based. At times he even managed to argue that it was essentially an antislavery measure: "There is but one possible way in which slavery can be abolished," Douglas told a northern audience, "and that is by leaving a State, according to the principle of the Kansas–Nebraska bill, perfectly free to form and regulate its institutions in its own way. That was the principle on which this Republic was founded, and it is under the operation of that principle that we have been able to preserve the Union thus far." His Kansas–Nebraska bill, he hoped, would settle the slavery extension question for all time, allowing the country to concentrate on more pressing matters like economic expansion.

In truth, Douglas knew that there would be plenty of northerners who opposed the repeal of the Missouri Compromise, but he calculated that he could unite the Democratic Party behind the measure, which in turn would set the stage for his own nomination for the presidency. He was wrong. Thanks to Douglas's parliamentary skills and the heavy deployment of presidential patronage to wavering northern Democrats, the Kansas–Nebraska bill became law. But it provoked outrage in the North, split the Democratic Party, hastened the collapse of the Whig party, and created the conditions for the rise of an exclusively Northern party, the Republicans. Across the free states, public meetings were held to protest the repeal of the Missouri Compromise, and the author of the bill was attacked as a lackey of the slaveowners. Douglas disconsolately told a friend that he could have traveled home to Chicago by the light of his burning effigy.

That southern political leaders, with their millions of dollars invested in slaves and their conscious and subconscious fears for the preservation of the southern racial order, should seize this chance to demand, as they saw it, equality of respect within the Union is not surprising. Southern whites, whether or not they were slaveowners, almost all agreed that slavery promoted equality among white men and ensured liberty by making capitalist exploitation of white workers unnecessary. But their demand was not that slavery should be extended to the North, merely that no artificial restraints should be placed on their ability to develop their own society. In their eyes they were not the aggressors.

What Douglas was trying to do in 1854 was to resolve the slavery question once and for all. By organizing the Kansas and Nebraska territories, Congress would have settled—at least in the sense of devolving to the local level—the status of slavery in all the land under American control in North America. Much criticized by historians who know in retrospect that it was a failure, Douglas' Nebraska policy was a logical outgrowth of the history and ideology of the Democratic Party and, in the context of the time, a perfectly rational, if risky, strategic response to the challenges it faced. Douglas consciously departed from the strategy of muffling discussion of slavery, but he did so in the hope of building a national coalition of southerners and northern Democrats that would marginalize northern antislavery advocates once and for all. Douglas himself appears to have been essentially indifferent to slavery as a moral problem and in this regard he undoubtedly spoke for many northerners. As events were to prove, however, even Douglas' charisma could not convince a majority in the North that the overturning of the

Missouri Compromise line was a price worth paying to secure national harmony. Popular sovereignty was a brilliant theoretical solution to the problem of slavery in American politics, but in real life it was a catastrophic failure. Up until the 1850s, slavery and freedom had been carefully segregated geographically. Douglas recklessly abandoned that circumspect policy, allowing free soil and pro-slavery forces to grapple with one another in the same territory and galvanizing into political action even those who had previously ranked the issue as low on their political agendas.

Abraham Lincoln was one of many Whigs who felt that the Kansas–Nebraska bill threw down a challenge that had to be faced. Having had a modest career in Illinois politics, and one term in the US House of Representatives, Lincoln had retreated to his law practice when the Nebraska bill was published. In a speech in Peoria, Illinois, in 1854 Lincoln expressed the shame and anger so many northerners felt at the expansion of slavery. "Our republican robe is soiled and trailed in the dust," he declared, "Let us repurify it. Let us turn and wash it white, in the spirit, if not the blood of the Revolution." He did not oppose slavery where it had always existed, in the southern states, but wanted it to be an exception to the general rule of freedom, on the path to eventual extinction. "Let us turn slavery from its claims of 'moral right,' back upon its existing legal rights, and its arguments of 'necessity.' Let us return it to the position our fathers gave it; and there let it rest in peace." He continued with words that, with their evocation of the universal mission of the American republic, foreshadowed his later wartime speeches and set out a clear narrative of where the nation had come from and where it should go in the future:

> Let us re-adopt the Declaration of Independence, and with it, the practices, and policy, which harmonize with it. Let north and south—let all Americans—let all lovers of liberty everywhere— join in the great and good work. If we do this, we shall not only have saved the Union; but we shall have so saved it as to make, and to keep it, forever worthy of the saving. We shall have so saved it, that the succeeding millions of free happy people, the world over, shall rise up, and call us blessed, to the latest generations.[2]

A journalist for the *Chicago Tribune* recalled that the 45-year old lawyer's speech "went to the heart because it came from the heart . . . Mr. Lincoln's eloquence was of the higher type which produced conviction in others because of the conviction of the speaker himself. His listeners felt that he believed every word he said, and that, like Martin Luther, he would go to the stake rather than abate one jot or tittle of it."[3]

Two Free Soilers from Ohio, Senator Salmon P. Chase and Representative Joshua Giddings, issued a manifesto entitled *Appeal of the Independent Democrats* which condemned the repeal of the Missouri Compromise as a "gross violation of a sacred pledge [the Missouri Compromise]" and warned that Douglas was conspiring with southerners to convert free territory which was rightfully open to northern free laborers into a "dreary region of despotism, inhabited by masters and slaves." The *Appeal* was a highly effective piece of political propaganda masterfully targeted not at the already sympathetic antislavery constituency but at a broader audience of northerners who had been brought up to believe that republics could only be maintained by constant vigilance against the threat of tyranny. They made clear that their purpose was not the abolitionists' aim of immediate extermination, but to place slavery back on the course of ultimate extinction. "Whatever apologies may be offered for the toleration of slavery in the States," wrote Chase and Giddings, "none can be urged for its extension into Territories where it does not exist." Veterans of the Free Soil party of 1848, Chase, Giddings and their supporters hoped to stimulate a massive electoral realignment. If the two-party system of Whigs and Democrats could be broken down, they hoped, then a new, sectional party could be created in the North that might be powerful enough to halt the spread of slavery.

At first that was exactly what seemed to be happening. The anti-Nebraska protest meetings and resolutions in state legislatures united partisan foes as no other issue had done. "Thank God," one Bostonian wrote to Charles Sumner, "the chains that have bound the people to their old organizations have been snapped asunder."[4] An encouraging sign for the advocates of realignment was the disarray in the northern Democratic Party. A majority of New England and New York Democrats refused to back Douglas' bill, and even in his own state of Illinois a sizeable minority of his own party opposed him. The defection of a large number of northern Democrats over the Nebraska bill not only weakened the party in states like Illinois where they had hitherto been dominant, but it increased the power of southerners within the party, further alienating antislavery northerners.

Over the next two years "fusion" conventions were held by factions of Whigs, Democrats and Free Soilers to nominate joint tickets. They called themselves by many names—anti-Nebraska tickets, People's parties and Republicans. The latter was the name popularized by Horace Greeley of the *New York Tribune* and first adopted by a fusion convention of Free Soilers and Whigs in Michigan in July 1854. The name "Republican" was appealing because, unlike the Liberty and Free Soil Parties, it suggested that their concern was with republican liberty not the fate of black slaves per se. Like the 1848 Free Soilers, the anti-Nebraska fusion movements fused antislavery language with an appeal to northern whites' self-interest and the assertion that they were the conservative protectors of the inheritance of the Revolution from the evil designs of the Slave Power.

Despite their fury at the Nebraska bill, some Whigs, including Lincoln and the antislavery New York Senator William H. Seward, initially kept their distance from fusion movements, hoping that the Whigs could capitalize on Democratic splits, and use the anger created by the repeal of the Missouri Compromise to revitalize their party. Three factors made such hopes futile. The first was that in many parts of the North, the Whigs had been severely weakened by defections and a lack of organization even before the Kansas–Nebraska Act. The second was that while northern Whigs could run strong campaigns against the Kansas–Nebraska Act in local and state elections, when the all-important 1856 presidential election arrived they would face the same problem they had faced in the previous two elections of having to negotiate with the southern wing of the party, and, tellingly, the last two Whig presidential candidates had been southerners. The third reason why the northern Whig party was essentially dead by 1854 was that anti-Nebraska fusion movements were not the only groups challenging for the anti-Democratic vote. In 1854 and 1855 an even more powerful challenge arose in the form of the anti-immigrant American party—or, as it was popularly known due to the secret pledge that members took, the Know-Nothing Party.

Know-Nothingism was the most powerful political manifestation of anti-immigrant—or more precisely anti-Catholic—sentiment in nineteenth-century America. It was especially strong in the northeast where the majority of the three million immigrants from Ireland and Germany who came into the United States in the late 1840s and 1850s settled. It was a much weaker force in the Midwest, but gathered strength in the South as well, largely among Whigs who, like their former copartisans in the North, were searching for a new anti-Democrat alternative. Know-Nothingism was a grassroots populist movement that exploited the anxieties of Americans in the 1850s about the pace of social change and the perception that politicians and the existing party system were hopelessly corrupt. It promised to renew and purify the republic, to return virtue and honor to public life through the power of popular mobilization. Stephen Miller, one of the leaders of the movement, explained that its purpose was to "take from the professional politicians the government of States and cities." Whig and Democratic leaders alike, Know-Nothings charged, had treated "this country as the mere skittle ground of gambling politicians."[5]

REPUBLICANISM AND THE SLAVE POWER

By the time of the 1856 presidential election, the new Republican Party, defined by its absolute opposition to the extension of slavery into the territories, had overtaken the Know-Nothings as the primary anti-Democratic force in the North. Faced with the collapse of the old Whig party, important local leaders like Lincoln and Seward joined the new movement. In areas where the Know-Nothings were strong, Republicans co-opted their anti-Catholic prejudices wholesale. Republicans also borrowed an antiparty political style from Know-Nothings, promising to purify sordid partisan-ridden Washington. The Know-Nothings' status as grassroots insurgents was also compromised by their nomination of the former Whig President Millard Fillmore as their candidate in 1856. Ultimately, Republicans were more successful than Know-Nothings in forging a coherent message which convinced a majority of northern voters that the republic could only be preserved by uniting behind a truly sectional party. The Republican campaign in 1856 was ignited by indignation at a brutal assault on antislavery Senator Charles Sumner in the chamber of the US Senate by a South Carolina congressman, Preston Brooks. To Republicans this act of violence encapsulated the barbarity of the South, the poisonous cultural consequences of slavery. Southerners rejoiced, presenting Congressman Brooks with ornamental canes to replace the one he had broken on Sumner's head. The Republican presidential candidate, the western explorer John C. Frémont, held firmly expressed antislavery views which endeared him to the new party's core supporters, but he did not have a sufficiently broad appeal to win the election. Once again, the Democrats won the White House by deploying their old trick of nominating a "northern man of southern principles"—in 1856 it was James Buchanan—who could hold the disparate wings of their party together. The new Republican movement had established a powerful base from which they could launch their next bid for national power. Moderate southerners were alarmed by the appearance of a powerful block of Republican congressmen in Washington.

Meanwhile events in Kansas were further inflaming sectional opinion. The consequences of popular sovereignty, it became clear, was a low-level civil war among settlers. Many of the free state settlers who rushed into the new territory were funded by antislavery groups in New England. Pro-slavery settlers from neighboring slave state Missouri were actively supported by guns and money from the South. Acts of appalling brutality were committed on both sides but newspapers in each section blamed the other for instigating the violence (Republicans linked the Kansas Civil War to Preston Brooks' attack with the slogan "Bleeding Sumner, Bleeding Kansas"). Probably the worst single atrocity was committed on the night of May 24, 1856, by a little-known abolitionist from New England, John Brown, and a posse of men, several of whom were his own sons. In what Brown later claimed was retribution for earlier attacks on free state settlers, Brown's party descended on a small group of cabins at Pottawatomie Creek and massacred in cold blood five pro-slavery settlers with heavy cavalry broadswords.

Pro-slavery settlers won the first round, establishing a provisional government in Lecompton and writing a pro-slavery state constitution which they then "ratified" with dubious legality in the face of a boycott from free state settlers who had established their own rival government in Lawrence. Even Stephen Douglas was appalled by this blatantly undemocratic process and opposed the admission of Kansas as a slave state on the basis of the Lecompton constitution. His objection was primarily procedural—the pro-slavery settlers were making a mockery of popular sovereignty as Douglas had, perhaps naively, envisaged it—but his stance incurred the wrath of his former southern party allies. Once again the northern Democrats were split, some siding with their most charismatic leader, Douglas, and others with the Buchanan administration which, to the surprise of some, backed the Lecompton constitution.

Serious as Bleeding Kansas was for the prospect of finding a compromise settlement of the slavery extension issue, the most fateful blow was struck by the southern-dominated Supreme Court in the notorious *Dred Scott* case of 1857. *Dred Scott* was a slave who sued for his freedom on the grounds that his master—20 years earlier—had taken him into a US territory where slavery was prohibited by the terms of the Missouri Compromise. The Court decided by a majority of seven to two against the plaintive. A majority of the justices argued that since Scott was black he was by definition not a US citizen and was therefore not allowed to bring suit in a federal court. Chief Justice Roger B. Taney of Maryland argued that at the time of the ratification of the Constitution—and, implicitly, ever since—blacks were "so far inferior that they had no rights which a white man was bound to respect." That was a provocation to antislavery politicians like Charles Sumner, who, while hardly free from the racism of his age, was a genuine advocate of equal rights. But this was not the most momentous, surprising or dramatic part of Taney's judgment. Having decided that Scott was not eligible to bring a suit at all, Taney nevertheless went on to examine the substance of the case, determining quite deliberately to use the authority of the court to intervene in the political row over the status of slavery in the territories. Using arguments that satisfied even the most die-hard Calhounite, Taney ruled that Scott was not entitled to freedom because the now-overturned Missouri Compromise itself had been unconstitutional. The most important argument he used to make this case was that since slaves were just another kind of property a slaveowner could not be deprived of his slaves without the "due process" guaranteed by the fifth amendment to the Constitution. In other words, a man could no more have his slaves confiscated than he could his cattle or his land, whether by an act of Congress or a territorial legislature, unless he had committed some crime and been fairly tried in a court of law. This was an astounding line of argument, not least because, as Republicans were quick to point out, the next logical move would be to declare that the ability of states to exclude slavery was contrary to the due process clause as well. What was beyond doubt was that if Congress had no right to ban slavery in the territories then Douglas' popular sovereignty formulation was as much under threat as the desire of northerners to restore at least the Missouri Compromise line—or, in the case of the Republican Party, to exclude all further expansion of slavery.

If one of Taney's aims in preemptively declaring that the entire raison d'etre of the Republican Party—no more slavery—was unconstitutional had been to undermine the electoral position of the party, then his judgment was completely counterproductive. Republicans felt vindicated in making their case that they were the only protectors of northern interests. Northern state legislatures with Republican majorities fell over themselves to pass resolutions condemning the judgment. The *Dred*

Scott decision was yet more grist for the mills of the Republican conspiracy theorists. Slavery, argued the inaugural edition of the New England literary journal *Atlantic Monthly*, was like "the evil fairy of the nursery tale" present at the nation's birth to "curse it with her fatal words." Every generation had to rededicate the nation to freedom; this was a challenge comparable to that faced by their Revolutionary forebears. Will "we who broke the sceptre of King George . . . surrender ourselves, bound hand in foot in bonds of our weaving, into the hands of the slaveholding Philistines?" asked the *Atlantic Monthly,* rhetorically.[6]

The biggest loser from the *Dred Scott* decision (apart from Scott himself) was Stephen Douglas. Throughout his political career Douglas had walked a high-wire act, balancing the demands of slaveowners for reassurance and protection with the fear of northerners that the expansion of slavery threatened their own free labor society. Popular sovereignty had seemed to him to be a way of achieving that balance, but the Lecompton fight and the *Dred Scott* decision had made his case far harder to make. Douglas, the "Little Giant" of Illinois politics, was tested as never before in seven public debates in 1858 with Abraham Lincoln, encounters that have acquired a mythical status as the apogee of public engagement in rational critical discourse. The debates were reprinted verbatim in newspapers across the country and avidly commented on in the editorial columns.

Lincoln's main theme was the idea that the Slave Power, abetted by its northern Democratic accomplices, had corrupted the white south and was now attempting to maintain and expand its control of the national government at the expense of the millions of free white northerners who would no longer have access to economic opportunity in the west. "A house divided against itself cannot stand," Lincoln warned. In a world in which nations were being consolidated and slavery was disappearing throughout the Atlantic world, this was an issue which had to be confronted. Ultimately, Lincoln argued—not necessarily soon, but ultimately—the United States would become either a slave nation or a modern free-labor nation. The time had come to be clear about the final destination.

Douglas' response was essentially that Lincoln was being absurd: the nation had survived for 70 years without any one group imposing their moral sentiments on another, and that if the heat was taken out of the conflict, there was no reason why it could not continue to do so. Douglas had already made clear his opposition to the Lecompton constitution, and in response to Lincoln's probing in these debates he developed an ingenious means of reconciling the *Dred Scott* decision with popular sovereignty. Slavery, he pointed out, required positive legislation—a slave code, the creation of slave patrols, laws about the treatment of slaves—in order to survive. In effect he was saying that Taney might be right on a point of law about the unconstitutionality of banning slavery in a territory (and after all it had been Douglas who had been willing to overturn the Missouri Compromise in the first place), but that the de facto position was that settlers would have to take positive action if slavery was to exist. These debates, then, were not between antagonists at opposite ends of the argument. Both men thought the Lecompton constitution in Kansas was illegitimate; both agreed that slavery could not be touched in the states where it already existed. Lincoln, of course, was completely opposed to any extension of slavery, but in practice Douglas came close to that position as well, at times appearing to argue that since Kansas and Nebraska were unsuited to slavery, popular sovereignty was a different route to the same end.

The debates were all the more fascinating because these points of agreement forced the two men to uncover the underlying moral question that divided them. Douglas repeatedly said that he personally did not care whether slavery was voted up or down. In his concern for the economic advancement of the white man's republic, slavery was a distraction. It was not the threat to republican institutions that Lincoln claimed; it was simply, as southerners asserted, a peculiar species of property, a perfectly valid way of organizing race relations. In a line of attack that would be used again and again by Democrats throughout the Civil War, Douglas accused Lincoln of favoring racial equality. Lincoln was at pains to deny that charge—"I do not understand that because I do not want a negro woman for a slave I must necessarily want her for a wife. My understanding is that I can just let her alone," he said—and he made clear that he was opposed to "negro citizenship."[7] But he also insisted that all that he said and did about the question of slavery was based on a firm moral conviction—clearly not shared by Douglas—that slavery was simply wrong. Invoking an international liberal movement, the battle over slavery, he said, was part of

> the eternal struggle between these two principles—right and wrong—throughout the world. . . . The one is the common right of humanity and the other the divine right of kings. . . . No matter in what shape it comes, whether from the mouth of a king who seeks to bestride the people of his own nation and live by the fruit of

their labor, or from one race of men as an apology for enslaving another race, it is the same tyrannical principle.[8]

In a narrow sense, Douglas won the debates because the Democrats retained their majority in the Illinois legislature, which therefore returned him, rather than Lincoln, to Washington as senator. But two years later it was Lincoln, not Douglas, who became president. Lincoln captured the Republican nomination at the Chicago convention in 1860 in part because his better-known chief rival, William H. Seward, was reputed to be more radical. Building on the name he had garnered for himself in the debates with Douglas, Lincoln had carefully positioned himself as essentially a conservative, a man motivated not by a desire for revolutionary change but to preserve the republic. More effectively than any other Republican, Lincoln countered the old charge that antislavery politicians were dangerous extremists by reclaiming the founding fathers for his cause. In a magnificent, closely argued speech at the Cooper Union in New York on February 27, 1860, he displayed his mastery of history to the full, countering Douglas and southerners' claim that opposition to slavery extension was a radical departure. Lincoln pointed out that at least 23 signers of the Declaration of Independence had voted for Congress's right to regulate slavery in the territories, contrary to the doctrine of the *Dred Scott* decision. "We stick to, contend for, the identical old policy on the point in controversy which was adopted by 'our fathers who framed the Government under which we live,' " insisted Lincoln, while southerners and northern Democrats "with one accord reject . . . and spit upon that old policy, and insist upon substituting something new."[9] Northern Democrats were left in the position of trying to persuade voters that American freedom included the right to enslave. The incongruity of slavery in a nation dedicated to freedom and individual equality ultimately sapped northern Democrats of some of their popular support and propelled the Republicans to power.

THE RISE OF THE SECESSIONISTS

While Republican politicians built their party in the free states, the dome of the Capitol building in Washington was still being constructed. In the final months of the Pierce administration, while the Kansas–Nebraska act was convulsing the North, another dispute was taking place over a much more minor matter—the design for the statue of freedom that was to be placed on top of the dome when it was completed. In the original plans, the goddess of liberty was shown, with a sword in hand, and a liberty cap on her head. To Secretary of War Jefferson Davis, the liberty cap, the symbol of popular liberty in the American and French revolutions, and originally the symbol of the emancipated slave in ancient Rome, had worryingly radical connotations. It was a symbol, argued Davis, which was "inappropriate to a people who were born free and would not be enslaved." He demanded that it be replaced by a Roman helmet. And so it was.[10] In microcosm, this episode revealed how deeply the need to defend slavery had altered the political consciousness of leading southern politicians. While Republicans like Lincoln appropriated a nationalist discourse to legitimize Republican opposition to the extension of slavery, southern slaveowning politicians like Davis became highly sensitive about those elements of the American national tradition that were anything other than a clear-cut endorsement of slavery.

The political realignments of the 1850s revealed that, as George Rable has put it, "the triumph of both democracy and political parties in the Old South was far from complete."[11] If antipartyism was a widespread public sentiment in the North, it was far more potent in the South, where a suspicion of party hacks and "wire-pullers" was coupled to a far more overt elite disdain for democratic government. Slavery did indeed color political culture in the antebellum South. The vision of social harmony projected by southern leaders like John C. Calhoun did not allow space for party competition, still less class tensions among whites. To an even greater extent than the North, the 1850s saw a collapse of southern faith in the capacity of parties to defend fundamental values, like freedom and defense of honor. Yearning for a return to an idealized eighteenth-century gentleman's republic, the Virginian Muscoe R. H. Garnett looked back with dismay at the general drift "in the direction of democracy" across the nation for the previous 50 years. "Democracy, in its original philosophical sense," he wrote, "is, indeed, incompatible with slavery, and the whole system of Southern society."[12] Such statements were seized upon by northern newspapers and circulated as yet more evidence that the South was an alien political culture.

With Calhoun dead, the case for the superiority of "southern institutions" was put most vigorously by James H. Hammond in a speech to the Senate in 1858. With northern newspapers bemoaning the economic hardships of the sudden economic downturn that had gripped the North the previous year, Hammond lauded the "harmony" of the South's "social and political institutions" which "gives her . . . an extent of political freedom, combined with entire security, such as no other people ever enjoyed upon the face of the earth." Hammond was blunt that "in all social systems there must be a class to do the mean duties, to perform the drudgery of life." In the South this "mud-sill" class were an inferior race. The North's democracy, in contrast, was an absurd hypocrisy: "Your slaves are white, of your own race; you are brothers of one blood."[13] The classic pro-slavery tract was George Fitzhugh's *Cannibals All or Slaves Without Masters* (1857), which argued that capitalism was a war of all against all, whereas slavery was paternalistic, socially cohesive. Northern workers, asserted Fitzhugh, "labor under all the disadvantages of slavery, and have none of the rights of slaves."[14]

While Republicans were building a sectional party in the free states, southern-rights advocates were gaining ground in the South as well. They were aided by the collapse of the Whig party, which left southern Whigs without a natural political home. At one end of the southern political spectrum in the 1850s were the "fire-eaters"—men who persistently called for the breakup of the Union and the creation of a separate southern nation. The quintessential Southern nationalist was Edmund Ruffin of Virginia, a sometime agricultural reformer, slaveowner and pro-slavery publicist whose long mane of white hair and wild eyes reinforced his public image as an extremist. Ruffin, who had been orphaned as a boy and submitted himself to a lifelong regimen of self-improvement and physical exercise, was obsessed with the idea of controlling one's own destiny. He was such a committed southern nationalist that he even refused to support John C. Calhoun for the presidency in 1824 on the grounds that Calhoun was too much of a Unionist. Ruffin pronounced that "as a body, the majority of the northern members of Congress are as corrupt, & destitute of private integrity as the majority of southern members are the reverse."[15] The fight over slavery was viewed through this classical republican lens. The tactics of negotiation and compromise which are the essence of democratic politics came to be seen as dangerous to the preservation of honor, which, by definition, was a matter of principle that could not be compromised.[16] Another famous "fire-eater," William Lowndes Yancey of Alabama, argued in a famous letter in 1858 that the time had at last arrived to "fire the Southern heart—instruct the Southern mind—give courage to each other, and at the proper moment, by one organized, concerted action we can precipitate the cotton States into a revolution." Neither political parties, nor electoral politics, nor the safeguards of the federal Constitution, could save the South, Yancey argued. Only a recreation of the spirit of 1776 could do that. He predicted that the time had come when southerners, realizing that the only way to preserve their freedom was to return to a purified republican vision of the Founders, would "organize Committees of Safety all over the cotton states."[17]

What kept secessionists at bay in the late 1850s was the continued ability of the Democratic Party to wield national power. The party retained its function as a mechanism that magnified southern influence in Washington, as revealed by the pro-southern stance of Pierce and Buchanan and a patronage policy that favored southerners with plumb jobs. Southerners continued to exert a disproportionate influence in the Senate. Even so, the center of gravity of southern politics was continually radicalizing. The *Dred Scott* decision pulled the rug from under the Whiggish southerners who had been prepared to support popular sovereignty even if it led to more free states. Why now demand less than the Supreme Court mandated? For a generation, southern politics had been a contest over which men, or which strategy, would best protect southern rights. More and more southerners began to give a hearing to those who argued that the Union had become so corrupted by Yankee influence that the only solution was to break free.

One event, above all, intensified this view. In October 1859, the messianic abolitionist John Brown launched an amateurish raid on the Federal arsenal at Harpers Ferry, a village nestled in a bend of the Potomac River in Virginia. His aim was to distribute the arms to local slaves and spark a general insurrection. He was quickly apprehended by US troops under the command of Colonel Robert E. Lee. Brown's raid struck at southern society at its weakest point, but shocking as it was for white southerners that violence had been used on their home soil, the most frightening aspect of the whole affair was the northern response. While most mainstream politicians—including Republican leaders like Lincoln—condemned Brown's acts, there was also, in some quarters, an unmistakable admiration for his bravery. In antislavery strongholds like Massachusetts, funds were raised for Brown's legal defense and to support his family. Brown played the part of martyr to perfection. Republican newspapers reported his well-aimed final words as he was led to the gallows: "I, John Brown, am now quite certain that the crimes of this *guilty land* will never be purged away—but with *blood*."[18] Ralph Waldo Emerson said that Brown's death would make the gallows as glorious as the cross. Brown's raid reinforced southerners' conception of themselves as victims. It was *their* honor and rights which were at stake, they asserted. All they demanded was equal protection for their property. Can we "live under a government, the majority of whose subjects regard John Brown as a martyr and a Christian hero?" asked *De Bow's Review*.[19] It was a rhetorical question, of course. The *Richmond Whig* concluded that "thousands of men who, a month ago, scoffed at the idea of a dissolution of the Union . . . now hold the opinion that its days are numbered."

LINCOLN'S ELECTION AND THE SECESSION OF THE DEEP SOUTH

The one national institution which could prevent a sectional rupture in 1860 was the Democratic Party. Another victory by a candidate supported by northerners as well as southerners would have kept southerners in power in Washington and bolstered the position of southern Unionists. But when the Democratic convention met in Charleston in April 1860, this last bond of Union finally ruptured. With Kansas's application for statehood still blocked in Congress by wrangling over the legitimacy of the pro-slavery Lecompton constitution, the delegates bitterly fought over the issue, with southerners demanding not only the immediate admission of Kansas as a slave state, but that Congress should pass a federal Slave Code for the territories (a tacit admission, incidentally, that there was validity to Douglas' claim that slavery could only exist if there was positive legislation protecting it.) Southerners promoted the candidacy of Vice President John C. Breckinridge of Kentucky, a fervent supporter of the Lecompton constitution, while most northerners championed Stephen Douglas. Each side was convinced, with some justification, that the nomination of the other's candidate would be electoral suicide in their own section. There was an impasse, the convention reconvened six weeks later in Baltimore, and there, after a fight over the credentials of some pro-Douglas delegates from southern states, the party broke up. Angry southern delegates bolted and nominated their man Breckinridge on a southern-rights platform, while Douglas was nominated by the remainder of the delegates on a platform that endorsed popular sovereignty.

The Republicans' platform was less radical than in 1856. They condemned Brown's raid, and a provocative reference to slavery as a relic of barbarism was removed. In a determined effort to broaden their base, Republicans courted the economic interest of different regional groups, including supporting a tariff on imports of (mainly British) manufactured goods in order to protect American industry, an issue that was especially important in Pennsylvania, a key electoral state. The nomination of Lincoln rather than Seward was part of the same strategy of broadening their appeal. A group of former Whigs and Know-Nothings calling themselves the Constitutional Union Party nominated the 64-year-old John Bell of Tennessee for president on a platform that avoided specific pledges but placed itself firmly in the compromise tradition of Henry Clay.

A summer of drought heightened the febrile tension in the South. Rumors of slave insurrections and reports of poisoning and arson attacks by slaves were rife. Almost unanimously, southern politicians—even the leaders of the Bell and Douglas factions in Deep South—warned that the election of Lincoln and the "Black Republicans" would result in secession. Republicans refused to take this threat seriously. Downplaying the slavery extension issue—especially in closely contested districts—their campaign promoted their plans for a homestead bill that would give free land to free laborers in the west and a Pacific railroad, as well as the higher tariff—all measures which had been defeated in the last session of Congress by a Democratic majority. With the backing of large numbers of evangelicals who saw the party as a moral crusade to redeem the nation, and with the use of spectacular campaign events and colorful marching clubs, Republicans mobilized lots of young voters, including many English, Scottish and Welsh immigrants, and some Germans. Unlike southern radicals, Republicans cast their sectionalism—as Lincoln had done in his Cooper Union address—as nationalism. Shorn of the albatross of having to placate a southern wing, they could do this with a clarity that none of the other parties could match.

Even had the Democrats not split, Lincoln would probably still have won. He polled 54 percent of the vote in the free states and took the Electoral College votes of every free state except for New Jersey and the new far west states of California and Oregon. Although nationwide he won only 40 percent of the vote, he had a clear majority in the Electoral College. The 1860 election reflected the depths of sectional polarization. It had not been in any genuine sense a national campaign. Lincoln and Douglas contested the free states and Bell and Breckinridge the slave states. Lincoln was not even on the ballot paper in most of the slave states. Breckinridge had little support in the North beyond a few Democratic machine politicians. Bell's strength was mainly in the upper South and the Border Slave States—in fact the Constitutional Union Party polled less than 3 percent of the vote in every free state except Massachusetts, Vermont and California. The only candidate who to any extent muddied the picture of two separate sectional presidential races was Douglas. Ever the astute politician, Douglas quickly came to the conclusion that Lincoln was going to win, but that only made him redouble his efforts to try and convince the voters that in surging toward the most sectional candidates—Lincoln and Breckinridge—they were playing with fire. Breaking with the convention by which presidential candidates refrained from campaigning on their own behalf, Douglas undertook a heroic speaking tour of the South, breaking his health in the process, and delivering impassioned attacks on secession even on the steps of the state capitol in Georgia. At the same time, his strenuous efforts to assuage southern fears alienated moderate voters in the North. He did attract voters in every section, but in such small numbers that he won Electoral College votes in only New Jersey and Missouri. The election was proof, if any were needed, that not only was the nation divided but that the South was now in a minority. Northerners had just demonstrated that they could select the president without regard to southern opinion.

Antislavery men welcomed Lincoln's election as a decisive break with the past. The patrician Bostonian Charles Francis Adams was elated that "the great revolution has actually taken place" and that "the country has once and for all thrown off the domination of the slaveholders."[20] In the South the reaction was ominous. Fire-eaters were galvanized into action by the expected result. To no one's surprise, the South Carolinians were the first to make a move. On November 9, only two days after the election results were known, the South Carolina legislature called for elections to a secession convention. The only issues now were timing and strategy. Remembering the bathetic outcome of the Nashville convention in 1850, die-hard secessionists successfully resisted calls for a southern convention. Urging immediate action in case popular indignation at Lincoln's election faded, fire-eaters in the Deep South captured the political momentum. One of the declarations adopted by the South Carolina secession convention justifying their departure from the Union denounced the free states for defeating the "ends for which this Government was instituted," for denouncing "as sinful the institution of Slavery," permitting "the open establishment among them of societies, whose avowed object is to disturb the peace of and eloign the property of the citizens of other States," and inciting slaves to runaway and rebel. By February 1, 1861, Mississippi, Florida, Alabama, Georgia, Louisiana and Texas had passed secession resolutions similar to South Carolina's. By February 9, commissioners from the seven seceded states, meeting in Montgomery, Alabama, had adopted a provisional constitution. Jefferson Davis became the provisional president.

Much of the secessionists' rhetoric mixed self-righteous indignation with a defensiveness that had a more-in-sorrow-than-in-anger tone. "We have never aggressed upon the North," complained a Louisiana newspaper plaintively. "Yet," it continued,

> every appeal and expostulation has only brought upon us renewed insults and augmented injuries. They have robbed us of our property, they have murdered our citizens while endeavoring to reclaim that property by lawful means, they have set at naught the decrees of the Supreme Court, they have invaded our States and killed our citizens, they have declared their unalterable determination to exclude us altogether from the Territories, they have nullified the laws of Congress, and finally they have capped the mighty pyramid of unfraternal enormities by electing Abraham Lincoln to the Chief Magistracy, on a platform and by a system which indicates nothing but the subjugation of the South and the complete ruin of her social, political and industrial institutions.[21]

Robert M. T. Hunter, a moderate Virginian, warned that the Republican Party was dedicated "to ends and purposes not only different from, but hostile to, those for which this political organism was created. They will destroy the Union as it was framed by the fathers, and seek to substitute another for it."[22] Other Confederates frankly acknowledged that secession was not envisaged by the founding fathers, but claimed legitimacy from the revolutionary origins of the United States. "Each state has the right of revolution, which all admit," explained Senator Alfred Iverson of Georgia in his valedictory speech before leaving Washington in 1861. By this argument, secession was the true conservative policy. Using remarkably uniform language evoking codes of masculine honor and republican liberty, southerners echoed each other in protesting that the election result was a humiliation which the South could not be expected to endure. "The election of Lincoln," wrote a southern correspondent of Caleb Cushing, a rare Massachusetts supporter of Breckinridge, "has placed *our* necks under *their* heels."[23] Calvin H. Wiley, a North Carolina politician protested that "we are charged, before the Bar of Nations, with being an inferior people."[24] A correspondent of Alabama Senator C. C. Clay declared that it was "far better to die a free man than live a slave to *Black Republicanism*."[25] In short, in the words of a Vicksburg, Mississippi, editor, to submit to "Lincolnism would betray the spirit of a slave."[26]

At the core of all these arguments was an anxiety about the preservation of their racial order from newly empowered meddlesome Yankees. Southern newspapers speculated that Lincoln would appoint Yankee postmasters in the heartland of slavery who would distribute abolitionist material to slaves. Wealthy slaveowners exercised a disproportionate influence on southern political life, and, naturally enough, they dominated secession conventions. Some historians have argued that these southern elites feared that a Republican administration would stir up resentments among lower-class southern whites. There is evidence that the prospect—however theoretical—that the administration would use its patronage power to build up the Republican Party in the South based on nonslaveholding whites was certainly a cause for concern among some southern politicians. Some historians have argued that southern elites' fears of the possibility of nonslaveholding southern whites being persuaded by antislavery arguments were a major factor in convincing them of the need for secession.[27] Such fears had been intensifying since 1857 when *The Impending Crisis of the South,* an antislavery tract by Hinton Rowan Helper, was published. As David Brown has recently shown, Helper's case—that slavery was holding back southern economic development and in particular was harmful to the economic interests of nonslaveholding whites—adopted the free labor ideology that was being used by Republicans to attack slavery and southern society. What made Helper's book especially terrifying to southern elites was that he was a southerner himself—a North Carolinian from poor, nonslaveholdng stock.[28]

Loyalty to the Union remained strong in some parts of the Appalachian South among poor nonslaveholding whites. But ultimately, most common folk of the South shared the same emotional response to the prospect of outside interference as the slaveowners. On the face of things, uneducated poor whites in remote parts of the South far from a great plantation had little in common with the sons of wealthy planters, but what they usually did share was a determination to protect their way of life. For many, secession was the right response to the election result.

It was an attempt to solve through political means a political problem: the not inaccurate perception among many southerners that they were losing—or perhaps had already irrevocably lost—control of the national government, and that a northern sectional majority would undermine slavery, and therefore the southern social order, if not immediately, then in time.

The South was by no means united. Rapid and deft political maneuvering by secessionists was critical to the speed with which secession was effected across the Deep South. The vote in some of the Deep South states had been very close, and, in Louisiana and Alabama if not elsewhere, severely tainted by corruption, intimidation of known Unionists, and vote rigging. The tide of secession was held back by Unionists in the Upper South states of Virginia, North Carolina, Tennessee and Arkansas. In parts of the Upper South and Appalachian mountain region the Whig party revived its local organization in 1860 which partly explained the success of the Constitutional Union Party. Across the South, counties with a larger number of slaveowners were more likely to support secession than those with few slaveholders. But this was not always the case. In Virginia, still the state with the largest number of slaves, secession was opposed by a majority of the slaveowning political elite, who argued that the Union, notwithstanding the election of a "Black Republican" president, still provided more security for slavery than an untested Southern Confederacy. Conscious that Lincoln's election had been entirely legitimate, some urged that the South wait for an "overt act" of aggression by the new administration. In North Carolina on January 10, 1861, Thomas Crumpler, a Unionist delegate to the state legislature from Ashe County, passionately attacked the logic of secessionism. Attacking northern abolitionists as a "leprous spot upon our body politic" as well as the self-interest of South Carolina, who had been "wishing herself out of the Union" for years in order to reopen the slave trade, Crumpler argued that secession would be counterproductive. By leaving the Union, the South would "surrender to our enemies the very charter by which [southern rights] are secured, as well as . . . all the physical and moral power by which they are to be enforced."[29] As Crumpler understood, the Constitution made it impossible for any Republican president, or even a Republican Congressional majority, should there ever be one, to abolish slavery where it currently existed. Southern Unionists like Crumpler were to be proved right by events. They shared with northern abolitionists the prescient understanding that the only circumstance in which the existence of slavery could be threatened would be a war.

The idea of creating an independent South spoke to a deep emotional and psychological need in many southerners. For many, secession was a catharsis for ten years or more of pent-up frustration and indignation, a populist solution to a political crisis that was felt at the level of a personal insult. Drunk on their own rhetoric, delegates to secession conventions often engaged in serious-minded debate, but they also gave vent to a rising excitement, a sense that finally they could take control of their own destiny. Before his state seceded, the Georgia Whig, Alexander H. Stephens—who argued passionately that the time was not yet ripe for so risky a move as secession—despaired that the people had become "wild with passion and frenzy, doing they know not what."[30] If their rhetoric was at times histrionic, it was far from irrational for southerners to see Lincoln's election as a threat to the power of slavery. But it did not follow that immediate secession was the most prudent response. Understandable as it may have been, secession was ultimately a gamble that rested on a mistaken faith in northerners' lack of will to fight.

THE NORTH'S WAR FOR THE UNION

President Buchanan's New Year's Day reception in 1861 must have been the most unhappy such event in the history of the White House. Southern congressmen wearing the blue cockade of secession refused to shake the president's hand. Buchanan's dilemma was acute. He denied any right of secession but insisted that he had no constitutional authority to stop it. In his December 1860 Message to Congress, he argued that

> the power to make war against a State is at variance with the whole spirit and intent of the Constitution ... Our Union rests upon public opinion and [can] never be connected by the blood of its citizens in civil war. If it cannot live in the affections of the people, it must one day perish.[31]

Angry northerners warned him that he was a traitor for not confronting secession with force while southerners wrote to him claiming that coercion would "result in the ruin of liberty in the western world."[32] Adrift amid events that he could not or would not control and assailed from all sides, Buchanan ended his presidency a hapless figure.

If Buchanan had little of substance to offer in the way of compromise proposals, some in Congress were working hard to find a peaceful way out of the crisis. In December 1860 Senator John J. Crittenden of Kentucky, a self-conscious heir to Henry Clay, proposed a series of constitutional amendments which would restore the Missouri Compromise line, prohibit the interstate slave trade and provide federal compensation to slaveowners for runaways. The most attractive part of the package for the South was the promise that slavery would be guaranteed by constitutional amendment south of the Missouri Compromise line in all future as well as existing territories. This opened the possibility of the acquisition of Cuba, or more of Mexico, or other parts of Central America as additional slave states, a long-term dream of southern leaders which would violate the Republicans' pledge to oppose all slavery expansion. Republicans blocked the Crittenden proposals at every stage.

Even so, Lincoln's defeated rival for the Republican nomination, William H. Seward, let it be known that the new administration was open to negotiation. Lincoln had invited Seward to be his Secretary of State and many, including Seward himself, expected him to be a de facto "Prime Minister" controlling the policy of the inexperienced President. Seward was a charming figure with long experience of Washington politics and good contacts with moderate southerners who he worked hard to reassure about the essential conservatism of the incoming administration. Never one to underestimate his own importance, Seward explained to his wife that "I am the only hopeful, calm, conciliatory person here."[33] Seward, however, despite his ill-deserved reputation as a radical, was not representative of his party. The man whose election had precipitated the secession crisis remained at home in Springfield, Illinois. Lincoln was happy to repeat assurances he had already made that he had no intention of interfering with slavery where it existed, and was even prepared to support a constitutional amendment (which had been secretly drafted by Seward) formally protecting slavery in the states since he believed that that was already the constitutional position. But on the critical question of slavery in the territories, he was unyielding. "Stand firm," he told a fellow Republican, "The tug has to come, & better now, than any time hereafter."[34] Lincoln argued that the time for compromise had passed. Once the seven Deep South states had seceded, the issue that northerners focused on was no longer slavery extension but the defiance of the Constitution and the treasonous threat to the integrity of the Union. The question became whether Lincoln would stand up to the secessionists and insist on collecting customs duties and protect federal property in the South.

Had the incoming Lincoln administration incurred the wrath of its party base and given in to pressure for compromise by endorsing the Crittenden proposals it is just conceivable that the momentum toward secession could have been halted. Part of the problem, though, was the relative speed with which the Deep South acted. By the time the Crittenden bill reached the floor of the Senate, the representatives from the seven seceded states had already departed. To use a metaphor that Civil War Americans were fond of, the Deep South had already crossed the Rubicon. Even so, without the Upper South, particularly North Carolina and Virginia, the Confederacy would be highly vulnerable in the event of war, and the reluctance of the Upper South to secede gave false hope to some in the North. Many people north of the Mason–Dixon line, including the Kentucky-born Lincoln, misinterpreted the highly conditional nature of Upper South Unionism. Those who urged delay before passing secession ordinances did so only for tactical reasons and hardly anybody in the South disputed the right of secession or failed to assure their fellow southerners that even if they opposed secession now, they would not be found wanting if it became necessary to defend their state against Yankee invasion. In truth, the only way that the secession of Virginia, Tennessee, North Carolina and Arkansas could have been avoided was if Lincoln effectively acknowledged the de facto reality of secession. The overwhelming majority of northerners would never have accepted such a policy, even had Lincoln been willing to consider it.

At first, even some antislavery campaigners in the North—notably veteran abolitionist William Lloyd Garrison and *New York Tribune* editor Horace Greeley—agreed with these Upper South Unionists (and with President Buchanan) that it was impossible to coerce a state back into the Union without destroying republican principles. But by the time Lincoln left Springfield for his rail journey to Washington on February 11, the day before his 52nd birthday, the popular mood in the North demanded firmness from the new president. As the Southern states seceded they took federal property with them, including economically and strategically valuable forts and mints. A host of complex problems immediately pressed themselves on the federal government: would they try to recapture lost property by force? Would they try to deliver the mails? Attention focused in particular on the two remaining federal forts that had not yet fallen into the hands of secessionists: Fort Pickens near Pensacola, Florida, and Fort Sumter, in the harbor of Charleston, South Carolina. The latter was an especially taxing problem because it was in range of artillery batteries on the shore that were manned by increasingly impatient militia. The garrison in Fort Sumter was commanded by Major Robert Anderson, a Kentucky slaveowner who was already, by mid-February 1861 acquiring the unsought status of a patriotic hero in the North for his brave defiance. The symbolism of a federal fort flying the star-spangled banner in full view of the city where secession originated made Sumter the most likely flashpoint in the uneasy standoff between the seceded states and the federal government.

Crucially, it was not just Republicans who wanted a stern show of force against the rebels. Many Democrats invoked the memory of their great hero, Andrew Jackson, who had threatened to send troops to crush South Carolina's efforts to "nullify" federal laws in the early 1830s. As southern members resigned from the government, Buchanan promoted nationalist Democrats in the Jacksonian mold—northerners like John A. Dix and Edwin Stanton, both of whom had supported Breckinridge in the election and who felt personally betrayed by secession. In the final chaotic months of the Buchanan administration, these men tried to put some backbone into the lame duck president and offered bipartisan support to Lincoln.

Northerners had grown up in a culture imbued with romantic nationalism, in which the greatness of their Union had been extolled, not just because it was the freest nation on earth, but also because it was the greatest—a magnificent empire of liberty stretching across a continent, an unimaginable source of wealth, opportunity and dreams. The notion of dismembering this nation was repugnant. "We love the Union," explained a New York editor, "because already in commerce, wealth and resources of every kind, we are the equal of the greatest."[35] A Philadelphia newspaper predicted that secession would mean that

> this proud Republic . . . would dwindle into insignificant States, more contemptible than those of Germany or of Central America . . . Like Mexico, we should either become a prize for some military adventurer to grasp at, or keep up a petty show of distinct sovereignties, continually warring against each other, or adopting foolish and injurious restrictions to check each other's progress. The proud title of a 'citizen of the United States' could be claimed no longer, and having no nationality commanding the respect of the world, our persons and property would be secure in no part of the globe.[36]

Beneath such reasoning was a gut feeling that, as Lincoln put it in his inaugural address, "physically speaking we cannot separate." Although the ideological components of American nationalism are often understandably emphasized by historians, there was also a strong territorial element as well. By the 1860s, many factors—including the circulation of newspapers, improved communication by railroad and the telegraph, the expansion and definition through treaty of the nation's borders, and the rapid migration to the far west after the discovery of gold—had all helped to generate a greater-than-ever sense that American nationalism was defined not just by a commitment to democracy and freedom but also, like other nations, by the *patria*, the unified national space. A separate Southern confederacy would violate the ideal of a territorially defined continental nation-state. "That portion of the earth's surface which is owned and inhabited by the United States, is well adapted to be the home of one national family," Lincoln told Congress in December 1862; "it is not well adapted for two or more."[37]

Like other nineteenth-century nationalists, Lincoln was convinced of the supreme value of the Union for its own sake and assumed, unquestioningly, that sovereignty resided in the people as a whole, who had collectively elected him president. To secede in the face of that election result was therefore to challenge democracy and the rightful sovereignty of the people. Secession, in Lincoln's words, was "the essence of anarchy," a challenge to due process and an act of defiance against American institutions. It was an act that disregarded the "the judgment of this great tribunal, the American people." Cast in such a way, secession was a direct challenge to the principle that nationhood rested in the sovereignty of the people would be defeated. For one to triumph the other must be defeated. This was an idealistic romantic nationalism that fused the nation with the idea of freedom and the practice of representative, constitutional government. Indeed, like liberal nationalists in Europe, Lincoln assumed that democracy and nationalism were not only reconcilable, but integral to one another and mutually reinforcing; defeat one and you defeat the other. If the rebels won, and proved that "discontented individuals" could "arbitrarily . . . break up their Government" it would "practically put an end to free government upon the earth."[38] This was the bedrock of Lincoln's understanding of the great crisis, one he repeated in a number of different formulations almost every time he made a speech, and from it he never wavered. Significantly, the nationalist arguments made against secession seemed to validate and reinforce decades of arguments by antislavery activists that slavery had corrupted republican government in the South. Even hitherto Democratic and conservative journals like the *Philadelphia*

Press, which had supported Douglas in the 1860 election, now warned its readers that "the leaders of the Disunion cabal are men of the most aristocratic pretensions," and that, "South Carolina, which is at the head of Secession, is almost a monarchy herself."[39]

The mood in Washington—which was, after all, a southern city in which slavery was still a legal institution—was deeply hostile to the new "Black Republican" president. Lincoln delivered his inaugural address on March 4 in an atmosphere of fear and anxiety, with sharpshooters on the rooftops on the watch for secessionist troublemakers. To no one's surprise, his speech offered no new concessions. In his peroration, he deftly attempted to make secessionists take the responsibility for any war that might follow. "In *your* hands my dissatisfied fellow countrymen and not in mine is the momentous issue of civil war," he argued. "The government will not assail *you*. You can have no conflict, without being yourselves the aggressors." He ended with a memorable appeal to national sentiment:

> We are not enemies but friends. We must not be enemies. Though passion may have strained, it must not break our bonds of affection. The mystic chords of memory, streching from every battle-field, and patriot grave, to every living heart and hearthstone, all over this broad land, will yet swell the chorus of the Union, when again touched, as surely they will be, by the better angels of our nature.[40]

The speech was evasive about the practical issues facing the country. What exactly did he mean by pledging that the government would not "assail" the rebels? Would the government reassert control over federal mints, arsenals, forts and customs houses now in the hands of the rebels? Yet even in a speech designed to reassure wavering southerners and suspicious northerners that the issue at stake was not slavery but Union, Lincoln was clear about the moral crux of the dispute. "One section of our country believes slavery is *right* and ought to be extended, while the other believes it is *wrong*, and ought not to be extended."[41] There was no doubt about the new president's own stance on that issue, but much uncertainty about what would ensue.

Few presidents in American history have come into office with as little experience of national politics or executive decision-making as Lincoln. None have faced so serious a challenge to the survival of the Union. Harriet Beecher Stowe compared the nation to a ship on a perilous passage. At its helm was a plain working man of the people, with no more culture, instruction, or education than any such working man may obtain . . . The eyes of princes, nobles, aristocrats, of dukes, earls, scholars, statesmen, warriors, all turned on the plain backwoodsman . . . watched him with a fearful curiosity, simply asking, "*Will* that awkward old backwoodsman really get that ship through?"[42]

THE SUMTER CRISIS

Lincoln probably hoped that his conciliatory inaugural address would buy him some breathing space. But when he walked into his White House office on the morning of his first full day as president, he was confronted with unmistakable evidence that time was running out. A dispatch from Major Anderson informed him that if action were not taken immediately his garrison at Fort Sumter would be starved out. The issue of whether to reinforce this last remaining bastion of federal authority in South Carolina could not be put off. Seward, still in close contact with moderate Virginians, urged the president to quietly abandon Sumter and make his symbolic stand at Fort Pickens. Seward was right that the moment of last resort had not yet arrived, at least for the federal government. If Sumter were surrendered there would still be more time for peace feelers, emissaries, and negotiation. Lincoln appears to have paid serious attention to Seward's suggestion that he abandon Sumter if, in return, the Virginia secession convention dispersed, but the idea came to nothing. Meanwhile the new Treasury Secretary, the antislavery Ohioan Salmon P. Chase, backed by Secretary of the Navy Gideon Welles and Postmaster General Montgomery Blair, urged Lincoln to reinforce Sumter at once. In their view, the surrender of the fort would be unacceptable to northern public opinion. A stand had to be taken. Making abundantly clear that, contrary to Seward's confident expectations, he had no intention of ceding control of his administration to anyone else, Lincoln sided with Chase, but with an important caveat that, he believed, gave him the moral high ground. Fort Sumter would be resupplied with food and provisions, but not arms. An unarmed relief expedition was ordered, and Lincoln telegraphed his decision to South Carolina Governor Pickens. Throughout his life, Lincoln was a man who instinctively prepared for the worst, and he must have feared that even an unarmed relief vessel would be seen as a provocation by the South Carolinians. But Lincoln's actions ensured that if war was to come, it would be the rebels who fired the first shot. And so it was to be.

In Montgomery, Alabama, on April 9, Jefferson Davis' cabinet heard news of Lincoln's decision and they duly ordered the commander of the Confederate garrison in Charleston—a dashing French Louisianan called Pierre Gustave Toutant Beauregard—to demand Anderson's surrender or else level the fort. The Confederate government knew that attacking Sumter would inaugurate war, but they were under enormous public pressure to act. Weeks of waiting were irritating southern newspapers who clamored to bring the conflict to a head. At 4.30 in the morning on April 12, 1861, the Confederate batteries ringing Charleston harbor opened fire on the low dark island, built to guard Charleston from the sea, but now an outpost of an enemy power. The first shot was fired by the Virginia fire-eater Edmund Ruffin, who had been transformed from a slightly ridiculous marginal figure to a Southern hero. Word of the impending showdown had spread around Charleston and the shore was crowded with onlookers who loudly cheered the bombardment. Anderson surrendered, without having lost a single man. It was an oddly bloodless beginning to the bloodiest war of the age.

By opening fire on Fort Sumter, the Confederates played into Lincoln's hands by making the issue a test of whether a free government could defend itself. The image of the stars and stripes under fire rallied the North in defense of the Union, overshadowing the slavery issue entirely. Newspapers which the day before had called for compromise and a cooling of passions called for vengeance and urged their readers to rally behind the flag. On April 15 Lincoln called for 75,000 volunteers under the 1792 Militia Act to serve for 90 days, the maximum amount prescribed by the law. This was the "overt act" that conditional Unionists in the Upper South had been waiting for. On April 17 the Virginia secession convention—still in session after two months of inconclusive discussion—adopted a secession ordinance. Arkansas followed on May 2, North Carolina on May 20, and in Tennessee the legislature's decision to join the confederacy was ratified by a popular vote on June 8.

Once the first shot had been fired—fittingly in the state that had long been in the vanguard of calls for secession—Lincoln had no choice but to respond with force, irrespective of the consequences for the secession of the Upper South. Volunteers were rushing to join hastily created militia units even before the call for troops reached the desks of state governors, so it was in a sense only a response to popular demand. In New Britain, Connecticut, the first war meeting, as in so many other northern towns, was the church service held on April 14, the Sunday after Sumter. Three days later the town had a full company of 78 men ready for orders, even before Lincoln's call for troops.[43] "Men cannot think or attend to their ordinary business," reported Oliver Wendell Holmes from Boston in 1861. The war consumed all. "How long it is since Sumter!" wrote Jane Woolsey, only three weeks after the war began. "I suppose it is because so much intense emotion has been crowded into the last two or three weeks that the 'time before Sumter' seems to belong to some dim antiquity. It seems as if we never were alive till now; never had a country till now."[44]

Some in the South went to war with, at best, a divided heart. Jonathan Worth, a Whig from North Carolina who had opposed secession, joined the army as soon as his state seceded, but did so with grave forebodings that he expressed in a letter to his brother. "I have been forced by surrounding facts to take sides, or rather front with my section . . . but I do not have a particle of confidence in the new rulers to whom we submit," confessed Worth on May 15, 1861.

> I leave the flag of the Union and the flag of Washington because I am subjected and forced to submit to my master—democracy, detesting it with more and more intensity as I become better acquainted with its objects. . . . I think the South is committing political suicide, but my lot is cast with the South and being unable to manage the ship, I intend to face the breakers manfully and go down with my companions.[45]

With the Upper South out of the Union, attention turned to the four remaining slave states that had not yet seceded: Missouri, Kentucky, Delaware and Maryland. These Border States were microcosms of the nation at large, divided internally between slaveholding counties and large numbers of free laborers. The loss of any one of them would have been a huge blow to the Union. Maryland had a particular strategic importance since if it had seceded, the federal capital, Washington, would have been cut off from the North. Maryland had a relatively small slave population concentrated in the South and the eastern shore, but a unionist north and west and the large city of Baltimore, which, like New York and Boston, had an immigrant population that was largely opposed to antislavery politics but had no political ties to secession. Of the

50,000 Marylanders who fought in the war, an estimated 20,000 fought for the South. The state's Unionist Governor, Thomas H. Hicks, refused to call a secession convention. On April 19, 1861, the sixth Massachusetts Volunteers entered Baltimore, Maryland, on route to Washington. No railroad lines passed through the city so they had to leave the train from New York and march through the streets to the southbound train station. On the way, the inexperienced troops were attacked by a secessionist mob and responded by firing into the crowd. Four soldiers and a dozen civilians were killed. In response, the secessionist police chief of Baltimore approved the tearing up of railroad lines and telegraph poles in an attempt to stop Union troops passing through the city in the future. Lincoln responded with force. On May 14, the Union army occupied Baltimore, habeas corpus was suspended and suspected secessionists were arrested and locked up in Fort McHenry without trial. Governor Hicks summoned a special session of the state legislature, which, under heavy pressure, voted against secession. The infringement of civil liberties in Maryland prompted outrage from some quarters in the North, including from the Chief Justice of the Supreme Court, Roger B. Taney, who, sitting as a federal circuit judge, issued a judgment, known as the *Merryman* case, which condemned Lincoln's actions as unconstitutional. Throughout the war, Lincoln would have to balance civil liberties with security, just as the nation at large would have to weight the price of war, with its demands and losses, against the goal of reunion.

FIRST BULL RUN

The events of the first few months of 1861 can only be fully understood if we remember that the vast majority of Americans were not trying to seek an accommodation; they wanted a fight. A few wise heads on both sides knew that once war came, it would be long and costly, but for many, resorting to violence was not a sign of failure, but a manly, healthy, possibly even a purifying way of resolving an otherwise intractable conflict. In retrospect the complacency of both sides seems astonishing. "You may slap a Yankee in the face and he'll go off and sue you," sneered one southern politician, "but he won't fight!"[46] Northerners were no less cocky that the "rebs" would be routed in one decisive battle. After Virginia's secession, the Confederate government moved from Montgomery to Richmond, only a hundred or so miles due south of Washington. Newspapers like the *New York Tribune* emblazoned "Forward to Richmond!" atop their editorial pages. Volunteer troops gathered in Washington in their makeshift uniforms. The army quartermasters' department hurriedly located what arms and ammunition they could. The time for the phony war was over. On both sides of the Mason–Dixon line, Americans wanted resolution.

On July 16, Union general Irvin McDowell, a 42-year-old West Pointer with good political connections but no previous field experience, ordered 35,000 troops, mainly raw, untrained volunteers, together with a small unit of professional troops to advance. With no proper command structure, or effective means of communication among the officer corps, the amateur army moved at a leisurely pace, taking two and a half days to march 20 miles into Confederate Virginia. Warned of the ponderous advance of McDowell's men by locals, General P. G. T. Beauregard's 20,000 Confederates massed near Manassas junction and waited for what everyone assumed would be the contest that would determine whether the southern bid for independence would live or die. The southerners were also overwhelmingly volunteers, militia groups with names like the Tallapoosa Thrashers, the Bartow Yankee Killers, the Chickasaw Desperadoes, the Racoon Roughs and the Lexington Wildcats.[47]

In preparation for a Yankee attack, the Confederates followed the rule book of Napoleonic warfare and moved immediately to concentrate their forces. A second Confederate army under the command of Joseph E. Johnston was concentrated in the northern Shenandoah Valley. On July 17, Beauregard sent a message to Johnston asking him to join him and help "crush the enemy." Similar orders arrived from Richmond the next day from President Jefferson Davis, a military man himself who had an active conception of his constitutional role as commander in chief. A railroad line ran directly from near where Johnston's army was encamped to Manassas, although less than a third of his troops that went by rail got there in time, hardly an auspicious start to what is often known as the first modern war. The ones that marched on foot arrived in time for the battle.

Beauregard had placed his forces on the western bank of Bull Run, a rocky stream to the north and west of Manassas Junction. The federal troops named the battle by the river, the Confederates by the nearest town, a pattern that was repeated throughout the war. As word spread of the impending battle, Washington society packed picnic hampers and rode in carriages to watch the action. On the morning of July 21, federal troops attacked forcing the rebels to retreat to defensive lines on Henry Hill, a small mound west of Bull Run. It was there that the brigade of five Virginia regiments led by General Thomas J. Jackson made their stand. Another Confederate commander, in an effort to rally his own troops, was reported to have cried, "Yonder stands Jackson like a stone wall; let's go to his assistance." The South's first military hero, "Stonewall Jackson," a fanatically devout man who compared the South's struggle to Cromwell's puritan crusade against the tyranny of King Charles, was born.

The battle was chaotic. Neither side had proper maps, or knew the lie of the land, or had reliable intelligence. The undulating hills prevented anyone from having a clear view of the battlefield. The cavalry on both sides operated seemingly at random, certainly without any proper coordination with infantry attacks. Troops mistook units on their own side for the enemy, and on several occasions opened fire. Commanders on both sides had little control over their own troops. At one point, Jefferson Davis appeared in person and tried to lead an attack as if he were a Tudor monarch, confusing Confederate command structure even further. Adding to the sense of pantomime, even 67-year-old Edmund Ruffin turned up at Bull Run as a volunteer with the South Carolina Palmetto Guards, and was allowed to fire an artillery round at the fleeing Union troops. In the words of the historian Marcus Cunliffe, Bull Run was "a zone between a dream and a nightmare, a black comedy of errors."[48] At one point in the afternoon, federal artillery destroyed a wooden clapboard house atop Henry Hill, killing outright its owner, the blind and bedridden widow, Judith Henry, who despite desperate pleas by Confederate soldiers had refused to leave the home in which she had been born. At about 4 p.m., the battle reached its climax. Having withstood the attacks of the morning, Beauregard's men counterattacked, screaming like banshees, unleashing the rebel yell on the enemy for the first time in the war. "There is nothing like it on this side of the infernal region," recalled a northern soldier after the war. "The peculiar corkscrew sensation that it sends down your backbone under these circumstances can never be told. You have to feel it."[49] While Union officers desperately tried get their men to regroup, the retreat degenerated into a disorganized, panic-stricken rout. "The men seemed to be seized simultaneously by the conviction that it was no use to do anything more," observed a northern officer, "and they might as well start home."[50] Congressman Alfred Ely of New York, who was there as a spectator, was captured and taken prisoner. Carriages, wagons, cannons jostled for position on the way back to Washington.

The Confederates were criticized by some at the time and many since for not making even more of this victory, but they were barely more organized than the Yankees. The following day McDowell had recovered his position and concentrated his forces again. The chance for a decisive Confederate victory had vanished. The casualty figures in this first great conflict were tiny compared to the carnage of later battles, yet at the time, the deaths of 1982 Confederates and 2896 Federal soldiers shocked both sections profoundly. While Southerners rejoiced at their victory, Northerners were forced to confront for the first time the scale of the undertaking they had so blithely embraced. Some of the Union's 90-day volunteers, the 4th Pennsylvania and the 8th New York Artillery, marched home on the very morning of the battle because their time was up. Others disbanded a couple of days later. They felt no shame in doing so because they had done their duty as they had conceived of it. War, they thought, was about a show of force, a blend of theater and sport with the romance of a duel in a Russian novel. Both sides would now have to learn to fight a real war.

3 The Failure of Limited War, 1861–1862

THE MILITARY BALANCE SHEET, 1861

For every inhabitant of the Confederate states, there were more than two Americans who lived in loyal states. There were thousands of citizens of loyal states, especially in the two largest border slave states, Kentucky and Missouri, who actively supported the Confederacy. But they were more than counterbalanced by the white southerners, especially in the mountainous areas of east Tennessee, western North Carolina, western Virginia and northern Alabama, as well as parts of Texas and Arkansas, who remained loyal to the Union. And then there were the more than three and half million slaves and 130,000 free blacks in the Confederacy who were at best a double-edged sword to the Confederacy. On the one hand, their labor freed white men to serve in the Confederate army, allowing for one of the most complete mobilizations of the military-age population in history (more than 80 percent). On the other, about 150,000 black men from the Confederacy were eventually to serve in the Union army.

A glance at a few figures from the 1860 census gives a sense of how far the North outstripped the South in almost every economic measure. The lack of indigenous raw materials was a major problem for the South, which until the war had relied on the North and Britain for the iron and steel it needed for railroad construction. There were 110,000 manufacturing establishments in the North—some of them very small—employing an average of ten workers each. The South had roughly a tenth of the number of factories and a tenth of the numbers employed (110,000 workers in the Confederate states against 1,300,000 in the North). More than 85 percent of capital invested in industry was invested in the North, and more than 80 percent of the nation's bank deposits were there too. The North had more than twice as much railroad mileage as the South. Of huge significance was the fact that in 1860, the nonseceding states produced 15 times as much iron as the Confederacy, and 97 percent of the firearms. In terms of agricultural production, the North also seemed to have a decisive advantage. In 1862 and 1863 the loyal states grew more wheat than the whole country had grown in 1859. No less important was the greater number of horses available to the Union army. Less easy to measure, but no less significant, was the mechanical and industrial expertise available to the Union army. The Army Corps of Engineers performed technical miracles that were invaluable in every theater of war. Southerners who had disparaged the "greasy mechanics" of the North had their own railroad engineers and bridge-builders, but they scrambled to keep up with federal armies in these respects. The North also had a banking and credit system that, chaotic as it was in many ways, was much superior to anything in the South. President Lincoln could draw on the support of private financiers to help fund the war in a way that was simply not possible for President Davis.

The US navy in 1861 was a relatively small outfit, with almost no experience of the sort of coastal in-shore fighting that would be required of it during the war. Of the 42 ships in arms, only three were initially available to enforce the blockade that Lincoln declared against the Confederacy in the spring of 1861. Since the South had more than 200 harbors and navigable river mouths, not to mention a long land border with Mexico, the capacity of this small naval force to implement an effective naval blockade seemed dubious in the extreme. But in comparison, the South began with no navy at all and apparently no industrial capacity with which to create one. The most valuable industrial and agricultural regions of the South were also the most vulnerable to attack. Missouri and Kentucky's failure to secede deprived the Confederacy of two major southern cities, Louisville and St Louis, and the fertile agricultural lands of Kentucky which would have been invaluable in supplying the Confederate army. The capital, Richmond, was on the frontline throughout the war. New Orleans, four times the size of any other city in the South and the only large port, fell into Federal hands after scarcely a year of war. Other southern port cities such as Charleston, Galveston, Savannah, Mobile and Wilmington were all vulnerable to a combination of naval and land attack.

By most measurable standards—population, industrial and agricultural capacity, financial infrastructure, transportation—the North therefore appeared to start with a decisive advantage. "In view of the disparity of resources, it would have taken a miracle" to enable the South to win, concluded the historian Richard N. Current, "as usual God was on the side of the heaviest battalions."[1] This manpower and material imbalance, especially when read with the advantage of hindsight, have led to the widespread view that the South faced such overwhelming odds that it never had a serious chance of victory and that it lasted as long as it did only because of the brilliance of its generals. But as countless examples in history show, war is not determined by industrial output alone. The South had strengths that, many felt, outweighed its weaknesses. Most important was the basic strategic calculus of the war. The North had to subdue an area larger than Western Europe. Supply wagons—as many as thirty or so for every thousand troops—had to accompany the armies wherever they went. Lines of communication had to be protected. When areas of rebel territory were taken, troops had to be diverted from frontline fighting duty to pacify and secure the countryside. In theory, the South had all the logistical advantages of interior lines and a friendly population from which they could harass and frustrate the invaders. The American war of Independence had been won in this way, with the rebel colonists dragging out the fighting until the British, for all their military superiority, no longer had the will to continue the fight. The bacterial challenge facing Civil War soldiers also had a big impact on the fighting capacity of the armies and the capabilities of the leaders. The frustratingly slow pace of Union armies which so exasperated Lincoln was partly due to the debilitating effects of disease. Sherman despaired that "our armies disappear before our eyes, they are merely paper armies."[2]

Not all the technological and industrial advantages the North possessed could be applied in any straightforward way to winning military campaigns. Few army officers on either side had much of an idea of how railroads could help the war effort, for example. And in any case, there was nothing resembling a proper rail network in the South. More than ten different gauges were in use; even a single railroad company often owned rolling stock of several different gauges. There was no rail link between North and South since no rail company had yet built a bridge across the Potomac or Ohio rivers.[3] Geography helped the South in other ways too. The deep rivers flowing west to east across Virginia presented serious obstacles to the federal advance on Richmond, while the Shenandoah Valley offered a protected corridor that led directly from the Confederate heartland to within reach of Washington DC. On closer inspection, even some of the North's numerical advantages began to look like weaknesses. The northern white population was much more diverse than in the South. Almost one in five northerners, or four million people, were foreign-born. A hetero-geneous society like this might be harder to bind together for a long war. And although, on paper, the Union had the advantage of begin-ning the war with a professional army in place, in fact the 14,000 or so professional soldiers, scattered across the frontier, who remained in the Union were too few for the task at hand. Both sides therefore had a similarly daunting logistical challenge in building huge volunteer armies. The US regular units were initially kept together, while the bulk of the army was made up of volunteer units manned and officered by civilians with little or no military experience. Above all the Confed-erates had the advantage that they knew what they were fighting for. "Those who . . . console themselves with the reflection that starvation and want will bring [the rebels] to their knees are verry [*sic*.] much mistaken," wrote an Ohio officer in 1862, "[t]hey are united & common danger cements them."[4]

These balance sheets of Union and Confederate strengths and weaknesses could have been transformed by foreign intervention. Formal diplomatic recognition would have been a powerful signal that the Confederacy was a permanent creation and not a mere internal rebellion. Substantial financial aid to the South would have tied foreign economies and governments into the success of the South, making military intervention more likely. French intervention in the American War of Independence had been the decisive factor in the defeat of the British, and had European powers—specifically Britain and France— been prepared to intervene they could easily have tipped the balance in the Civil War as well. The great bargaining chip available to the South was their cotton exports. One southerner boasted to a British newspaper reporter in February 1861 that "we have only to shut off your supply of cotton for a few weeks and we can create a revolution in Great Britain."[5] The Union blockade of southern ports was too porous to have cut off the supply of cotton to Europe, but the southerners completed the job themselves. An embargo on cotton exports was effectively imposed in the summer of 1861. Bales of cotton stacked up in New Orleans harbor were set alight rather then be shipped to Britain. By 1862, the supply of cotton to Britain from the southern states had been cut off almost completely. Even so, the Civil War remained an American affair. No foreign government intervened militarily, or even offered diplomatic recognition to the Confederacy. The faith that southerners placed in King Cotton proved to be an illusion. Existing stockpiles of raw cotton in Britain meant that it took more than a year before the embargo affected the mills of Lancashire and Yorkshire. And unfortunately for the Confederates, the Civil War coincided with a concerted effort to develop new sources of raw cotton in the British Empire. By 1864, textile manufacturers were importing from Egypt and India nearly three-quarters as much cotton as they had from the United States in 1860. The American South never fully regained its European markets, and the price of cotton was never again as high on the world commodity markets as it had been before the war. Confederates who had relied on political pressure from unemployed textile workers and bankrupt mill owners overestimated the importance of textiles to the mid-Victorian British economy, which boomed in the early 1860s. Sympathy for the Confederate cause in Britain had two main sources, neither of them influenced by the economic blackmail of the cotton embargo. Some Tory politicians in particular relished the prospect of the failure of the American republican experiment and supported the South from simple schadenfreude or from a conviction that a divided United States would allow the reassertion of British power in the western hemisphere. Others, like William E. Gladstone, were sympathetic to what appeared to be the legitimate nationalist aspirations of the southern people.

The greatest danger of war between Britain and the United States came not as a result of the economic effects of the cotton embargo, or an abstract political preference for one side or another, but from a conflict over the rights of British shipping. When the United States declared its neutrality during the Napoleonic Wars, the British government had quickly become infuriated by what it had seen as American violations of the Royal Navy's blockade of French ports. In previous conflicts, Britain had developed the doctrine of "continuous voyage" to justify seizing ships bound for a neutral port if they believed the cargo was to be transferred to a blockaded port afterwards. At the time, the Americans had bitterly protested the injustice of this position. Now the roles were reversed. The US navy tried, and on occasion, succeeded in seizing British merchant vessels bound for neutral ports near the Confederate coast such as the Bahamas or Cuba, on the grounds that the cargo was then to be transferred to southern blockade runners. On November 8, 1861, Captain Charles Wilkes of the USS *San Jacinto* boarded a British ship, the *Trent*, 300 miles east of Havana and removed two Confederate envoys, James Mason and John Slidell, on route to Europe to press for diplomatic recognition. Wilkes became the Union hero of the hour when he delivered his Confederate captives into federal custody in Boston, but the British government was furious at the violation of its flag. The diplomatic row was defused after Secretary of State Seward apologized and released Mason and Slidell, insisting as he did so that the case proved that the British had finally accepted the United States' conception of neutral shipping rights.

STRATEGY AND TACTICS

The political objectives of each side set the parameters within which military strategy—the best deployment of available resources—was formulated.[6] The seven Deep South states had seceded, adopted a consti- tution, elected a provisional Congress and president, designed a national flag and formed a navy and an army—in short they had achieved de facto independence—in just 60 bloodless days; thereafter their task was preservation. The South simply did not have the logistical capacity for a full-scale invasion of the North. Lee's two incursions into Maryland and Pennsylvania in the summers of 1862 and 1863 were really grand raids. Even had the Confederate forces not been repelled at the battles of Antietam in September 1862 and Gettysburg in July 1863, Lee had little room for maneuver in the North. At the other end of the spectrum, the most defensive option—a large-scale guerrilla strategy—was never seriously considered. Guerilla warfare depended on conceding large swathes of territory to the enemy, something that was never politically possible. The need to protect the southern homeland from the threat of slave rebellion as well as the incursions of Union troops impelled the Confederate government to pursue a strategy of maintaining territorial integrity.

There is a venerable historiographical tradition which, taking the Confederates at their word about their fundamentally defensive aims, questions why they nevertheless made so many apparently offensive moves. "We seek no conquest, no aggrandizement, no concession of any kind," insisted Jefferson Davis. "All we ask is to be left alone." This was not quite true because Davis had hopes of bringing Kentucky, Maryland, and the southwestern territories of Arizona and New Mexico into the Confederacy. More importantly, even insofar as Confederate war aims were fundamentally defensive, most historians agree that they were pursued by offensive tactics. One grim indicator of this is the astonishing fact that 55 percent of Confederate generals were to die in battle, many of them in offensive actions.[7] There were three main reasons why a purely defensive strategy could not have been pursued. The most important was that independence could not simply be declared; it had to be won and conceded if it was to be real and enduring—as the rebels in the War of Independence had proved. The only way Confederates could do that was by forcing the north to stop fighting. And to do that they had to undermine the northern public's appetite for war. It was northern public opinion that was the real target of the Confederate army. The second reason was that the material advantages of the Union would take time to marshal. So it made sense for the South to strike out while they had the momentum. The third reason was that southern public opinion demanded it. Davis attempted to create a defensive barrier around the South, but inevitably the Union army broke through, first in the western Virginia mountains and along the Atlantic seaboard, then in Tennessee, then down the Mississippi corridor. The response of the leading southern general, Robert E. Lee, was to seize the initiative and to engage the enemy wherever possible, distracting the Union troops from the task of conquest, buying time. Lee sought a clear decision in the South's favor; he did not believe that the Confederacy had the luxury of just waiting, attempting to avoid defeat. He understood that the longer the war dragged on, the greater the chance that the North's manpower and materiel advantages would be brought to bear.

For the Lincoln administration and the vast majority of northerners, no military outcome which left the Confederacy in place was acceptable. Once the war had begun, the South was equally unwilling to compromise on its basic objective of independence. But neither side was clear about how these political objectives could best be realized on the battlefield. And at the outset, each fell into the trap of underestimating the other's will to fight and overestimating the number of sympathizers they had in the other section. While southern politicians confidently predicted that the North would never stomach a long fight and that the Democratic Party would reassert itself and its traditional alliance with the South, northern political leaders clung to the myth that secession was a ploy by a small slaveholding elite.

The popular faith that the war would be over in 90 days was in part the bravado of a people mobilizing for martial combat. It also reflected the ignorance and inexperience about the reality of warfare— and serious assessments of the military situation seemed out of place amid the popular enthusiasm for a cause which most took for granted. A short war could be managed within existing frames of reference. Many feared the impact of a long war on the institutions and moral character of the republic. In any case, if secession lacked popular support in the South then the rebellion could be put down with comparative ease. Martial valor was related closely, in good republican fashion, to the *virtue* of the combatants. If force could not subdue them, the rebellion must be respected as legitimate. "A brave, martial people, of eight or nine millions, cannot be subdued; an usurping, domineering, terrorizing faction may be," the *New York Tribune* declared. In his July, 1861, message to Congress, Lincoln argued that ordinary southerners possessed "as much of reverence for ... their common country, as any other civilized and patriotic people."[8] If the Southerners had never really left the Union, the war was analogous to using the army to put down a riot. This analysis seemed logical enough given the Republican Party's denunciation of a sinister unrepresentative "Slave Power" over the preceding five years. Northerners clung to this seductive theory with stubborn persistence because it enabled them to evade the central ideological dilemma posed by the war: how to coerce unwilling southerners back into a Union that was supposed to be based on government by the consent of the governed.

The assumption among Unionists that support for secession was weak and shallow underpinned the strategy developed by the aging and long-serving General-in-Chief Winfield Scott in the weeks after Sumter. Scott, a former Whig presidential candidate and Mexican War hero, was a native of Virginia, but his loyalties remained firmly with the Union. Known as the "Anaconda Plan," Scott's strategy was to strangle the young Confederacy by blockading its ports, closing its borders and taking control of the Mississippi river. In the end, all of these things were done, but the underlying assumption—that encirclement would revive southern Unionism and undermine secession from within the white South—was a chimera. The Anaconda plan did not take into account the argument that if the political institutions of the Confederacy could be established for a few months unmolested by a direct military assault, their chances of long-term survival would be greatly enhanced, not least because of the message that it would send out to foreign governments.

The patience and passivity of the Anaconda plan was also wildly at odds with the public mood. Northerners wanted a fight and politicians and newspaper editors were convinced that the capture of the Confederate capital would end the war. This was a questionable assumption, but it had massive consequences for the way the war was fought. In this most democratic of wars, public opinion was the final arbiter of military strategy. The press reporting of the battles in Virginia focused northern public attention on the eastern theater even when the Union army was making much more progress in the west, and consequently helped shape the strategic thinking of politicians and generals. Military historians have often bemoaned the obsession with the eastern theater, but the truth is that if public opinion on both sides believed that the war would be determined in Virginia then to a large extent that became the strategic reality. The concentration on the east is justified by the concentration of bloody battles that were fought there. James M. McPherson has calculated that of the 50 southern regiments with the highest percentage of battle casualties, 40 fought with the Army of Northern Virginia in the east, while more than half of all the men killed in battle on the Union side fought with the Army of the Potomac. Furthermore, men from New England and the mid-Atlantic were 23 percent more likely to be killed in battle than their comrades from western states.[9]

On a tactical level, the background and experience of Union generals did not prepare them for a war to destroy the Confederate willpower and war-making capacity. In the Mexican War, the tactic of frontal assaults—as at Palo Alto and elsewhere—had succeeded. In contrast, the advantage appeared to lie with the defense in the Civil War. Only one in eight frontal assaults succeeded. This shift is often attributed to technological change, in particular the introduction of rifled muzzle-loading cannons and muskets that were more accurate than the old smooth-bore weapons, and the invention of the minie ball—a conical shaped bullet that expanded as it was fired. The sense that frontal assaults were ineffective, even suicidal, was enhanced by officers on both sides who quickly acquired the habit of ordering their men to build field fortifications, and by generals who—with a few stunning exceptions—tended to make cautious, defensive decisions about the placement of their troops whenever they could. Even so, Civil War battlefields rarely, if ever, resembled the Western Front in the World War I. As Paddy Griffith has argued, "attacking formations were not mown down before they arrived close to the enemy, but managed to instill themselves at highly 'Napoleonic' ranges and slog it out until all ammunition was used up."[10] In this era before the widespread use of an effective machine gun, offensives against well-defended positions could succeed when commanders not only had a numerical advantage but were also prepared to be persistent and flexible—as Grant and Sherman proved in 1864 and as British generals on the Western Front learned after 1916.

In the first year of the war a huge constraint on the North's freedom to launch an assault was the importance of not alienating the Border States. It was here in these four slave states that remained in the Union that the Civil War was genuinely a brothers' war. Kentucky and Missouri in particular were very divided, with members of the same family serving in different armies. Kentucky, after all, was the native state of both Lincoln and Davis, as well as the home state of the "Great Compromiser," Henry Clay. These Border States were strategically vital. Maryland and Delaware mattered because their secession would have forced the federal government to abandon Washington. The loss of Missouri would have given control of the Mississippi and Missouri river networks to the South, while Kentucky's secession would have added to the Confederacy a white population larger than any other southern state save Virginia, economically valuable farmland and livestock, and in the Ohio River, a formidable natural barrier on their northern border. While Lincoln was prepared to use force to keep Maryland in the Union, in Kentucky, which was so internally divided that it declared its neutrality in the conflict, a more circumspect approach was needed. Both the Union and the Confederate authorities sought to bolster the position of their supporters in the state by trying not to be seen as the aggressor. In the end, it was Confederate forces under General Braxton Bragg who blinked first and crossed over into Kentucky, giving Unionists the excuse they needed to invite Union troops into the state to repel the "invasion." Even after this event, the pressing need to prevent Kentucky following North Carolina or Tennessee and seceding in protest at the North's attempt to "subjugate" a fellow southern state decisively shaped Union policy. Lincoln promised in his initial call for troops that "the utmost care will be observed to avoid any devastation, any destruction of or interference with, property, or any disturbance of peaceful citizens any part of the country."[11] In December 1861, Lincoln told Congress that he did not want the war to "degenerate into a violent and remorseless revolutionary struggle."[12] Had the president done anything other than promise to respect slave property rights in 1861 or early 1862, the North would have been so divided that its capacity to continue the war would have been seriously threatened. Certainly it would have made it hard to keep the Border States, even Maryland and Delaware, with their relatively small slave populations on side.

In the heady early months of the war, then, slavery was an issue that almost everyone tried to avoid, but which was unavoidably present.

Paradoxes abounded. Slavery was protected by the Constitution, and the North was fighting to preserve the Constitution. But this simply pointed to an irony at the heart of the northern war effort: the Constitution could not be adequately defended using solely constitutional means. In fact, the barely whispered truth was that the Constitution had not only failed to prevent a civil war, its ambiguities may even have made one more likely. James Buchanan's narrow reading of the Constitution had left him naked and unarmed in the face of the secession crisis. Ulysses S. Grant, who had been rejuvenated by the war and had reentered military service as a colonel, expressed views on the relationship between slavery and the war that were probably typical of a majority of northerners. "My inclination," he wrote to his father in November 1861,

> is to whip the rebellion into submission, preserving all constitutional rights. If it cannot be whipped in any other way than through a war against slavery, let it come to that legitimately. If it is necessary that the Republic may continue its existence, let slavery go. But that portion of the press that advocates the beginning of such a war now, are as great enemies to their country as if they were open and avowed secessionists.[13]

The number of public voices advocating an attack on slavery grew after the defeat at Bull Run in July 1861. Many abolitionists had expressed pacifist ideas before the war, but as Henry Ward Beecher, perhaps the most influential minister in the North, put it in a sermon the day after the firing on Fort Sumter: "I hold that it is ten thousand times better to have war that to have slavery."[14] Frederick Douglass encapsulated the view point of the abolitionist movement: *The simple way to put an end to the savage and desolating war now being waged by the slaveholders, is to strike down slavery itself*, the primal cause of the war."[15] But it was not just abolitionists who linked the crushing of the rebellion with the end of slavery. Horace Greeley's *New York Tribune* summed up each day's war news under the heading "The Pro-Slavery Rebellion." The radical antislavery senator Charles Sumner was confident that the defeat at Bull Run had "done much for the slave." He told Lincoln that the defeat was "the worst event & the best in our history; the worst, as it was the greatest present calamity & shame—the best, as it made the extinction of Slavery inevitable."[16]

THE UNION ARMY ADVANCES: DECEMBER 1861–MAY 1862

The core institutional identity for Civil War soldiers was their company and then their regiment. Five or so regiments were combined into a brigade, commanded by a brigadier general, and two or more brigades formed a division, commanded by a major general. The next tier in the organizational pyramid was the corps. By the summer of 1861, Union and Confederate forces had been organized into separate armies consisting of two or more corps. Each side created armies with specific geographic strategic responsibilities, the Union side often naming them after rivers (such as the Army of the Potomac and the Army of the Cumberland) and the Confederates after geographical areas (the Army of Northern Virginia, the Army of Tennessee). The Army of the Potomac was the Union army given the most important responsibility— leading the assault on the new Confederate capital, Richmond, Virginia, against the Confederate Army of Northern Virginia.

In the wake of Bull Run, Lincoln appointed George B. McClellan as Commander of the newly created Army of the Potomac. In addition to this field command, McClellan replaced Scott as General-in-Chief. "I can do it all," he assured the president. He described the soldiers of McDowell's shattered army as "a collection of undisciplined, ill-officered and uninstructed men, who were, as a rule, demoralized and ready to run at the first shot." McClellan was a dapper, self-regarding man. He viewed his fellow officers and his political leaders with ill-concealed contempt. On one occasion, returning home to find Lincoln and Seward waiting to see him, he ignored them and went upstairs, sending word, 30 minutes later, that he had gone to bed and would see them another time.[17] McClellan convinced himself that he would need at least 200,000 fully trained and equipped men in order to have any chance of defeating Joseph E. Johnston's 45,000 Confederates in northern Virginia. The withering judgment of generations of historians is that McClellan lacked the resilience to fight the war that had to be fought. His overcaution bordered on paranoia, and for all his organizational ability, this rendered him ultimately a failure as a general. Through the late summer and autumn of 1861, Lincoln unsuccessfully pressed McClellan to attack. Rumors abounded in Washington that the conservative Democratic officers surrounding McClellan were secret sympathizers with the rebellion.

While McClellan painstakingly drilled and built up much-needed supplies, General Henry W. Halleck was in charge of Union forces in

Missouri and southern Illinois. A career army officer, with a reputation as a scholar of the theory of warfare that earned him the slightly mocking nickname "Old Brains," Halleck set about devising a plan to force Confederate forces out of Kentucky and Tennessee, and then to take control of the Mississippi River. His subordinate commander, General Ulysses S. Grant, was stunningly successful at putting this strategy into practice. He captured Fort Henry on February 6 and Fort Donelson ten days later, opening up to the Union the southward-flowing Tennessee and Cumberland rivers and with them an invaluable entry route into the South. Don Carlos Buell maneuvered the Confederates out of Nashville with its crucial manufacturing capacity and transport links on February 25. Grant stumbled into the first big battle of his Civil War career at Shiloh on April 6–7, 1862. His army was surprised by a Confederate force under Albert Sydney Johnston and P. G. T. Beauregard, although, in the bloodiest battle of the war to that point, the Union forces held their ground, in part because of the timely arrival of General Don Carlos Buell's reinforcements. The outcome of Shiloh was that a Confederate counteroffensive had been thwarted, albeit at heavy cost. When Lincoln was urged to remove Grant from command after the battle, he replied, "I can't spare this man, he fights."[18] On May 30, Halleck led a huge federal force that captured Corinth, Mississippi, another key strategic target because of its railroad links. In a few short months, the Union army had captured a vast swathe of the most economically and strategically vital territory in the heart of the Confederacy, from Kentucky down to Mississippi. Critical progress had been made toward implementing a central plank of Scott's Anaconda Plan, splitting the Confederacy in two by taking control of the Mississippi River. The failure to muster all available troops to defend Middle Tennessee before the fall of Henry and Donelson, wrote Josiah Gorgas, the head of the Confederate Ordinance Bureau, on June 12, 1862, "was the great mistake of the War."[19]

The backdrop to the launch of McClellan's spring offensive was therefore one of unremitting failure for Confederate arms. Even relatively small engagements outside of the main theaters of war went against them. In northwestern Arkansas, the rebels lost the battle of Pea Ridge at the beginning of March and in the far west, on March 28, a small Confederate invasion force was repulsed at the battle of Glorietta in New Mexico. In February, March and April, on the coast of North Carolina, the US navy helped capture a succession of islands and harbors: Roanoke, New Bern, Fort Macon. Most depressing for southern morale was the scuttling on May 11 of the CSS *Virginia*, an extraordinary iron-clad warship, popularly known by its former name the *Merrimac*, which a couple of weeks earlier had astonished and delighted the southern public by destroying a number of northern wooden vessels. The fact that the Confederacy with its meager ship-building and manufacturing base had created an iron-clad at all was truly impressive, but the life of the low-slung warship was never likely to be long once the Union navy countered with an iron-clad of its own, the *USS Monitor*. Nevertheless, the sinking of the *Merrimac* helped reinforce, on the eve of McClellan's great offensive, the sense that the military initiative which had so clearly lain with the South in the previous summer and autumn was slipping rapidly away. The good news that southerners clung to in May 1862 was the daring victories of Stonewall Jackson in the Shenandoah Valley. The *Richmond Whig* leapt on Jackson's success, enthusing that his "little army is the pride of the South and the terror of the North. . . . Oh, for a dozen Jacksons!"[20] In boosting Confederate morale the Valley Campaign was of great value, but the big picture was that McClellan appeared to be closing in on Richmond.

In the North, the hopes invested in McClellan's new, disciplined army were immense. Typical of the hyperbole in the northern press was *New York Times*' assurance to its readers on March 12 that the "final blow may now be struck which shall annihilate the rebel army as an organized force, and crush the Government of the rebel Confederacy at its Capital."[21] Newspaper reporters who witnessed the marching and logistical preparations lauded, with justifiable enthusiasm, the "most magnificent army ever assembled on American soil." In such circum-stances, anything less than the rapid fall of Richmond and the collapse of the Confederacy would seem like failure. The spring offensive was intended to end the war once and for all, and for McClellan it was an extraordinary opportunity to test his self-confidence in his own military leadership. His plan avoided a direct approach to Richmond, the Confed-erate capital which lay about 90 miles south of Washington. Instead, in what became known as the Peninsular Campaign, the Army of the Potomac was to be transported by sea to the mouth of the James River, from where they would attack Richmond from the east, evading, or so they hoped, Confederate defenses. Lincoln was reported to be highly skeptical about this scheme, but did not feel he could take the respons-ibility for overruling his popular and supremely confident general.[22]

In Washington, Benjamin Brown French, a clerk in the House of Representatives, noted in his journal in April that "the Nation has been wonderfully excited, & Washington has, of course, been in a tumult. The news of victory after victory over the rebels has come and over them we have all rejoiced, and appearances indicate that the game of secession is nearly played out."[23] Secretary of State Seward concurred with this assessment. He told Charles Sumner at the start of May that he was utterly confident that the war would be over in 90 days.[24] Joseph E. Johnston, who was the highest-ranking officer in the old army to join the Confederacy, delayed McClellan's advance at the old Revolutionary war battle-sites of Yorktown and Williamsburg, but by May, he was backed up within sight of Richmond. On May 14, John B. Jones, a clerk in the Confederate War Department in Richmond, noted glumly in his diary that "Our army has fallen back to within four miles of Richmond. Much anxiety is felt for the fate of the city. Is there no turning point in this long line of downward progress?"[25]

CONFEDERATE VICTORIES IN THE EAST: MAY TO SEPTEMBER 1862

On May 31, the rebels attempted a counterattack at the battle of Seven Pines and among the wounded was General Johnston. At this point, Robert E. Lee, the Colonel who had arrested John Brown and had until then been a military advisor to Jefferson Davis, took field command of the rebel armies for the first time. Just two months earlier, Lee, who had opposed secession, had been offered command of the federal army, but had refused to lead a force that would invade his home state of Virginia. Lee was at first regarded with suspicion by southern press and public. "I do not much like him," wrote the North Carolinian diarist Catherine Edmondston, on hearing the news that Lee was to take charge of the defense of Richmond, "he 'falls back' too much. His knick name last summer was '*old-stick-in-the-mud*' . . . There is mud enough now in and about our lines, but pray God he may not fulfill the whole of his name."[26] But Lee, a taciturn undemonstrative man, was about to prove himself one of the wiliest, most courageous, and most effective commanders of the war. In contrast to Johnston's concern with conserving his forces' strength against a stronger foe, Lee believed that the Confederacy could counter the manpower advantage of the Union army only by seizing and keeping the initiative. In a stunning series of victories known as the Seven Days battles, Lee's leadership transformed the Confederacy's position in just one, spellbinding week. The Seven

Days battles were characterized by not only great bravery and daring, but also some tragic, futile frontal assaults, such as that by A. P. Hill's division at Mechanicsville on June 26 and the following day at Gaines's Mill. Most appalling of all was the assault led by General Daniel Harvey Hill on July 1 at Malvern Hill, where, against a superb natural defensive position, more than 5000 southern soldiers were killed in one afternoon. High as Confederate casualties were, it was exhilarating to southerners to be on the offensive. Some Union officers urged a counterattack at Malvern Hill against an obviously weakened enemy. But McClellan made what he described as a "tactical" withdrawal down the James River to Harrison's Landing where he energetically set about requesting more men and supplies. The Peninsular Campaign that was meant to seize Richmond had ground to an ignominious and bloody end. More than 50,000 men had died, and, given the soaring expectations of Union success, a stalemate was tantamount to a Confederate victory.

Lee's first great foray in the field had succeeded completely in his larger strategic objective. Richmond had been saved to fight another day, and Confederate morale lifted. Union General Philip Kearny, the millionaire scion of a New York banking family, fumed that "McClellan's want of Generalship, or treason, has gotten us into a place, where we are completely boxed up. . . . And out of which nothing short of most bold and dashing moves can extricate us to be of any service."[27] In Washington, Benjamin Brown French was sardonic: "Our generals call it a strategic movement of McClellan to obtain a better base of operations! Two or three such strategic movements would anni-hilate our army."[28] Privately, Senator Zachariah Chandler of Michigan called McClellan "an imbecile if not a traitor" who had "virtually lost the Army of the Potomac."[29] Lee, meanwhile, was on the path that would make him the ultimate embodiment of Confederate nationalism. In Columbia, South Carolina, Grace Brown Elmore thanked God for Lee's success. "Thou hast answered our prayers," she wrote, "and given us one who is well able to guide us through this fearful time, and lead us on to freedom."[30]

Some historians have argued that the Peninsular Campaign was an example of how Lee's offensive strategy merely sapped critical manpower from the South for no long-term strategic gain. Herman Hattaway and Archer Jones, for example, see the Seven Days battles as "attrition distinctly favorable to the Union" which effected "little real change in the strategic situation."[31] But this underestimates the political consequences of McClellan's failure. The Seven Days battles were the first great watershed of the war. Never again did northern newspapers expect such an easy victory. Officers and men in the Army of the Potomac developed what almost amounted to an inferiority complex.[32] Had Lee not taken command in place of Johnston the war may well have come to a swift end in the summer of 1862. Johnston always retreated and might have been maneuvered into a siege in Richmond by McClellan, who, in such circumstances, would eventually have prevailed. This was the moment when a limited war, one that respected the inviolability of slavery, could have been won. McClellan's failure inaugurated a new kind of war, one that he was unprepared to fight.

As McClellan's star faded, John Pope became the next in a series of generals who took command of the Army of the Potomac, only to be outwitted by General Lee. On August 30, a smaller Confederate force, which Lee had audaciously divided into two divisions headed by Stonewall Jackson and James Longstreet, forced a confrontation with Pope near the site of the previous year's Bull Run battlefield. In the year since the first battle in this rolling hill country, the armies had been transformed from enthusiastic, disorganized amateurs into seasoned, well-drilled units capable of inflicting sustained damage on the enemy. This second battle of Bull Run was an even more decisive Confederate victory than the first and cost the lives of almost twice as many Union soldiers as Confederate soldiers. Emboldened, Lee then launched the first of his two grand raids into the North. He wanted to keep the Army of the Potomac out of Virginia, collect food and forage for his own Army of Northern Virginia in Maryland and Pennsylvania, and allow Virginia farmers to gather the harvest in peace. In a broader strategic sense, Lee recognized the advantages of taking the war to the North. Having rebel troops in a northern state would make it difficult for Republicans in the upcoming midterm elections to argue that the project of military subjugation of the rebellion was working. In their more optimistic moments, Confederate leaders hoped that Lee's invasion might perhaps persuade Maryland slaveholders to support the Confederacy and foreign powers to recognize it.

The Army of Northern Virginia crossed the Potomac on September 4. Lee had divided his forces once again, ensuring that he could not be caught in a pincer movement by sending Stonewall Jackson to preemptively deal with Union troops stationed at Harpers Ferry. Jackson did so with barely a shot fired, capturing over 12,000 Union troops; one of the largest ever surrenders of US troops in history. Thereafter, little went right for the Confederates. By an extraordinary chance,

Lee's secret battle plans, dropped accidentally by a messenger, were discovered by a Union soldier and delivered to McClellan, who, after Pope's failure, was back in full command of Union forces. Using the intelligence that had so serendipitously fallen into his lap, McClellan caught up with Lee. The battle that the rebels would know as Sharpsburg and the federals as Antietam began at first light on September 17. Like so many encounters, Antietam was a fluid, confused and messy fight, with "friendly fire" compounding the difficulties of communication on a large battle area where no one had more than a partial view of the fighting. Here, as elsewhere, particular spots on the battlefield acquired an especially gruesome reputation—Miller's cornfield, the epicenter of fighting in the first few hours of the battle which changed hands 15 times in a couple of hours; the old sunken road, thereafter known as the "bloody lane," from which the rebels held the attacking federals at bay for three hours in late morning. At about 1 o'clock in the afternoon the Confederate line at Bloody Lane collapsed and, amid heavy fighting, Lee's army retreated in disorder back across a narrow bridge over Antietam Creek and into the town of Sharpsburg. The Union army now had an opportunity to cut off Lee's line of retreat and destroy his army, but despite pleas from his officers, McClellan refused to allow thousands of uncommitted Union troops to join the fray. Having been thrown a lifeline, the Confederates counterattacked, bolstered by the timely arrival of reinforcements led by General A. P. Hill, whose troops had marched 17 miles in eight hours from Harpers Ferry. By nightfall, the rebels had retaken the narrow bridge over the creek. For all the carnage, the Confederate line had been pushed back only a few hundred yards.

The following day, both armies remained on the field of battle amid the bodies of the 23,000 men who had fallen—more men killed in one day than the Americans had lost in the Revolution, the War of 1812 and the Mexican War combined. Astonishingly, McClellan permitted Lee, to recross the Potomac into Virginia unmolested. McClellan's dwindling band of defenders celebrated the "Little Napoleon's" success in turning back Lee's army, which, since the Seven Days battles, had seemed invincible. Many others, including the president, fumed that he had missed a tantalizing opportunity to crush the rebel army decisively. McClellan, while moaning that his achievements were not being recognized in Washington, was typically unstinting in the praise he lavished on himself. "I have the satisfaction of knowing that God has in His mercy a second time made me the instrument for saving the nation," he told his wife.[33]

The spring and summer of 1862 had been a three-act drama for the South. In the spring Confederate fortunes looked bleak, but a combination of Lee's brilliance and McClellan's failure of nerve turned the tables in the Seven Days battles. Then came the high point with the dramatic victory over Pope's army at the second battle of Bull Run. Then, the third stage, hubris: the invasion of Maryland culminating in the carnage at Antietam. To southerners whose optimism had been sky-high in August, the retreat from Antietam was a disappointment. Lee had hoped to remain in the North for much longer, and there was some muted criticism of his recklessness with his soldiers' lives. Lee had marched his men beyond endurance prompting rising desertions and sickness. There was little to be gained from confrontation at Antietam, and only a supreme confidence in his army's ability to beat a foe with twice as many men could have induced him to make a stand there and then. Furthermore, his successful retreat had been entirely dependent on McClellan's astonishing failure to follow up his victory. Yet the gains of the summer more than offset these problems. The losses in the west were obscured by the heroism and audaciousness of Lee's men. From the summer of 1862 onward, hope for the future of the Confederate republic rested on Lee and his army. The people's confidence in him, and the aura of invincibility that surrounded him even after Antietam, did more than any other single factor to prolong the Confederate fight for survival. The bloody stalemate at Antietam may have been regarded on both sides as tantamount to a defeat for the Army of Northern Virginia, but the Confederate cause remained very much alive and spirits in the South high.

EMANCIPATION

On July 7, 1862, with his army forced back to Harrison's Landing on the James River, McClellan, who had never suffered from an overly narrow conception of his role, decided to set out, in a letter to the president which he also released to the press, his "general views concerning the state of the rebellion; although they do not strictly relate to the situation of this Army or strictly come within the scope of my official duties." His letter—known as the "Harrison's Landing Letter"—laid bare the divisions within the North over the purpose of the war. McClellan argued that the war "should be conducted upon the highest principles known to Christian Civilization," by which he meant that it "should not be a War looking to the subjugation of the people of any state, in any event." Private property should be respected, and, in particular, McClellan insisted that "military power should not be allowed to interfere with the relations of servitude." He concluded that

> a system of policy thus constitutional and conservative, and pervaded by the influences of Christianity and freedom, would receive the support of almost all truly loyal men, would deeply impress the rebel masses and all foreign nations, and it might be humbly hoped that it would commend itself to the favor of the Almighty."[34]

McClellan was in effect mounting a preemptive attack on what he knew was the rising support within the Lincoln administration for a formal declaration that the emancipation of the slaves should become an official northern war aim. The irony is that had McClellan's assault on Richmond succeeded, he would not have needed to issue the letter. McClellan was arguing for a continuation of the limited war that had been tried and now, it appeared, had failed. While McClellan made his impassioned plea that the war should not escalate, President Lincoln was coming to the opposite conclusion.

McClellan's conception of a limited war died on the field of Antietam. The limited Union victory in that fight was to be the final battle of the first phase of the war. Just days later, on September 22, 1862, the president issued a proclamation stating that if, by January 1, 1863, the rebel states had not returned to the Union, the United States would, from that date onward, regard slaves held in rebel areas as free. This Preliminary Emancipation Proclamation had an incendiary effect. It was an ultimatum to the South: return to the Union within 100 days with slavery intact, or face total destruction. Jefferson Davis called it "the most execrable measure in the history of guilty man." The three-month delay was not because Lincoln thought it likely that the rebels would throw down their weapons, but it sent a clear message that emancipation was a tool of war rather than an end in itself. Like a riot policeman warning that if a mob didn't disperse they would be fired upon, Lincoln was giving fair warning that the Confederates should not mistake the seriousness of northern intent.

On January 1, the president duly issued the Emancipation Proclamation. As the preliminary proclamation had promised, it applied only to those areas of the United States still up in arms against the government, and much of the document was taken up with a list of counties in rebel states which, because they were now occupied by the Union army, were exempted from the proclamation. Then came the central point: "I do order and declare," wrote Lincoln, "that all persons held as slaves within said designated States, and parts of States, are, and henceforward shall be free; and that the Executive government of the United States, including the military and naval authorities thereof, will recognize and maintain the freedom of said persons."[35]

The black community reacted with jubilation. A bishop in the African Methodist Episcopal Church in Washington DC recalled that while the proclamation was being read aloud from the first edition of a newspaper,

> every kind of demonstration and gesticulation was going on. Men squealed, women fainted, dogs barked, white and colored people shook hands, songs were sung, and by this time cannons began to fire at the navy-yard. . . . Great processions of colored and white men marched to and fro and passed in front of the White House and congratulated President Lincoln on his proclamation. The President came to the window and made responsive bows, and thousands told him, if he would come out of that palace, they would hug him to death."[36]

Frederick Douglass told supporters, "we shout for joy that we live to record this righteous decree." At a public meeting in Boston, the veteran white abolitionist Wendell Phillips wept for joy in the belief that his life's work had come to fruition.

Pressure on the federal government to abandon its initial declarations that it would not touch slavery in the South came in part from the actions of slaves themselves. In March 1861, even before Sumter had fallen to the Confederates, eight runaway slaves appeared at a federal garrison in Florida apparently in the belief that the Union troops would protect them and give them their freedom.[37] Over the next year this trickle grew to a steady stream. In May 1861, General John C. Frémont, the antislavery politician who had been the first Republican presidential candidate in 1856, issued an order declaring free all slaves in Missouri, the military district under his command. Abolitionists were delighted at this evidence that the war would strike at the heart of the hated institution, but Lincoln, concerned about the impact on the Border States and determined not to let individual officers take control of a fundamentally political question, countermanded the order. Meanwhile, General Benjamin F. Butler, a former Breckinridge Democrat politician, developed a more subtle approach. He announced that any fugitive slave who sought refuge in Union-held Fortress Monroe in Virginia would be held as "contraband of war." Butler's declaration was supported by politicians from all parts of the Republican Party. Montgomery Blair, who was later to arouse the hostility of radicals for his presumed leniency toward southern rebels agreed on the grounds that "secession niggers" had been used by rebels to "do all their fortifying." Blair's approach was strictly pragmatic however. He suggested that Butler might "improve the code" by making sure that the Union army only offered protection to slaves able to work. He should "let the rest go" in order "not to be required to feed unproductive laborers, or indeed any that you do not require or cannot conveniently manage." For Blair the "contraband policy" was not tantamount to a policy of emancipation by stealth. "The business you are sent upon", he reminded Butler, was "war not emancipation." The ultimate solution to the slave question, Blair argued, was "a renewal of Mr. Jefferson's idea" of colonization. He was confident that for the majority of southerners who were nonslaveholders, and who therefore had no financial incentive to hold on to their slave property, "the removal of the negroes from among them will make them all emancipationists. It is the idea of negro equality alone that embitters them against the North."[38]

General Halleck issued a general order prohibiting Union officers from accepting any more contrabands into their camps and requiring them to eject any currently under their protection. Halleck's order only applied to Union armies in the west, but it represented a direct challenge to Butler's approach. In November 1861, General William T. Sherman instructed a subordinate that "we have nothing to do with [runaway slaves] at all and you should not let them take refuge in Camp. It forms a source of representation by which Union men are estranged from our cause."[39] This became an ever-harder position to maintain. During the winter of 1861–1862, the practical difficulty of fighting a war against a slave society without infringing slaveowners' property rights was illustrated by the experience of the Tenth Massachusetts Volunteers who were encamped in Northern Virginia. Runaway slaves—"contrabands" as they were now known to Union troops—arrived each morning at the gates of the camp, and officers eagerly employed them as personal servants. "I have got a 'Contraband,' " wrote a delighted Captain Charles Brewster in January, 1862.

His master whipped him in the morning for something or other and he took leg bail in the evening and landed here night before last. . . . He is quite smart for a nigger though he is quite slow but he is willing and I think has improved a good deal since I got him. I have not heard anything of his master, and if I do I shan't give him up without a struggle."[40]

Brewster came from an antislavery family and he defended his acquisition of a cheap black servant as a blow against the peculiar institution. But shortly afterwards, a fellow officer, Captain Miller, who was apparently a "proslavery" Democrat complained about the presence of blacks in the camp to a superior officer, Major Marsh, who in turn ordered the Tenth Massachusetts to return their "contrabands" to their masters. A running battle ensued with the "contrabands" fleeing the camp whenever pro-slavery officers entered to search for them, and antislavery officers and men posting placards and holding meetings to protest about the effort to drive the slaves back into the hands of their masters. The majority of soldiers held antislavery views and, according to Brewster, the regiment was

almost in a state of mutiny on the Nigger question . . . the men did not come down here to oppress Niggers and they are not quite brutes yet, as some of their officers are. . . . Major Marsh well knows that the slaves masters are waiting outside of camp ready to snap them up, and it is unhuman [*sic.*] to drive them into their hands, if you could have seen strong men crying like children, at the very thought as I did yesterday you would not blame me for standing out about it nor can one blame the men for showing sympathy for them, for they are from Massachusetts and are entirely unused to such scenes, and cannot recognize this property in human flesh and blood.[41]

Encounters with runaway slaves had a dramatic impact on some Union soldiers. Black people were exotic and fascinating to rural farm boys from the North. An Illinois private wrote home to his young children in 1862, "I have seen lots of Negroes which are black people and little Negroe children. A Negroe woman got me some water to wash my feet. Their skin is dark brown and their hair is short and black and curly."[42] Northern soldiers may not have met many black people before, but many of them had grown up in antislavery households, and they interpreted their encounters with freed slaves in the light of what they had heard and read of the cruelties of slavery. Private Chauncey Cooke wrote to his mother in Wisconsin about "a toothless old slave with one blind eye" who told him horrific stories of his wife and children having been sold, of whippings and being hunted by bloodhounds when he tried to escape. When Cooke reported the tales to his comrades they told him "it was all bosh, that the niggers were lying," but Cooke was certain of the truth of what he had heard: the stories were "just like the ones in Uncle Tom's Cabin and I believe them."[43]

Some Union troops were convinced by evangelical preachers and antislavery propaganda that expunging the sin of slavery would redeem their country in the eyes of the Lord. Some simply wanted black troops to be placed in the front line instead of them. Most were probably convinced by the much more pragmatic case that if the rebels hated emancipation, then it must be a good thing. Emancipation was a weapon which, whatever its merits on its own terms, struck at the heart of southern society. Slavery was the "tap-root" of rebellion. Pull up the root, and you kill the rebellion. Union soldiers commonly used terms such as "darkie" and "nigger" in their letters. Even proudly antislavery soldiers exhibited an unquestioning racism. There was no contradiction in holding racist views while also thinking that a war against seces- sion was inherently a war against slavery, that the Confederacy was a repressive society that challenged basic American values of freedom and opportunity. "This war is killing slavery," wrote Charles Francis Adams, Jr, the grandson of former President John Quincy Adams, in April, 1862, while on a visit to the Union-occupied sea islands of South Carolina.[44] Captain Brewster of the Tenth Massachusetts agreed that "this war is playing the Dickens with slavery and if it lasts much longer will clear our Countrys name of the vile stain and enable us to live in peace hereafter."[45]

The political pressure for emancipation in the North had been rising throughout 1862. Congress had already taken a lead. The departure of congressmen from seceded states had left the Republican Party with a large majority in both houses of Congress, which it used to abolish slavery in the one area where Congress had clear constitu- tional authority: the District of Columbia. In jubilant defiance of the *Dred Scott* decision, Congress then outlawed slavery in the western territories as well. The controversial Second Confiscation Act, passed by Congress in July 1862, had already declared the slaves of rebels "forever free of their servitude" and required the Union army to regard slaves who came to their lines as free men, so long as their masters were rebels. On the basis of this act, Lincoln had penned an executive order for Union officers instructing them to "seize and use any property, real or personal, which may be necessary or convenient for military purposes." In effect this gave legislative sanction to General Butler's "contraband" policy by declaring that the slaves of rebels should be considered free when the Union army came into contact with them. A Militia Act had already decreed that freed slaves could be employed by the Union army (though not enlisted as soldiers). In terms of the relationship between Union soldiers and the slaves they encountered, therefore, the president's proclamation was not breaking new ground.

The arguments against issuing a presidential proclamation of emancipation were, given the racist assumptions of the time, powerful. Few military leaders were calling for such a move. It would divide the North and intensify southern resistance. Its impact on foreign powers was uncertain. Given the racism of most northern soldiers, the prospect of enlisting black troops would have, at best, an ambivalent effect on the already battered morale of the Union army. In the face of these well-rehearsed objections, Lincoln's decision to issue the proclamation reflected the president's own understanding of the need to face up to the fundamental problem the nation faced.

Lincoln's private views on the subject of slavery are reasonably clear. His conviction that slavery was wrong had steadily grown as he had confronted the implications of the Slave Power. That did not mean, however, that he was always inclined to support emancipation as a tool of war. Lincoln's conception of politics involved a very clear division between his private views and his public duties. "I am naturally anti-slavery," Lincoln wrote in 1864,

> If slavery is not wrong, nothing is wrong. I cannot remember when I did not so think, and feel. And yet I have never understood that the Presidency conferred upon me an unrestricted right to act officially upon this judgment and feeling. . . . I have done no official act in mere deference to my abstract judgment and feeling on slavery."[46]

Contrary to McClellan's pleas for respect for rebel property, the president was announcing that the gloves were coming off. As General Halleck put it, "perhaps with us now, as in the French Revolution, some harsh measures are required against the 'slave power' "[47] Lincoln himself put it less dramatically when, on July 13, he first aired his plans to issue an emancipation proclamation to Secretary of State Seward and Secretary of the Navy Gideon Welles. "We must free the slaves, or be ourselves subdued," said Lincoln.

The Emancipation Proclamation did not alter Lincoln's basic proposition that the preservation of the Union was the moral purpose of the war. Indeed, for him, the Union, as Alexander Stephens was later to remark, was elevated "to the level of religious mysticism." A delegation of Chicago Christians came to the White House to petition the president to transform the war into a crusade against slavery only a few days before Lincoln made the Preliminary Proclamation public. Lincoln did not reveal his plans, but assured them that that he viewed the issue of emancipation "as a practical war measure, to be decided upon according to the advantages or disadvantages it may offer to the suppression of the rebellion."[48] He had said much the same thing in a widely published letter to Horace Greeley a couple of weeks earlier in which he had stated that

> If I could save the Union without freeing *any* slave I would do it, and if I could save it by freeing *all* the slaves I would do it; and if I could save it by freeing some and leaving others alone I would also do that. What I do about slavery, and the colored race, I do because I believe it helps to save the Union; and what I forbear, I forbear because I do *not* believe it would help to save the Union.[49]

This practical justification for emancipation was backed up by the concern among Lincoln and his supporters that the Proclamation not be regarded as an incitement to rebellion. The final Emancipation Proclamation explicitly enjoined "the people so declared free to abstain from all violence, unless in necessary self-defense."[50]

The historian Richard Hofstadter once famously described Lincoln as a "delicate barometer" of public opinion. Lincoln himself once claimed that he was "shaped" by events. And it is certainly true that Lincoln was a deft politician, who was unusually good at calculating the mood of the many different political constituencies on which he depended. His decisions were always circumscribed by his judgment about what was politically and constitutionally possible. Yet he was a shaper of events as well. The Proclamation irrevocably altered the terms on which the war would be discussed and conducted. It did not settle the future of slavery—only Union military victory and ultimately the Thirteenth

Amendment could do that. Nor did it signal that Lincoln believed that only a forcible emancipation could end slavery in America—in his message to Congress in December 1862 and in later letters and statements, he reiterated his plea to slaveowners in the Border States (which were not covered, of course, by the Emancipation Proclamation) to accept with emancipation in return for federal compensation. Southern planters, whether in rebel or loyal areas, notably refused to cooperate in this way, in stark contrast to slaveowners in Brazil or the British Empire, or the Russian nobility, who ensured that they salvaged as much as they could from the decision of Tsar Alexander II to free the serfs in 1861.

The future status of slaves depended on the Union army, and on the commitment of northerners to the emancipation policy. When the Confederate army was in the ascendant, for example during Braxton Bragg's invasion of Kentucky in 1862, and the army of Northern Virginia's march into Maryland and Pennsylvania in 1863, the tide of emancipation was not merely stopped but reversed, as thousands of blacks were re-enslaved. Indeed, since it applied only to rebel-held areas and not to those slaves under Union control, the proclamation did not actually free anyone; as Secretary of State William H. Seward wryly conceded, "we show our sympathy with slavery by emancipating slaves where we cannot reach them and holding them in bondage where we can set them free."[51] Building on the apparent logic of Seward's comment, it has become conventional to dismiss the proclamation as just a piece of paper, at best incidental to the real-life story of slaves freeing themselves. In explaining emancipation, scholars such as Leon Litwack and Ira Berlin have turned the spotlight away from Lincoln and toward the agency of slaves.[52]

The desire of slaves to be free was indeed the basic reality with which the slave society of the South had to contend, but it would be a serious mistake to underestimate the significance of the Emancipation Proclamation to the eventual abolition of slavery. The declaration that all slaves in rebel-held areas would be forever free was a statement of intent rather than of fact. But it sent out a very clear message, with the authority that only a presidential proclamation could bring, that the terms of engagement had changed. By themselves, the raw truth was that African-Americans in the South lacked the numbers and the power to overthrow slavery. Lincoln, the Republican-controlled Congress, and the Union army, removed the legal bulwarks of slavery and neutralized the military power of the white South. Even as a stopgap measure, which could still, in theory, have been rescinded by a future president or countermanded by a court, the Emancipation Proclamation transformed the legal status of slaves.[53] It is true that, had President Lincoln resisted the pressure on him to issue a proclamation of emancipation, the process of abolition would have continued anyway. Slaves would still have sabotaged the Confederate war effort where they could, and they still would have run away wherever Union troops came within marching distance. But the Proclamation dramatically altered the context in which slaves took decisions to run away. It was a bold recognition that this was not a war to restore the old Union, but to create something new. "Just a little while since," wrote a black abolitionist, "the American flag to the bondman was an ensign of bondage; now it has become a symbol of protection and freedom. Once the slave was a despised and trampled on pariah; now he has become a useful ally to the American government."[54]

It is important not to lose sight of the political and strategic risks that Lincoln was taking in coupling together the fate of the Union with the fate of slavery. In terms of the political position of the administration, emancipation was a highly dangerous move. In some Union regiments there were near-mutinies at the news. Lincoln's mailbag was filled with letters urging him to make a public declaration of support for emancipation, but there was also no shortage of warnings from Republicans in key states who argued that making the abolition of slavery a war aim would be devastating for the president's friends in the midterm elections due in September, October and November 1862. The black abolitionist Frances Ellen Watkins Harper thanked God that the president had not failed the slaves. "The fierce rumbling of democratic thunder" had not shaken from his hand "the bolt he leveled against slavery."[55] But Lincoln's old Illinois friend Orville Hickman Browning was one of many political allies who told him that the emancipation proclamation had been "disastrous to us." Before it had been issued, "all loyal people were united in support of the war and the administration," wrote Browning. Now, the North was divided.[56]

The delegation of Chicago ministers who visited Lincoln a couple of weeks before he issued the Preliminary Emancipation Proclamation, argued that such a move "would secure the sympathy of Europe and the whole civilized world, which now saw no other reason for the strife than national pride and ambition, an unwillingness to abridge our domain and power. No other step would be so potent to prevent foreign intervention."[57] They were right that the British political class had thus far been generally dismissive of the idea that slavery was at stake in the Civil War. In October 1861, Foreign Secretary Lord John Russell dismissed the idea that North and South were "contending, as so many States of the Old World have contended, the one for empire and the other power."[58] The Emancipation Proclamation did not immediately alter British perceptions, though. Russell feared it would lead to "acts of plunder, of incendiarism, and of revenge" and worried that the war would descend into a barbaric struggle.[59] The conservative *Spectator* magazine stingingly, and accurately, observed that the principle asserted by the Emancipation Proclamation "is not that a human being cannot own another, but that he cannot own him unless he is loyal to the United States."[60] Two weeks after the Preliminary Emancipation Proclamation had been issued, Gladstone made a famous speech in Newcastle in which he declared

> that Jefferson Davis and other leaders of the South have made an army; they are making, it appears, a navy; and they have made what is more than either—they have made a nation. We may anticipate with certainty the success of the Southern States so far as their separation from the North is concerned."[61]

But in the long run, the Union's official endorsement of emancipation prevented whatever slim chance there may have been of British intervention on behalf of the South. The British abolitionist tradition may have been attenuated by the 1860s, but the Anglo-American connection that linked antislavery organizations and churches across the Atlantic was still strong enough to be energized in support of the Union after the Emancipation Proclamation.[62] In January 1863, a public meeting of Manchester workingmen sent a formal message to Lincoln assuring him of their support now that it was clear that "the war which has so sorely distressed us as well as afflicted you, will strike off the fetters of the slave."[63]

The Emancipation Proclamation paved the way for the use of black troops on a grand scale. The 179,000 African-Americans who took up arms against the Confederacy shaped the war decisively. The sight of former slaves in arms against their former masters was terrifying and enraging to southern whites and inspirational to slaves who remained in bondage. It was the most tangible evidence that the power structures on which the Old South had depended were being turned upside down. In the Border States, the enlistment of black troops was a massive blow to slavery. More than half of all black men in Kentucky enlisted. The emancipation policy raised the stakes. "There is now no possible hope of reconciliation with the rebels," concluded Halleck. "The north must either destroy the slave-oligarchy, or become slaves themselves."[64] One did not need to be an antislavery Republican to understand this hardheaded reality. "I am no *abolitionist*," wrote a Kentucky lady in late 1862, but "I am for closing this war as quickly as possible and if [it] can [only] be done by freeing all the niggers, let them go."[65] The promise of black freedom inaugurated and symbolized the end of the limited war approach. By taking the moral high ground from which he would not retreat ("the promise being made, must be kept," Lincoln later said), emancipation legitimized the escalation of the war.[66] The sacrifice of white southerners in their pursuit of independence gave the lie to the widespread assumption of so many northerners, including Lincoln, that secession was an elite trick that belied the underlying Unionism of the ordinary southern people. Ultimately it was the strength of Confederate resistance which mandated the shift from a limited war to one that encompassed emancipation.

4 Emancipation and Hard War, 1862–1864

CONFEDERATE HIGH TIDE: DECEMBER 1862–JULY 1863

McClellan's caution at Antietam was enough to seal his fate once and for all with Lincoln. For the second and final time, he was relieved of command. The president appointed General Ambrose E. Burnside to replace McClellan as the new commander of the Army of the Potomac and urged him to launch a fresh assault on Richmond immediately. Burnside certainly looked the part. The Rhode Islander wore a soft, wide-brimmed hat with the crown pushed out, a style that became known as a "Burnside" after the war. Burnside left an even greater etymological legacy thanks to his distinctive arrangement of luxuriant facial hair combined with a clean shaven chin that is presumed to have been the source of the term "side burns" which came into American usage in the 1880s. Sadly for the Union cause, Burnside's impact on men's fashion was more impressive than his military prowess. He had been reluctant to assume command, and his lack of confidence showed.

Burnside's immense army, well supplied and with hot-air balloons for surveillance, should have been able to outgun the Confederates, but it seemed that they could not outmaneuver them. Burnside's plan was to cross the Rapahannock River above the town of Fredericksburg, which lay on the direct route from Washington to Richmond. A delay in the arrival of the pontoon bridges meant that before the Union army had even crossed the river, General Lee had time to concentrate his troops on the heights behind Fredericksburg, leaving sharpshooters in the town itself to pick off the Federal engineers as they positioned the pontoons. Eventually a combination of artillery shelling and an advance party that cleared the Confederates from the town enabled the vast Union army to cross the river on December 13. The odds were never high that the Union army, despite its greater numbers, would overcome the rebel defenses. In repeated assaults on the gentle rise up to Marye's Heights, the Army of the Potomac suffered terrible losses. "We might as well have tried to take Hell," wrote a New York infantryman.[1] Watching line after line of Union soldiers advance up the hill only to be cut down by the Confederate defenders, General Lee was reported to have turned to an aide and commented, "it is well that war is so terrible or we should grow too fond of it."[2] More than twelve and a half thousand Union soldiers were killed in the day-long battle on 13 December, and they had gained no ground and inflicted only relatively minor damage on Lee's army.

Burnside's brief tenure as commander of the Union's most important force, the Army of the Potomac, was over and the northern press descended into a furious rage. The people of the Union, cried *Harper's Weekly*, had "borne, silently and grimly, imbecility, treachery, failure, privation, loss of friends and means, almost every suffering which can afflict a brave people. But they cannot be expected to suffer that such massacres as this at Fredericksburg shall be repeated."[3] Lincoln was succinct: "If there is a worse place than Hell, I am in it,"[4] he told a visitor when the news of the December 13 debacle came through. The news from Fredericksburg inaugurated the bleakest period of the war for the North. The future Supreme Court Justice Oliver Wendell Holmes, a captain in the Union army at the time and usually an irrepressible optimist, wrote in his diary,

> I've pretty much made up my mind that the South have achieved their independence. The Army is tired with its hard, & its terrible experience & still more with its mismanagement & I think before long the majority will say that we are vainly working to effect what never happens—the subjugation (for that is it) of a great civilized nation.[5]

Advocates of an armistice and a negotiated peace became more vocal not only in their Democratic strongholds, but in New England and the big eastern cities as well. Any military advantages that Lincoln hoped would come from the Emancipation Proclamation were hard to discern. The prospect of foreign intervention on behalf of the South had receded, but northern opposition to the war had immeasurably increased. The attempts to recruit men, to sell bonds that funded the war effort, and, above all, to keep up the spirits of the men in arms and their families at home depended utterly on the faith in the possibility of military victory. By the gloomy Christmas of 1862, that prospect seemed to dim.

In the aftermath of the debacle at Fredericksburg, the Army of the Potomac duly got its fourth commander in five months. After McClellan, Pope, and Burnside came Joseph Hooker, a hard-drinking, fast-living West Pointer, who surrounded his headquarters with prostitutes ("Hooker's girls" or "hookers" for short.)[6] Under Hooker's influence, sniffed Charles Francis Adams, Jr, army headquarters "became a place to which no self-respecting man liked to go and no decent woman could go. It was a combination barroom and brothel."[7] The new commander may have offended the sensibilities of Bostonian men of letters, but he raised the morale of the troops. Sanitary conditions in camp were improved, he insisted that fresh vegetables and soft bread be included in the men's daily rations, and even succeeded in getting his men the six months' back pay due to them. Lincoln wrote an astonishingly frank letter to his new commander, making clear his reservations about his character. In a direct allusion to a widely reported remark of Hooker's that he thought the country needed a dictator, Lincoln dryly observed that "Only those generals who gain successes, can set up dictators. What I ask of you now is military successes, and I will risk the dictatorship."[8] Hooker was confident of success, perhaps overconfident. The Army of the Potomac was the "finest on the planet," he boasted, and at that moment, before it moved against Lee that spring, it certainly looked that way.[9]

Four months later, Hooker put into action a far more imaginative plan than Burnside's frontal assault. His idea was to keep Lee occupied at Fredericksburg, while swiftly moving the bulk of the Army of the Potomac on a large-scale flanking movement upstream west along the Rappahannock River to attack Lee's left flank. If all went well, the Army of Northern Virginia would be trapped south of Fredericksburg, forced either to retreat toward Richmond while being attacked on both flanks, or to concentrate on repelling Hooker, which would expose their rear to attack at Fredericksburg. At first, Hooker's plans went well. On April 30, 70,000 Union troops forded the river and crossed into the scrubby woodland known as the Wilderness. Once again Lee responded with speed and daring. Anticipating Hooker's plan, Lee divided his army on May 1, leaving 10,000 troops at Fredericksburg and marching the remaining 50,000 to engage with the Army of the Potomac before they could execute Hooker's plan. The general who had hitherto been known as "Fighting Joe" appeared to take fright at his first engagement with Lee, ordering his troops to dig in near a small crossroads called Chancellorsville, against the advice of some of his subordinate officers who wanted to maintain the momentum of the offensive. From that moment, Hooker was beaten. Characteristically, Lee seized the initiative, and, ably supported by Stonewall Jackson, he divided his army again. On the morning of May 2, General Jackson's 28,000 men made an audacious flanking march along narrow roads in an attempt to attack the Federal right. The remaining 18,000 Confederate troops were left in a wary standoff against three times as many Federal troops. Had Hooker attacked Lee at that moment, the rebel army would have been hopelessly divided into two. But amazingly, when Hooker was told by Federal scouts of Jackson's movements, he complacently concluded that the Confederates were retreating. Consequently, the Federal right flank was totally unprepared when twice their number of Confederates charged toward them out of the woods, screaming the rebel yell. The following day, the two wings of Lee's army were reunited in hard fighting and with the loss of 9000 Confederate troops. At this point, Hooker added to his litany of tactical errors by withdrawing from one of the few patches of land in this woody countryside that was high enough and clear enough to be used effectively by artillery. Confederate General Jeb Stuart promptly seized the ground and the rebels used the heights to pound the Union troops into retreat. Despite a Union counterattack when Federal troops at Fredericksburg broke through the resistance of Confederate General Jubal A. Early on May 5, the Army of the Potomac was back on the left bank of the Rappahannock River by the evening of the following day. "My God! My God! What will the country say? What will the country say?" agonized Lincoln.[10]

The relief of victory was blackened for Confederates by the death of Stonewall Jackson. Jackson had a habit of riding with his left arm raised up, which he believed relieved the pain from a bullet wound in his hand. On the evening of May 2, 1863, Jackson was mistakenly fired on by his own men. Struck three times in his left arm, which may well have been raised at the time, Jackson was taken to the nearest field hospital where the Confederacy's most accomplished field surgeon Dr Hunter H. McGuire skillfully amputated his arm. (General Lee apocryphally remarked, "he has lost his left arm, but I have lost my right.") Transported by ambulance 25 miles to a safer location, the general developed pneumonia. Less than a week later, he was dead. His amputated arm was buried separately in a marked grave outside Chancellorsville.[11] Jackson's death was a momentous event in the history of the Confederacy, prompting an outpouring of grief that transformed the dead general into a martyred hero. In retrospect, it is clear that the battle of Chancellorsville was the high-tide mark of Confederate military success. It was certainly the apogee of Lee's military career. Once again, his army had comprehensively outsmarted and outfought a Union army that was more than twice the size and far better equipped. Hooker's inept generalship had been a major factor in the southern victory, and such incompetence could not be relied upon indefinitely. The Confederates had also suffered huge losses in their triumph, and the difference in the size of the armies could be disguised by smart tactics only for so long.

In the west, the prospects looked a little brighter for the Union. Halleck's victories in the winter of 1861–1862 had stalled in the spring, in part because the Union army now needed to advance beyond the safe lines of communication of the Cumberland and Tennessee rivers. But in late April, the Union navy under David Farragut had captured New Orleans, the largest city in the South and, given its location at the mouth of the Mississippi River and its industrial capacity, a strategic prize of immense significance. Unlike in the eastern theater, where, on Lincoln's advice, the object of the Army of the Potomac was always the Confederate army, in the west the Federals seemed more concerned with the gaining and holding of significant cities, railroad junctions, river systems and economically productive plantation areas. By the time the Preliminary Emancipation Proclamation was issued, the Union army had settled on two key objectives in the west: control of the Mississippi River and the expulsion of the Confederates from Tennessee, both to encourage the east Tennessee Unionists and as a bridgehead from which an invasion of Georgia and North Carolina could be launched. The Union army of the Cumberland was led in the winter of 1862–1863 by General William S. Rosecrans. His aim was to drive Confederate General Braxton Bragg's Army of Tennessee out of central Tennessee.

On the last day of December 1862, Union troops under Rosecrans encountered Bragg's Confederates at the battle of Stone's River, near Murfreesboro in Tennessee. This was one of the most brutally fought battles of the war. Each side lost almost a third of their men in the fighting, which gave this battle the dubious distinction of being, proportionately, the costliest of the war. At the end of the first day, on which the rebels had launched a ferocious assault on the Federals, Bragg telegraphed Richmond to say that he had won a great victory, and that the Federals were retreating. But to Bragg's amazement, Rosecrans (or "Old Rosy" as his troops called him) held firm, strengthened his defensive lines and called for fresh supplies from Union-held Nashville. After more fighting over the following two days, it was the Confederates, lacking supplies and with their commanding officers losing confidence in Bragg, who were forced to withdraw.

Bragg's retreat at Stone's River meant that although it was not a battle that resulted in any clear-cut strategic gain for the Union, it was received by the northern press as a triumph. Coming hard on the heels of the defeat at Fredericksburg, this was a blessed relief to the North. Indeed, Lincoln speculated that "had there been a defeat instead, the nation could scarcely have lived over."[12] In an equally brutal but less spectacular way, the Union was gaining ground further west, beyond the Mississippi River. Few newspaper correspondents covered the war on the frontiers of Missouri, Arkansas, Kansas and the Indian Territory, but the fighting there sapped Confederate energies, men and materiel, and weakened their capacity to hold or regain the strategically vital Mississippi River.

At the start of 1863, General Ulysses S. Grant had his sights on Vicksburg, a town on the Mississippi which had been so well fortified by the defending Confederates that it was known as the "Gibraltar of the West." Grant's efforts to move against Vicksburg had been frustrated by dazzlingly effective cavalry raids led by Confederate generals Nathan Bedford Forrest and Earl Van Dorn that cut railroad and telegraph lines, and forced the surrender of the Union garrison at Holly Springs. The Union army's reliance on long supply lines was being effectively exploited by the South. Grant eventually moved his army down the Mississippi to Milliken's Bend, just to the north of Vicksburg, but his chances of taking the city seemed stymied by topography. Vicksburg was built on a high bluff overlooking the river, well defended by Confederate artillery. To the south and the west, swamps and thick jungle-like forest made an infantry advance impossible. Grant's challenge was to get his army downriver past the Confederate batteries to attack the city from the South. The Union army spent the spring of 1863 expending enormous effort on a tragi-comic series of elaborate schemes, which involved blowing up levees, digging canals that might divert the river, and attempts to navigate through shallow swamp water where gun boats were either repeatedly run aground on sandbanks or had their chimneys smashed off by overhanging branches. Rebel artillery pounded Union gunboats whenever they had the chance, and when that was impossible, Confederate axmen felled trees across swamps to make them even more impassable than they already were. All the while, Grant's army suffered alarming death-rates from typhoid and dysentery.

On all fronts, the Confederates faced superior numbers. In the summer of 1863, Lee attempted once more to relieve pressure on Virginia by taking the war onto northern soil. He proposed marching his entire army down the Shenandoah Valley into Pennsylvania. By living off the rich Pennsylvania countryside, Lee could replenish his army's supplies. The Confederates might even be able to capture Washington. Even if this was not possible, he would draw Union forces out of Virginia and, with a dramatic show of military power, he would demonstrate to the wavering North that the policy of military subjugation of the South was futile. General Longstreet tried to persuade the Confederate cabinet of an alternative plan to send a portion of the Army of Northern Virginia to reinforce General Braxton Bragg, who was losing ground to Union General Rosecrans in Tennessee. But Lee's plan carried the day. He has been criticized since for his recklessness, but the logic of his offensive was sound. The fatal flaw was that he lost the critical battle.

True to form, the Army of Northern Virginia moved north with a speed that took the Federals by surprise. Once in Pennsylvania, they plundered the countryside and rounded up free-born blacks, to be marched south into slavery "just like we drive cattle," as one appalled Chambersburg woman expressed it.[13] The federal army, now under the command of General George Gordon Meade, marched north to protect Washington. Lee was handicapped by the absence of his principal cavalry detachment led by Jeb Stuart, which, rather then perform its function of shielding Lee's advancing army from attack and reconnoitering the enemy position, was out of communication on a spectacular but tactically self-indulgent raid. Without Stuart, and without Stonewall Jackson, Lee seemed to have lost some of his uncanny ability to predict his enemy's every move. The two armies collided at a place neither of them had chosen: the small college town of Gettysburg.

CONFEDERATE REVERSALS: GETTYSBURG, VICKSBURG AND CHATTANOOGA

Over three days, on July 1–3, 1863, Union and Confederate troops fought the battle that has since been mythologized, not without foundation, as the pivotal moment of the war. The first day saw Confederate troops, attacking from the northeast, push the Federals back more than two miles through the town of Gettysburg. Some have speculated that had General Ewell, now in command of Stonewall Jackson's old brigade, assaulted the hastily assembled Union line that night, as Jackson surely would have done, the rebels would have prevailed and the battle would have been won. But Ewell, given discretion by Lee to attack only if he thought it wise, hesitated. And in the meantime, Union reinforcements arrived and bedded the Union army behind stone walls and rail fences on Cemetery Ridge, a gentle hill that ran in a southwesterly direction. By the morning of July 2, General Longstreet had concluded that the Union lines were too strong to be breached and he desperately urged Lee to march south and try to get between Meade and Washington DC.[14] Confident in the prowess of his army, even against superior odds and against formidable natural defenses, Lee ignored this advice and ordered Longstreet to attack. Throughout the second day, the rebels made bloody and unsuccessful assaults on the Union lines, notably on the Union's left flank at Little Round Top. Once again, an increasingly histrionic Longstreet begged Lee to give up the direct assault and try to maneuver round the Federal left.

The culmination of the battle came on the third day. Lee ordered three divisions to attack the Federal center. They were to be led by General George E. Pickett, a dashing Virginian who resembled a romantic cavalier. According to General Pickett, Longstreet desperately warned Lee of the folly of a direct attack: "Look, General Lee, at the insurmountable difficulties between our line and that of the Yankees—the steep hills, the tiers of artillery, the fences, the heavy skirmish line—and then we'll have to fight our infantry against their batteries. Look at the ground we'll have to charge over, nearly a mile of that open ground there under the train of their canister and shrapnel." "The enemy is there, General Longstreet," replied Lee, "and I am going to strike him."[15] At midday on July 3, an eerie silence fell over the battlefield. Confederate guns were moved into position to pound the federal lines. Union troops waited apprehensively surveying the lines of gray-clad soldiers clearly visible in the woods less than a mile away. At one o'clock, the Confederate artillery began shelling the Union lines on Cemetery Ridge. Just before his division attacked, General Pickett penned a letter to his wife, which he delivered to another officer to be sent if he fell in the assault:

> The men are lying in the rear, my darling, and the hot July sun pours its scorching rays almost vertically down upon them. The suffering and waiting are almost unbearable.... My brave Virginians are to attack in front. Oh, may God in mercy help me as He never helped before! . . . It is almost three o'clock. My soul reaches out to yours.[16]

As he sealed his letter, Pickett ordered his 13,000 men to march in parade formation across the fields to the Union lines. As soon as they were halfway across, Union troops opened volley after volley against the advancing men, backed up by the federal artillery, cutting swathes through the rebel lines. All 13 colonels in Pickett's division were killed or wounded. Fewer than half of the Confederate attackers made it back to their lines. In total, Lee lost a third of his army in the three days at Gettysburg.[17] On July 4, Pickett wrote again to his wife:

> My brave boys were full of hope and confident of victory as I led them forth, forming them in column of attack, and though officers and men alike knew what was before them,—knew the odds against them,—they eagerly offered up their lives on the altar of duty, having absolute faith in their ultimate success. Over on Cemetery Ridge the Federals beheld a scene never before witnessed on this continent,— a scene which has never previously been enacted and can never take place again—an army forming in line of battle in full view, under their very eyes—charging across a space nearly a mile in length over fields of waving grain . . . —moving with the steadiness of a dress parade, the pride and glory soon to be crushed by an overwhelming heartbreak. Well it is all over now. The battle is lost, and many of us are prisoners, many are dead, many wounded, bleeding and dying. Your Soldier lives and mourns and but for you, my darling, he would rather, a million times rather, be back there with dead, to sleep for all time in an unknown grave.[18]

The sense of possibility betrayed was captured many years later by the southern novelist William Faulkner:

> For every Southern boy fourteen years old, not once but whenever he wants it, there is the instant when it's still not yet two o'clock on that July afternoon in 1863, the brigades are in a position behind the rail fence, the guns are laid and ready in the woods and the furled flags are already loosened to break out and Pickett himself with his long oiled ringlets and his hat in one hand probably and his sword in the other looking up the hill waiting for Longstreet to give the word and it's all in the balance, it hasn't happened yet, it hasn't even begun yet, it not only hasn't begun but there is still time for it not to begin against that position and those circumstances.[19]

Although its drama has made Pickett's Charge the most famous moment in a famous battle, in plain truth the Confederate army lost the initiative, and arguably the chance to win, the day before. On July 2, repeated assaults on the federal positions failed. Military historians have argued ever since about whether Longstreet's open reluctance to take the tactical offensive led to hesitancy and sluggishness especially on the second day that contributed to the Confederates' defeat, or whether, on the contrary, the fault lay with Lee's reckless determination to attack come what may. By the time it was nearly three o'clock on the afternoon of third, a frontal assault may have seemed to Lee to be his only chance of regaining the initiative.

Many battles to come were devastating in loss of life, but Lee's army never fully recovered from Gettysburg, in spirit or in numbers. His officer corps and command structure was especially hard-hit. Never again in the war was Lee able to rely on his officers as he had done in 1862 and in 1864 he had to appear in person on the frontlines to rally troops, something that would have been unnecessary before. More than ever, the slaughter at Gettysburg made the Army of Northern Virginia Lee's army.

In the weeks and months following the invasion of Pennsylvania, rates of desertion soared in the Army of Northern Virginia. If Gettysburg has become, in retrospect, the symbolic moment when the South lost the war, at the time, many in the North mixed their jubilation at the retreat of Lee's army with an agonizing sense that a golden opportunity had been missed to finish the rebellion once and for all. In an uncanny re-enactment of McClellan's caution after Lee retreated from Antietam the previous September, Meade, who had only been in command of the Army of the Potomac for six days, refused to order an all-out counterattack. Lincoln was beside himself with exasperation, desperately urging Meade to prevent Lee's devastated army from recrossing the Potomac. Under huge pressure Confederate engineers rapidly constructed pontoon bridges that carried the Army of Northern Virginia back over the river during the night of the 13–14 July with barely any losses. "We had them in our grasp," said Lincoln, "we had only to stretch forth our hands and they were ours. And nothing I could say or do could make the army move."[20]

Meanwhile, in the west, Grant had finally broken through at Vicksburg after a campaign lasting many months. Earlier in the spring, he had settled on a plan that evaded the swamps and artillery batteries defending the town by marching his army west and south and crossing the river at Bruinsberg where the ground was firmer, some 35 miles downriver from Vicksburg, from where he could march back upstream on the eastern side of the river and have direct access to the city from the south and east. Grant was cutting himself off from his supply lines. It was the sort of daring move that Lee might have made, but which had hitherto been rare among Union generals. And then, instead of marching directly for Vicksburg, Grant headed east to Jackson, the Mississippi state capital. His plan was to defeat Confederate forces under Joseph E. Johnston in Jackson, and then, having cut Vicksburg off from any source of reinforcements or supplies and eliminated the threat to his rear, Grant would turn back west toward his main goal. General William T. Sherman played a critical role in the successful execution of this plan, and he tested out the strategy that would later earn him his reputation for taking the war to the enemy home front, by burning the factories and railroads of the city of Jackson, in order to destroy the enemies' will and capacity to wage war. Grant's army won some spectacular victories and pushed the outnumbered and outwitted defending Confederates back to Vicksburg, which was now encircled by Union forces, on the river and on land. By the end of May, a siege had begun. Union engineers tunneled under the Confederate line and exploded a mine, but the follow-up attack failed. The city was well defended by one of the most intricate systems of trenches built during the war, but the civilians and soldiers inside were starving. On July 4, Vicksburg was surrendered. The next day, Sherman marched to Jackson and forced Johnston's outnumbered and badly supplied army to retreat, leaving federal troops in control of central Mississippi.

The capture of the Mississippi River after the fall of Vicksburg meant that the Confederacy was now split in two, and the loss of Jackson further weakened the logistical challenge of supplying Confederate armies. Confederate Ordinance Chief Josiah Gorgas reflected sadly on July 28, 1863, that "one brief month ago we were apparently at the point of success. Lee was in Pennsylvania threatening Harrisburg, and even Philadelphia. Vicksburgh [*sic.*] seemed to laugh all Grant's efforts to scorn . . . It seems incredible that human power could effect such a change in so brief a space. . . . The Confederacy totters to its destruction."[21] The Union army made continued progress in Tennessee. Union armies led by Rosecrans and Ambrose E. Burnside (who had been transferred to the west after Fredericksburg), maneuvered Bragg's Confederates out of east Tennessee and on September 3, 1863, federal forces entered Knoxville. Six days later, Braxton Bragg evacuated

Chattanooga, a major rail hub situated in a gap in the Cumberland hills. It was a crucial gain. The Union army now stood on the threshold of Georgia. The Confederates successfully counterattacked at the battle of Chickamauga on September 19–20, 1863, briefly lifting southern spirits—in Richmond, war department clerk John B. Jones was hopeful that "surely the government of the United States must now see the impossibility of subjugating the southern people, spread over such a vast extent of territory"—but the underlying balance of power was shifting to the North.[22] The Confederate victory at Chickamauga left them in control of the high ground—Missionary Ridge and Lookout Mountain—to the south and east of Chattanooga. The victory had come at a painfully high price. The rebels had sustained losses of nearly 30 percent, or nearly 19,000 men. The Union army had lost almost as many, but they could replace the losses as the South could not.

Over the next two months, the Union army consolidated its position in the west. On October 17, 1863, Lincoln appointed Grant commander of all the armies west of the Appalachian Mountains. The urgent need now was to reinforce and resupply Union forces in Chattanooga, which following the battle of Chickamauga were dangerously exposed. Union supply lines were so precarious that by mid-October, troops were reduced to quarter rations. Grant made an immediate impact. He replaced Rosecrans with General George H. Thomas, and went personally to Chattanooga. Under Grant's direction, Union forces put in motion a plan to dislodge rebels at Brown's Ferry, downriver from Chattanooga, and open a new supply line to the west, just out of range of the Confederate artillery that was lodged menacingly at Lookout Mountain to the south. During November 24–25 in a series of nasty, hard-fought engagements, the Union army drove the Confederates from their seemingly impregnable defensive positions on Lookout Mountain and Missionary Ridge and forced them to retreat 25 miles to the South to establish a new defensive line near Dalton, Georgia. The decisive federal breakthrough on November 25 was unplanned. Missionary Ridge was a 400 foot high ridge that ran roughly north–south for 400 yards and was defended with two lines of rebel trenches, at the bottom and at the top. Both sides knew from previous battles that a full frontal assault uphill against entrenched defenders would be suicidal folly. So Grant gave Thomas' division, which had suffered most at the battle of Chickamauga, the responsibility of distracting the rebels on Missionary Ridge by attacking the first line of trenches at the base of the hill in what would appear to be frontal attack but while the real work would be done by Hooker and Sherman's men who would flank the rebels and approach the ridge from the north and south. Thomas' men astounded Grant and Thomas by not only taking the first line of trenches but then storming up the hill and, against all the odds, storming the ridge. Unlike Pickett's men at Gettysburg, the attacking forces at Missionary Ridge were able to keep out of firing range as they climbed the hill by using gullies and rocks until they were close enough to storm the rebel trenches. The Confederates panicked and ran "wildly down the hill and into the woods, tossing away knapsacks, muskets, and blankets as they ran."[23] "My God, come see them run!" yelled a Union private to his comrades. It was one of the most spectacular routs of the war. "This is the death knell of the Confederacy," concluded a rebel officer as his men fled from Missionary Ridge. Even while blaming his own men for the defeat, Bragg resigned, and with great reluctance Jefferson Davis replaced him with General Joseph E. Johnston.

The significance of the battle of Gettysburg was heightened by the Union victories at Chattanooga and Vicksburg. Seen in retrospect, these three southern reversals are often taken as *the* turning point of the war. As great swathes of the Confederacy fell into federal hands, as the northern economy geared up for war and as the Union army drew on more and more men, the northern war machine seemed unrelenting and unstoppable. No one was any longer talking about the possibility of foreign intervention. The emancipation policy seemed to lock the Union into an all-out war on southern society. The North was gradually learning how to translate its greater manpower and industrial strength into victory on the battlefield. As ever, the path to southern victory lay in the hearts of northerners who had to sustain the war, even while there were disturbing signs of growing disaffection with the war in the South. Yet however bitterly southerners regretted the reversals of 1863, they did not give up. No one at the time knew for sure that Lee would not have the ability to audaciously push the war into the North once again in 1864. Southern newspapers minimized the scale of the defeats and in countless letters Confederates worked hard to convince themselves and each other that ultimate victory was assured.[24]

"HARD WAR" IN 1864

By 1864, the assumptions underlying Union strategy were changing. One military approach to the military defeat of secession was

McClellan's conception of a limited war conducted according to the highest principles of Christian civilization. This had been swept away by the emancipation policy. The limits of a second approach—the occupation of territory—were also now becoming clear. A strategy of gaining and holding territory was useful insofar as it bolstered Union morale and depressed the South—the fall of Vicksburg, Atlanta and ultimately Richmond are the best examples of the positive benefits of this approach for the Union. But Lincoln had long understood that the war would be won only on the battlefield and that Confederate armies, not Richmond or swathes of Confederate territory, were the ultimate target of the federal armies. This was the lesson learned by Generals Grant and Sherman in the west, where the strategy of taking territory had failed to quash the Confederates' capacity to wage war. After all, if it had taken the Union army two years simply to take control of eastern Tennessee where much of the population supported the Union, how long would it take to subdue Georgia or South Carolina unless the rebel armies were destroyed? Only the defeat of armies— and Lee's Army of Northern Virginia above all—would mark the war's end.

The northern economy was becoming more and more efficient at war production, the draft and more importantly the threat of the draft were dragging more men into uniform, and northern military and political leaders were slowly learning from experience. Two lessons in particular had a direct bearing on the conduct of the war in 1864. The first was the need for coordinated campaigns on all fronts simultaneously, preventing Davis from transferring troops from one battlefront to another as needed. The Napoleonic blueprint for military victory was to concentrate force against the enemy's weak point and win with overwhelming numbers. Whatever the tactical soundness of this approach at a battlefield level, Lincoln had long recognized that in order for the Union's manpower superiority to be felt, a broader strategic vision was necessary. The second lesson, a corollary of the first, was spelled out by Sherman. The Union army, he explained, was "not only fighting hostile armies but a hostile people, and must make old and young, rich and poor, feel the hard hand of war."[25] More spectacularly, General James Montgomery, whose experience of the merciless guerrilla warfare in Kansas and Missouri undoubtedly colored his vision of the kind of war that had to be fought, declared that the "Southerners must be made to feel that this was a real war, and that they were to be swept away by the hand of God, like the Jews of old." By 1863, Union commanders, especially in the west, confiscated provisions and livestock from the local population pretty much at will. In 1864, this approach was elevated to the level of general strategy. Some of Lincoln's opponents in the North, as well as southerners, condemned what they saw as a "war of subjugation".

This strategy of fighting a vigorous and hard war on the social and economic support for the military rebellion, as well as the rebel army itself, was conditioned by a clear political logic. Northern military and political leaders rarely if ever lost sight of their basic goal of reunion. They sought not to humiliate the South for its own sake, but to crush the rebellion.[26] For all its brutality, the Union army never eviscerated the distinction between soldiers and civilians. When judged by the standards of the history of the English efforts to suppress resistance in Ireland, especially under Cromwell—a parallel well known to Civil War generals—Sherman's "hard war" doctrine was, in the words of Archer Jones, "a humanitarian venture" in comparison.[27] Sherman said that he wanted to make the southern people feel that "war and individual ruin are synonymous terms."[28] Yet committed as Sherman's soldiers were to the idea of taking the war to the southern people, they still made clear distinctions between different categories of southerners. They deliberately targeted South Carolina, the birthplace of secession, more harshly than North Carolina, where there was considerable Unionist and antiwar sentiment.[29]

Ulysses S. Grant explained in his memoirs the evolution of his thinking about the war. The turning point for him was the Confederate counterattack at Shiloh in 1862.

> I gave up all idea of saving the Union except by complete conquest [he recalled]. Up to that time it had been the policy of our army . . . to protect the property of the citizens whose territory was invaded without regard to their sentiments, whether Union or Secession. After this, however, I regarded it as humane to both sides to protect the persons of those found at their homes, but to consume everything that could be used to support or supply armies . . . Their destruction was accomplished without bloodshed, and tended to the same result as the destruction of armies. I continued this policy to the close of the war.

The legal framework in which Union generals operated was fleshed out in April 1863 by General Order no. 100, otherwise known as the "Lieber Code" after its author, the scholar and German émigré, Francis Lieber. The code had the remarkable aim of attempting to define the moral boundaries of warfare in the modern age. It was later used as the basis of the Geneva conventions. It stated that military necessity allowed for "the destruction of all property . . . and of all withholding of sustenance of means of life from the country" as well as "the appropriation of whatever an enemy's country affords necessary for the subsistence and safety of the Army." But the General Order also reminded commanding officers that "men who take up arms against one another in public war do not cease . . . to be moral beings, responsible to one another and to God." Military necessity

> does not admit of cruelty—that is, the infliction of suffering for the sake of suffering or for revenge, nor of maiming or wounding except in fight, nor of torture to extort confessions. It does not admit of the use of poison in any way, nor of the wanton devastation of a district. It admits of deception, but disclaims acts of perfidy; and, in general, military necessity does not include any act of hostility which makes the return to peace unnecessarily difficult.

In practice, the Union army had been attacking the Confederate's fighting capacity since the start of the war. What had changed by 1863 was the language, the awareness of what was going on, and the single-mindedness with which that aim was pursued.

If at the start of the war, northern politicians and generals had assumed that the Union army would advance into the South in an orderly manner with little civilian resistance; such illusions had been shattered by the spring of 1862. Experience had shown that the Union army could control areas of rebel-held territory only by first establishing a defensible enclave, from which a continuous war of raids and counterraids was launched. Although it was the big battles that attracted the attention of the press, and accounted for a majority of the battlefield casualties, relatively minor military encounters between raiding Union troops and small detachments of regular or irregular Confederate troops were the most common type of warfare. More than 7000 such confrontations are recorded in the *Official Records of the War of the Rebellion*. Most southern civilians never saw a great battle, but, by 1865, most had encountered a raiding party, or some form of "irregular" or guerrilla action. Establishing beachheads in strategically important and defensible places was the only way in which the North could feasibly conquer the South. Maintaining hold of an enclave forced the Confederacy to expend valuable resources in containing it, combating Union raids and in usually futile and hugely costly efforts to expel the alien federal presence. The Union naval dominance allowed them to establish several such beachheads in 1861 such as Fortress Monroe in Virginia and Port Royal Sound in South Carolina. The South Carolina Sea Islands remained in federal control for the rest of the war, and slaves were left in charge of fertile plantations after their masters fled. Without a major battle, the North created a base from which raids could be launched into the surrounding countryside, Worried about the possibility that federal forces might be able to besiege Charleston or Savannah from the land as well as from the sea, the Confederates were forced to maintain a force of about 25,000 men in the region.

From federal-controlled enclaves on the coasts of North and South Carolina, Union troops conducted raids into the rich surrounding countryside, and, with the support of gunboats, made raids up the many rivers and inlets along the long, indented coastline of Georgia, the Carolinas and Florida. The aim of such raids was the destabilization of southern society and to inflict economic damage. Cotton gins were burned, food and livestock seized, and, most dramatically, slaves who had not already run away were taken behind Union lines. In April 1863, Union Colonel Benjamin Grierson led a raid (later made famous by John Ford's 1959 film *The Horse Soldiers* starring John Wayne) across 600 miles from Memphis to Baton Rouge. Slavery disappeared from the Mississippi Valley even before the fall of Vicksburg because plantation slavery could not be sustained in the midst of Union raids. In February 1864, Sherman demonstrated the even greater value of infantry as opposed to cavalry raids. Infantry could do more damage. He marched 21,000 men on a rapid 300-mile round-trip from Vicksburg to Meridan, Mississippi, not with the intention of occupying territory or defeating concentrations of rebel troops, but to undermine southern morale. Raids became more and more important to Union strategy as the war continued. Conceived of as a diversionary tactic to help Grant's advance on Vicksburg, his cavalry pillaged and destroyed warehouses, railroads, livestock, cotton gins and farm equipment, and liberated hundreds of slaves. By 1864, the strategy of raids had become the central weapon against a dying but still belligerent Confederacy.

GRANT TAKES COMMAND

In March 1864, Lincoln appointed Grant general-in-chief of all the Union armies. He chose to take field command of the Army of the Potomac (although General Meade remained its titular head), and left General Halleck in Washington to become chief of staff and coordinate the movements of all the Union armies in all theaters, a role that was better suited to Halleck's fastidious and uncharismatic personality. This was the beginning of a recognizably modern command structure—something that the Confederacy never developed. Grant was well prepared for his new enhanced role. To a much greater extent than his predecessors, Grant, having come from the western theater, had a grasp of the whole strategic picture. Moreover, Lincoln had at last found a general who would need no prodding to attack and act swiftly. Over the long bloody summer months of 1864 this attitude would earn him the nickname "butcher." The year 1863 had seen some critical and bloody encounters—at Chancellorsville, Gettysburg, Vicksburg and Chattanooga—but for most soldiers, life in the army had meant long periods of inactivity, routine picketing duties and occasional skirmishes. Full-scale battles were rare. Until the spring of 1864, armies had met for grand encounters and had then retreated to regroup. Now, with Grant in command, the tempo of life in the army was transformed: a new aggression and energy was injected into the Army of the Potomac. Grant recalled in his memoirs that in his first Civil War engagement when he was a colonel in 1861, he had discovered that the enemy colonel "had been as much afraid of me as I had been of him." This was a valuable lesson. "From that event to the close of the war, I never experienced trepidation upon confronting an enemy, though I always felt more or less anxiety."[30] His job now was to make Lee as afraid of the Army of the Potomac as the Army of the Potomac had so often been of Lee.

Despite an ongoing crisis of supplies, and the depletion of their armies, Confederates fought doggedly and with great spirit throughout 1864. The continued military viability of the South was especially frustrating to the North since, in spite of a potential manpower crisis in the spring of 1864 when some of the three-year volunteers, the veterans of 1861, came to the end of their service and opted to return home, the Union had finally managed to translate its greater population into field armies that were consistently far larger than those of their enemies.

It took the North a further 18 months of hard fighting, at immense cost in lives, to crush Confederate military resistance. Even in this final phase, though, the key strategic calculus—northern popular and political will—was tested again and again. There were to be no more offensive victories like Chancellorsville, but by stalemating the Union army in a bloody war of attrition, the Confederates came close to accomplishing their goal of wearing down northerners' will to fight. As late as August 1864, it seemed possible that some sort of armistice would be agreed, to the inevitable benefit of the South. The visible superiority of the Union armies made their failure to breakthrough against the southern defenders even more dangerous to the northern will to win since it made the task of military conquest seem even harder.

As ever, the Confederates were aided by staggering incompetence on the part of some Union generals, especially those who, like Benjamin F. Butler, Nathaniel P. Banks and Franz Sigel, were politicians rather than professional soldiers. Butler, a walrus-faced Democrat-turned-Republican congressman from Massachusetts was in command of 30,000 Union troops based near Fortress Monroe on the James River (near to where McClellan had retreated after the Seven Days battles in the summer of 1862). Butler's task was to launch an auxiliary movement against Richmond to distract the rebels from Grant's main assault. Had he moved quickly enough, he could have taken Richmond, or at least the railroad hub of Petersburg, to the South. Neither city was well defended when Butler first advanced. But he failed, and his troops ended up being trapped in the enclave between the Appomattox and James rivers, effectively neutralized as a useful military force. In the Shenandoah Valley, the scene of so much fighting already, General Sigel was also defeated by Confederate forces that were smaller and much worse equipped than his own. And in far-off Louisiana, General Banks' ambitious effort to invade Texas via the Red River and Shreveport also failed, leaving the Confederates still in control of almost all of Texas as well as northern Louisiana and southern Arkansas.

In two weeks in May, 1864, the Union army suffered more casualties than in any comparable period in the war. The Army of the Potomac moved south of the Rapidan River (a tributary of the Rappahannock) in an attempt to flank Lee's right, force the Army of Northern Virginia out of its trenches and fight an open battle against the Federals' superior numbers. Lee did not wait to be attacked but launched a preemptive assault on the Union lines. He did so close to the site of his great victory at Chancellorsville, in the impenetrably thick woodland known as the Wilderness, terrain that he knew would negate the Union army's numerical advantage. The ensuing battle was one of the most confusing of the war. The thick vegetation made it impossible for soldiers to move without hacking their way forward. Whole brigades got lost. Commanders had no way of knowing what was going on. Sparks from the muzzles of thousands of rifles set the woods on fire, and thousands of wounded men burned to death. In two days of fighting, in which the Union army lost 17,000 men and about 10,000 Confederates, General Lee appeared once again to have robustly deflected a Union advance. The memory of the defeat at Chancellorsville hung over the Army of the Potomac in this hellish, burning woodland, in which the skeletons of fallen soldiers from the battles of the previous year lay amid the undergrowth. Before the campaign began, Grant had promised Lincoln that "whatever happens there will be no turning back," and he was as good as his word.[31] On May 8, Grant ordered the battered Army of the Potomac to march—not north back across the river as Hooker had done in similar circumstances a year earlier—but south. Even though they had suffered terribly, battle-hardened Union troops cheered when they realized that they were not retreating. "We marched free. The men began to sing," recalled one.[32] Grant's objective was to force Lee out of the Wilderness and into open ground by placing his army between the Army of Northern Virginia and Richmond.

Over the next seven weeks, according to one military historian, the soldiers themselves experienced "one long battle" rather than a succession of separate encounters.[33] In spite of the huge cost in lives, Grant repeatedly ordered assaults on the Confederate lines, maintaining an unrelenting pressure in an attempt to lure Lee into a devastating confrontation. Time and again, Lee moved his army more quickly and established powerful defensive lines. The action moved in an arc east and south as Grant tried to get through Lee's defenses, and Lee maneuvered to keep his heavily outnumbered and outgunned army between Richmond and the Federals. At Spotsylvania Court House on May 12, the rebels repulsed the Federals in a particularly vicious battle famous for the intense fighting around the "bloody angle", a U-shaped line of Confederate trenches which, by the end of the day, were filled with a mixture of blood, mud and corpses. "The rebels are piled up in heaps 3 or 4 deep," reported one veteran Massachusetts infantryman. "The pit is filled with them piled up dead and wounded together[.] I saw one completely trodded in the mud so as to look like part of it and yet he was breathing and gasping."[34] Spotsylvania was essentially yet another Union defeat. Grant had attempted to seize an important crossroads, Lee had beaten him to it, and had then successfully, albeit bloodily, held off the federal assault. The difference was that Grant refused to treat it as a defeat. Once again he refused to retreat and instead attempted another large-scale flanking movement to try to get between Lee and Richmond. Again, Lee anticipated the move and on June 3, the Army of the Potomac was hurled against well-entrenched Confederate fortifications at Cold Harbor. More than any other Civil War battle, Cold Harbor was a harbinger of the horrors of the Somme. Of the 7000 Union troops who died in a vain attempt to storm the rebel trenches, most fell in only a few minutes. "I regret this assault more than any one I have ever ordered," Grant admitted afterwards.[35] The night before the battle one soldier wrote in his diary "June 3. Cold Harbor. I was killed." The diary was found on his dead body after the battle.

After Spotsylvania, confused newspaper reports obscured the scale of the Union losses, and the northern public was whipped up into an entirely unjustified expectation that the final breakthrough had come. News of the losses at Cold Harbor was devastating to civilian morale. Once again, the high hopes of the spring appeared to have been crushed by the superiority of Lee's army. Unlike in the previous two years, Lee, knowing he was outnumbered, and with limited resources to play with, did not have the option of going on the tactical offensive. This did not necessarily matter, though. His effective defense at Spotsylvania and Cold Harbor sapped the stock that the North needed to win: faith in the possibility of ultimate success. In retrospect, we know that this was the last hurrah of the rebel army, but at the time, many on both sides thought it the final evidence of the futility of armed subjugation.

Grant's plans were frustrated time and again by the swift maneuvers of the enemy and the failures of some of his own generals. General David Hunter, a radical antislavery man, was even less successful than Sigel had been in charge of Union troops in the Shenandoah Valley. By the middle of June, Confederate General Jubal Early had taken back control of the valley. Two weeks later he crossed the Potomac and launched a spectacular raid into Maryland and, on July 11, to the defenses of the City of Washington itself. He was turned back only when Grant diverted a division from the siege of Petersburg and ordered Union cavalry commander General Philip Sheridan to pursue Early back into the Shenandoah Valley and "follow him to the death." Sheridan's men also destroyed crops and livestock in the valley so that they could no longer be used to supply Lee's army. The "hard war" strategy was never more obviously in evidence than in this unforgiving final stage in the Shenandoah Valley's own very particularly tempestuous civil war experience.[36]

The Army of the Potomac, meanwhile, had moved south from Cold Harbor and crossed the James River, in another attempt to force Lee out his trenches by flanking his army and seizing Petersburg. Once again, before a full-scale assault on the thinly defended Petersburg defenses took place, Lee's army had realized what was happening and had marched there with astonishing speed. Once again, thousands of soldiers were killed in futile attempts to dislodge the rebels from their earthwork entrenchments. For the third year in a row, a Union army that set out in the spring with such high hopes of crushing Confederate resistance in Virginia appeared, by mid-summer, to be defeated. Lee still had fewer troops, but Grant had lost more men—64,000 casualties in a month—and morale in the Army of the Potomac was sinking once again. The Union army bedded in for a siege of Petersburg, extending a line of trenches south and west around the city. Romantic notions of valor were tested against the ever-present danger of being shot by snipers, and the constant artillery bombardment. As on the Somme 50 years later troops built "bomb proof" shelters and zigzag trenches. If at first, soldiers had resisted building sophisticated field fortifications on the grounds that, as historians Grady McWhiney and Perry Jamieson observed, "there was no glory to be gained from fighting out of a hole in the ground," they soon accepted them as essential.[37] As one Ohio soldier put it, "the spade is more powerful than the cannon."[38] The psychological advantages of entrenchments for the defending forces are undisputable, as is the impact of such defenses on the fluidity of battles. However, it is also true—as the Army of the Potomac eventually showed—that battlefield defenses could aid the offensive as well since they enabled attacking forces to be pushed close to the enemy lines, from which an overwhelming raid could be launched at great speed.[39]

It was there, in the frustrating trench standoff outside Petersburg, that one of the most terrible moments of the war occurred. Pennsylvania troops from the coal mining part of the state drove a mine shaft 500 yards under the rebel trenches, filled it with gunpowder and, before dawn on July 30, it was exploded, blowing up 300 Confederate soldiers and creating a crater that was 170 feet long, 60 feet wide and 30 feet deep.[40] This dramatic opportunity to smash through rebel lines was turned into a horrible disaster for the Union army, and for a corps of African American soldiers in particular. Bad planning by Union officers, including the bungling Burnside, meant that the infantry who were supposed to advance in the wake of the explosion were uncertain what to do. Many charged down into the crater itself, from where they were picked off by Confederate artillery. As James M. McPherson has aptly put it, it was "like shooting fish in a barrel."[41] Many of the Union dead were black troops, a fact not lost on Confederates. "I do wonder what the gentle, sympathetical and philanthropical Aunt Harriet Beecher Stowe thinks of this sort of emancipation," wrote one delighted Confederate officer, "of striking off the shackle of bondage one day and the next march the dear creature into a hole and have them shot down by the hundred. Poor Uncle Tom!"[42] The bloody events of July 30 did nothing for the tactical position of either side, other than in its impact on morale in the armies and on the home fronts. The battle of the crater, and in particular the killing of so many helpless black troops, was reported with exultation in the southern press. A young Virginian woman expressed the prevailing mood in her diary:

> Truly God was with our Nation then, and the enemy 'fell into the pit which they dug for another'. What a scene of chaos and confusion must have ensued, after the Fort was blown up; and their miserable negro Reg't in whose valor they had trusted, rushed back panic stricken and demoralized, crowding and hiding themselves in the chasm which had been made.[43]

The Confederate press and public took what satisfaction they could from Union fiascos like the Crater, but there is mounting evidence that the tenuous position of the Army of Northern Virginia was beginning to sink in. Military historians have agreed that casualties among officers in the 1864 campaign had devastated Lee's command structure, already severely weakened after Gettysburg.[44] On at least two occasions, at the battles of Wilderness and Spotsylvania, when Lee had appeared near the frontline to rally the shattered troops, the soldiers, fearing that the inspiration of the Confederacy should himself become a casualty, shouted "General Lee to the rear" and turned him back. These incidents have entered Confederate Lost Cause folklore as illustrations of the devotion of ordinary Confederates for their leader. And a recent historian of the Army of Northern Virginia has gone so far as to claim that by the summer of 1864, "most members of the army who managed to persevere seemed to be fighting as much for Lee himself as for the Confederate government, for the idea of a Southern nation, or even for their families and homes."[45] The very dependence of the army on one man was of course in itself a serious weakness, and Lee's inability to rely on his general officers as he had done so successfully at least until Chancellorsville, revealed how much the army had suffered since the previous summer. Neither was it simply the loss of officers that hampered the effectiveness of the Army of Northern Virginia. The full impact of the loss in battle, through disease or increasingly through desertion, of so many experienced soldiers was temporarily mitigated by the siege, but, as Lee put it in a letter to the Confederate Secretary of War in August, "without some increase of our strength, I cannot see how we are to escape the natural military consequences of the enemy's numerical superiority."[46]

While Grant was trying and failing to outmaneuver Lee in Virginia, a similar dance was taking place between Sherman and Confederate General Joseph Johnston south and east from Chattanooga through Georgia toward Atlanta. Unlike Grant, Sherman did not order many direct assaults with the exception of the battle of Kennesaw Mountain so casualties were lower and more evenly balanced between the offensive and the defensive force than in Virginia. Johnston proved skilful at avoiding the open battle that Sherman craved, using slaves to build lines of trenches for his army to fall back to in advance of each flanking movement by Sherman. By keeping the army intact and casualties to a minimum, Johnston became a popular commander to his men, but as the rebel armies were forced back to within artillery range of Atlanta, southern newspapers attacked the southern commander in the same way that northern newspapers had attacked McClellan for his retreat from Richmond in the spring of 1862. Jefferson Davis, who had never liked Johnston anyway, replaced him with John B. Hood, a general known for his pugnaciousness rather than his tactical finesse. Hood duly sought open confrontation but the only result was to bleed his army while leaving Sherman in the field. "The Confederate government rendered us most valuable service" by removing Johnston, Sherman later wrote.[47] Sherman had not scored a knockout blow, but, given Johnston's tactics, the Federals had achieved all that they could: in 90 days, the rebels had been driven back 90 miles and, thanks to Hood's assaults, had suffered more casualties than the attacking force. As the military theorist Sir Basil H. Liddell Hart was later to write, Sherman's "indirect approach" in his advance into Georgia was a model of how to avoid the bloody stalemate of trench warfare which could have provided a valuable lesson to World War I generals.[48] By the time the Army of the Potomac were digging in for the siege of Petersburg, Sherman's men had closed on Atlanta and were also preparing to wait it out.

August 1864 marked a new low in northern confidence that the war could be won. The fighting in Virginia and Georgia had cost

100,000 northerners their lives in just three months, a level of carnage that had not previously been seen. And with both Grant and Sherman apparently bogged down and Rebel armies still seemingly in tact, the sacrifice did not seem to have yielded any tangible results. At the end of August and the start of September, events began to move in the Union's direction once again. With a series of brilliant flanking movements, Sherman tore up Hood's lines of communication and threatened to surround the rebel army. During the night of 1–2 September, Hood evacuated Atlanta, burning everything of military value before he did so. The news of this important breakthrough reached the North at about the same time as the news that Admiral Farragut had taken Mobile Bay in the face of determined opposition, thus cutting off one of the Confederacy's last significant port cities. At the same time, Sheridan's men were completing their task in the Shenandoah Valley, leaving a trail of devastation—and thousands of homeless refugees—in their wake.

By the late summer of 1864, Confederates were hopeful, and with good reason, that Lincoln would be defeated in the presidential election in November. Having long recognized that wavering northern will was the route to southern victory, Confederates hoped that with a Democrat in the White House the North would be prepared to negotiate. The fall of Atlanta helped to transform Lincoln's political fortunes, however, and his reelection sent a clear signal of northern commitment to the military struggle. As winter closed in again on the armies outside Richmond and Petersburg, perennially optimistic southern newspapers predicted that the coming winter and the difficulties of suppressing a hostile population would frustrate and defeat Union forces just as the Russian winter had defeated Napoleon in 1812.

Instead it was the northerners who proved their ability to live off the land and fight without rest. After his troops had taken Atlanta, Sherman expelled most of the civilian population in order to be able to use the city as a military base without having to police a hostile local population. When General Hood wrote to protest at an action which he called "pre-eminent in the dark history of war," Sherman responded with a withering attack on the hypocrisy of rebels who had "in the midst of peace and prosperity, plunged a nation into war ... dared and badgered us into battle [and] insulted our flag." War was about cruelty, wrote Sherman, "and you cannot refine it." The exchange of letters was gleefully reprinted as a pamphlet in the North by the supporters of Lincoln's reelection campaign as evidence of the determination of Union arms.[49]

The expulsion of the civilian population was merely a precursor to the next stage in Sherman's campaign, his famous march through Georgia from Atlanta to the sea, and then on into South Carolina. Sherman was blunt about the importance of targeting the southern will to fight if the war was to be ended quickly. Civilians had to feel the hard hand of war because it was they who ultimately sustained the military resistance. "We cannot change the hearts of those people of the South," Sherman wrote, "but we can make war so terrible . . . [and] make them so sick of war that generations would pass away before they would again appeal to it." He proposed to cut loose from his supplies and "move through Georgia smashing things to the sea." The risk of Sherman's plan, while Hood's army and Nathan Bedford Forrest's cavalry were at his rear and could not only cut the rail supply lines back to Chattanooga, but mount damaging raids into Union-held northeast Alabama and Tennessee, was not lost on Sherman, nor on his superior officer Grant, nor on Lincoln. But after some deliberation, Grant and Lincoln authorized Sherman to proceed. The march broke all the rules of tactics taught at West Point. But Sherman was confident that his army was strong enough to remain intact and could survive by impressing supplies from the local population.

As events turned out, the march to the sea achieved all that Sherman hoped. It had a huge psychological impact on the South that went beyond the material losses it inflicted. Sherman's 60,000 men left Atlanta on November 15 singing "John Brown's Body" to make good on their commanders' promise to "make Georgia howl!"[50] Theoretically, only official foraging parties were supposed to commandeer food and livestock but in practice, discipline was not well enforced. "The Yankees come nearer every day and we lie in Sherman's path to the sea," wrote Susan Eppes, the wife of a Georgia plantation owner. "As they advance, they pilfer and burn; all valuables are stolen; all provisions are taken, of course, and the rest goes up in smoke." Desperate to avoid this fate, Eppes got her slaves to bury food, silverware and even the family portraits in the garden. To her horror and amazement, when a party of Union soldiers arrived, her slaves rushed to tell them where the valuables were buried.[51] A swathe of country 50 miles wide and nearly 300 miles long was left devastated. The destruction caused by Sherman became legendary. Some was caused by the rebel army, as they tried to burn anything of military value before Sherman's men arrived, but the legend is based firmly in reality. On the eve of the evacuation of Macon, Georgia, Eliza Andrews bleakly surveyed the scene:

No more gay uniforms, no more prancing horses, but only a few ragged foot soldiers with wallets and knapsacks on, ready to march—Heaven knows where. . . . All the intoxicating liquors that could be found in the stores, warehouses and barrooms, had been seized by the authorities and emptied on the ground. In some places the streets smelt like a distillery, and I saw men, boys, and negroes down on their knees lapping it up from the gutter like dogs. Little children were staggering about in a state of beastly intoxication.[52]

"We had a gay old campaign," reported one of Sherman's soldiers. "Destroyed all we could not eat, stole their niggers, burned their cotton & gins, spilled their sorghum, burned & twisted their R. Roads and raised Hell generally."[53] By Christmas, Sherman's army had taken Savannah, and reopened his supply lines to the North via the sea. With Lee penned in near Richmond, Sherman gathering his forces to march on again, and the ragged Confederate armies now hemorrhaging men to desertion and disease, the last stage on the long, twisted road to Appomattox was at last open.

5 Citizen Soldiers

When the war began, the old regular army was utterly inadequate to the task at hand. Just over 16,000 officers and men were stationed mainly in the west providing security to settlers from Indian attack. About a third of the officers resigned their commissions to fight for the Confederacy. Thus, while the trained professional military men were vital to the military leadership of both sides, North and South essentially had to create armies from scratch. By the end of the war, more than three million Americans served in the armed forces of the Union and the Confederacy, including 180,000 African Americans in the Union army. The presence of slavery made it possible for the South to achieve the extraordinary feat of mobilizing more than 80 percent of the draft-age military population. One in three of all southern soldiers, a total of 258,000 men, did not survive the war. The North mobilized about 2.2 million men, half its military age population, one in six of whom, or about 360,000, died. In addition, the Confederacy impressed thousands of young male slaves into military service, digging ditches and carrying out menial tasks for the army. Impressments removed from many plantations precisely those slaves who their masters felt were most likely to revolt or run away.

Initially, men signed up for three- or nine-month stints in the North, and usually twelve months in the South. The average age of Civil War armies was 24, much older than later American armies, which reflects the broad base of mobilization. Not surprisingly, younger, unmarried men were overrepresented in the first wave of volunteers. Martin Crawford's study of Ashe County, North Carolina has shown that less than a third of the volunteers in 1861 were married, whereas over half of the 1862 volunteers left wives and families behind.[1] The evidence also suggests that the men who felt able to respond to the call for volunteers in 1861 were from wealthier families, which presumably had the resources to be able to sustain the loss of one or more adult members. Confederate recruits seem to have come from progressively poorer families as the war continued.[2] No one had any comprehension of what the war would involve, and at first, particularly in the North, joining the army was regarded as only one form of patriotic citizenship. In many northern communities, the only people to be labeled "shirkers" or "loiterers" for not volunteering in 1861 were the "listless" unemployed or unskilled workers. At first, no stigma was attached to established men with families, property or a farm or business to run for not enlisting. Immigrants were underrepresented in the Union army. Those who had not yet taken out citizenship were excluded from the draft. Manual and unskilled laborers were slightly overrepresented, and the professional classes underrepresented, but not as strikingly as one would expect given the widespread protests that this was a "rich man's war and a poor man's fight."

Rather than expand the regular army, the thousands of volunteers who rushed to the colors were organized into brand-new volunteer regiments. Companies, theoretically of a hundred men, but in practice often many fewer, were the basic unit of both armies. Ten companies formed one regiment. Typically raised in one locality, regiments were usually officered by a prominent local figure, who had often also provided the money for uniforms and arms as well. To the everlasting frustration of West Point–trained generals, Civil War armies were filled with officers who had no military experience at all. In the 27th New York Volunteers, the lieutenant had been elected, commented a sarcastic private, because he had led "a company of Wide Awakes, armed with torches, in the Presidential campaign of 1860, so of course he knew all about war."[3]

Especially in the first year or so, Jefferson Davis and Abraham Lincoln—and state governors North and South—all dispensed commissions to ambitious politicians, to repay political debts, and to please particular constituencies. Since there were so few trained military men and so many potential posts which offered if not riches then certainly the chance for glory and public success, such practices were probably inevitable. Up to a point, it made sense, too, given the basic political imperative on both sides of creating a broad consensus behind the war, and it did not strike anyone at the time as strange. On one occasion, a staff officer reported hearing a conversation between Lincoln and Secretary of War Edwin Stanton about the appointment of Brigadier Generals. The president apparently told Stanton he wanted to consolidate the support of the influential community of German immigrants and therefore he "wanted Schimmelfennig appointed." He said the name with much relish. Stanton replied that there were other German officers who had a better record. "No matter about that," replied Lincoln briskly; "his name will make up for any difference there may be." The president went off chuckling and repeating "Schimmelfennig" to himself.[4] General Alexander von Schimmelfennig, a veteran of the German revolutions of 1848, and had a perfectly respectable if unspectacular Civil War career.

Some of the untrained officers proved themselves extremely adept at the business of war—a notable example on the Union side being Joshua Lawrence Chamberlain, a college professor from Maine whose connections secured him a commission from the state governor and who went on to be the hero of Little Round Top at Gettysburg. Civil War Americans evidently had good grounds for thinking that character rather than training was the better preparation for service. At the start of the war, after all, Lincoln had almost no knowledge of military affairs, and no experience of battle at all, in contrast to the West Point–trained Davis. Yet it was the Union leader who proved to be the more intuitive strategist. Nevertheless, on balance, the fact that so many senior officers owed their places to blatant patronage not battlefield prowess ensured that both armies experienced an even steeper learning curve than would anyway have been the case.

Volunteers were very conscious of their status as citizens. Throughout the war volunteers resisted being transformed into regular soldiers, by, for example, being compelled to sign up for the duration rather than for a specified time period. Efforts to fill up old units with new volunteers were fiercely resisted in both armies. Volunteers wanted to retain their community identity and to be commanded by a familiar figure, not to be subsumed under an anonymous military machine. The structure reflected the strength of community and ethnic loyalties. In the Union army, some companies and even entire regiments were dominated by men with Irish or German names. In Chicago, a company of Swedes was formed. In New York, the Garibaldi Guards were made up of Italian, Hungarian, Croat and Spanish veterans of the 1848 Revolutions. In South Carolina, Wade Hampton, reputedly the largest slaveowner in the South, recruited a regiment of cavalry, artillery and infantry and led it into battle himself. He was wounded at First Bull Run.

In the first spring of the war, mobilization was a matter of local celebration and effort. Companies of volunteers from each town and village would depart for the railroad cars in a rousing patriotic festival which invariably included the town brass band, speeches from the mayor, the presentation of a flag, parcels of food and clothing from the local women, and much cheering, singing and tears. These ceremonies reinforced the connection between the military unit and the hometown, links that would be maintained by newspapers which featured extensive reports of the movements of the local regiment, and featured public letters from soldiers. From Wisconsin to Florida, and Maine to Texas, young men felt the thrill of adventure and the sweet intensity of unfamiliar emotions. Suddenly they became instant heroes to local girls who had seemed impossibly remote only days earlier. They lined outside photographers' studios in their new uniforms, bowie knives or pistols thrust into their belts for fearsome effect. They were inspired by dreams of noble glory, by a sense of duty and by peer pressure. Some wanted to escape their old lives, some needed the money.

Men like Charles Harvey Brewster, a young store clerk from Northampton, Massachusetts, when the war began, found a new sense of purpose and dignity when he volunteered in April, 1861. In his new uniform, Brewster felt "quite like a free man once more."[5] Alvin C. Voris, a 34-year-old a lawyer, state legislator and abolitionist from Akron, Ohio, had a more complicated decision to make than the unmarried Brewster. A devout Christian and a graduate of Oberlin college, a center of evangelical reformism and antislavery activism, Voris was torn between his familial duties to his wife Lydia and their children on the one hand, and his desire to serve in the army on the other. Praising the "fires of military spirit" in Ohio, he speculated that the army offered great opportunities for distinction for both himself and his family.[6] After hesitating for a few months, he volunteered in September 1861 and was commissioned as an officer.

The basic strategy of all armies is to set men apart from society by giving them distinctive uniforms and haircuts and forcing them to submit to distinctive rituals and unquestioning obedience. The close relationship between the community and the units of the army undermined this function. Civil War regiments, unlike army units today or in, say, the British army in the 1860s, had no traditions or preexisting culture into which the new recruit had to adapt. Instead, Civil War soldiers fitted themselves into an American tradition of voluntary militia which connected military service closely to the community. Civil War armies were made up of amateur soldiers and amateur officers, but to northerners and southerners alike this was a virtue not a disadvantage. Americans were steeped in the republican doctrine that standing armies were the tools of tyrants. They believed that a virtuous citizen army, motivated by noble thoughts of preserving free government, would be more than a match for a miserable army of hirelings and slaves. Americans had been taught—with dubious historical accuracy—that a virtuous republican citizenry had won the Revolutionary War and ever since they had chosen to place their security and independence in hands of public virtue not a regular army. The previous wars in which this young republic had been involved—the War of 1812 and the Mexican War—had been fought largely using local militias. Faith in this tradition of citizens-in-arms was extraordinarily durable, even though, especially in the North, the militia system had become either honorific, nonexistent or a laughing stock. Given their limited experience of militia organization, never mind full-scale warfare, Americans in both North and South were highly militaristic. Young men formed marching clubs and paraded on July 4 or in election meetings. In the South, slavery gave a purpose to the arming of the white citizenry, and many poor nonslaveholding whites who joined the Confederate army had previous experience carrying a gun in slave patrols. If the war had broken out ten years earlier, massive volunteer armies would have been more difficult to arm. During the 1850s, guns became significantly cheaper, easier to use and more readily available, due in large part to the mass production of rifled muskets by the armory in Springfield, Massachusetts.

Blacks had served in American armies in previous wars, and had long been enlisted in the US navy, but there was widespread opposition to their being included in the new volunteer Union army. A federal law of 1792 had banned them from state militias. A black leader in Cincinnati later recalled the opposition he had faced when, with a group of friends, he had tried to organize a militia company in May 1861. The police broke up one meeting with the words "We want you d—d niggers to keep out of this; this is a white man's war."[7] But after the Emancipation Proclamation opened the way for black regiments most black leaders actively encouraged enlistment. Frederick Douglass argued that through service in the army they could shape what he always called "this Abolition war" to their own purposes. In early 1863, Lincoln advocated the enlistment of blacks into the army on the grounds that "the colored population is the *available* and yet *unavailed of*, force for restoring the Union."[8] But black soldiers were not enlisted on equal terms. At first they were paid at a lower rate and throughout the war their segregated regiments were officered by whites. Black regiments were usually deployed as second-class soldiers, often doing menial labor such as digging trenches and loading and unloading supplies.[9]

In the tradition of citizen militias in previous American wars, companies of new volunteers initially claimed the right to elect their lieutenants and captains. At the same time, regimental officers were appointed because of their political connections to state governors.

The new citizen army offered a plethora of new patronage opportunities. In one Massachusetts regiment the men were complaining of being drilled too hard, but their complaints were ignored until the wife of the colonel came to visit and chided her husband for working his neighbors and neighbors' sons too hard.[10] Soldiers knew that their behavior on the battlefield and in camp would be reported back home. The difference between these citizen armies and professional armies was that the home community never relinquished oversight of their men at war. Civil War armies were anything but anonymous places.

Very gradually, haltingly, and in the face of tremendous resistance, the federal government attempted to assert some measure of central control over the mobilization and organization of Union troops. The July 1862 Militia Act passed by the US Congress strengthened the rickety old militia structure, ordered the enlistment in state militias of men between the ages of 18 and 45 and gave the president the right to call these men into federal service. States were given a quota of volunteers, and states in turn divided up their quotas into each town. In early 1863, Congress passed the Enrollment Act, setting up the machinery for a federal draft.[11] If states failed to provide enough men, the threat of a compulsory draft was there. The complex system prompted complaints about the way that the quotas had been allocated, and the reliance on local officials to implement the draft led to charges of incompetence, inconsistency and corruption. The system of allowing drafted men to pay a $300 commutation fee or hire a substitute instead of serving themselves led to charges that the rich were able to escape their duty. To avoid having to resort to compulsion, states and localities offered ever-higher bounties to attract likely volunteers—or cynical bounty-jumpers—to enlist on their rolls rather than in a neighboring state or town. New York and Pennsylvania ended up a bidding war, each raising the level of its bounty in order to fill its quota. The absurdity of the system was that potential volunteers had a financial incentive to delay joining up until the bounty increased. In Jacksonville, Illinois, where there was a desperate determination to avoid the shame of the draft, a volunteer could receive over $500. By 1864, a volunteer in Springfield, Massachusetts, could receive $875 from a combination of local, state, federal and private sources—a sum equivalent to three years' wages for an unskilled laborer. In addition, Springfield raised $80,000 for the relief of wounded soldiers, many of them just passing through the town, and the Soldiers' Rest Association became a major inclusive and extensive community activity, unprecedented in the town's history.[12]

The town of Deerfield in Massachusetts, like many other northern towns, at first had no trouble filling volunteer companies with local sons. By 1864, Deerfield was filling its quotas by paying for recruits from poorer neighboring towns.[13] In many places the local recruitment effort was in effect privatized by relying on bounty agents to find men, often from among new immigrant communities, in return for a sizeable cut of the bounty.

On most measures, the Union draft was strikingly ineffective. Reports abound of the multiple ways in which a man could avoid being drafted, from fleeing the district when the enrollment officers were compiling their list, to giving false names and addresses, lying about their age, feigning an illness or simply resorting to bribery. Even among those whose names were pulled out of the enrollment officers' hat, a third disappeared ("skedaddled") and failed to appear as requested in front of the recruitment boards. Among the rest, a majority were exempted for mental or physical illness, or because they claimed alien status or family hardship. Only a quarter of men whose names were drawn were called to service, and many of those then hired a substitute. Some Quakers had conscientious objections to military service, or to supporting the war financially by paying for a substitute. Abraham Lincoln legitimized Quakers' exemption from the draft when he intervened to support the case of a Vermont Quaker, Cyrus Pringle, who refused to serve when his name was called.[14]

The result was that, although conscription proved to be one of the most controversial aspects of the Lincoln administration's war policy, it did not add much manpower to the army. In total, 46,000 conscripts served in the Union army and 118,000 drafted men hired substitutes in their place. This amounts to only 13 percent of the 1,260,000 new recruits enlisted after the federal draft took effect in March 1863, and a much smaller proportion of the total numbers of men who served in the war. In the South, the proportion of drafted men was slightly higher—about a fifth of all Confederate soldiers were compelled to serve. Conscripted men and substitutes were poor replacements for the three-year volunteers who were now veterans. Appalled by the "off-scourings of northern slums" who were sent to make up the numbers in depleted regiments in the winter of 1863–1864, one northern soldier concluded that "if these fellows are trusted on picket, the army will soon be in hell."[15]

The bottom line was that in both armies, most men who served wanted to. And especially in the North those who were determined to avoid being enlisted generally found ways of avoiding it. The Union and the Confederacy shared much in common in their experience of recruitment and conscription. In both sections, initial enthusiasm waned by the end of 1861, and both had to resort to a mixture of carrots and sticks, increasingly relying on sticks to dig ever deeper into the reserves of eligible fighters. But the differences are also instructive. Southern volunteers were much more likely to sign up for the duration rather than for a fixed period but even so the Confederacy had to resort to conscription a year earlier than the Union, and were more reliant on conscripted men for the rest of the war. Unsurprisingly, popular perceptions of the likelihood of victory had a clear impact on the capacity of the armies to recruit. When the war began to go badly for the South in 1863, the numbers of volunteers fell sharply whereas they stayed relatively constant in the North.[16] The relative health of the northern economy and the much greater number of men, including immigrants, meant that a market for substitutes thrived in the North whereas in the South the price of substitutes soon became prohibitive. Similarly, southern towns could not afford the bounties that northern towns paid. By the end of the war, the Confederate government ended all the exemptions available to southern white men, even the hugely controversial exemption granted to planters owning more than 20 slaves who, it was argued, needed to stay in order to maintain the slave system. As the war continued, the Confederate government became ever harsher in its efforts to recruit troops, and the level of national—as opposed to state—control became ever tougher. The North, in contrast, was able to relax its efforts toward the end of the war.

LIFE IN CIVIL WAR ARMIES

The reality of military life was a shock to most of these volunteers, many of whom bridled against the strictures of discipline and few of whom had traveled far from home before. "I have saw more since I left home than I ever expected to see," wrote Elijah DeBord of the 37th North Carolina Volunteers, in April, 1862. The Confederate capital, Richmond, was "the largest place that I ever thought be made," DeBord enthused to his parents.[17] For most soldiers the war consisted of long periods of boredom interrupted by episodes of sheer terror. Only in the final campaigns in 1864–1865 were soldiers engaged continuously day after day. Most of their time in uniform was spent in camps, living in tents or improvised huts. Typical days were spent drilling and doing picket duty. Hunger was a recurrent theme in soldiers' letters, especially when they were on the move, or far from supply lines. Union soldiers were generally much better fed than their southern counterparts. They could rely on a daily ration of hardtack (a hard bread made of flour and water), beef or pork, and occasionally vegetables. Tobacco, tea, coffee and sugar were luxuries that were harder to rely on, and, along with newspapers, were the goods most often exchanged illicitly across the lines.[18] Soldiers also took opium in great quantities, as a "remedy" for bowel disease and to cope with the fear of battle.

Planters, professional men and laborers, the devout and the profane, the young and the old, fathers and sons were thrown together in unfamiliar roles, with the social hierarchies of civilian life increasingly challenged as the war progressed. The rootedness of units in local communities set clear limits on the diversity and unfamiliarity of a soldier's immediate comrades, but their letters are filled with comments about the behavior and attitudes of men in other companies and regiments. Moralizing Yankee soldiers complained especially about drunkenness and prostitution. "Last night 'Bacchus' reigned all night long," complained a chaplain in a Pennsylvania regiment. "The demoralization from whiskey, beer, and strumpets is becoming fearful."[19] As in other wars, Civil War armies developed a grudging respect for each other, and there were moments when their shared experience transcended the conflict. Even after the battle of Spotsylvania, one of the most vicious of the war, a Union officer reported with amazement that pickets from the two armies who only an hour earlier had been killing and wounding each other shook hands during a lull in the fighting one night. "The great staples of conversation are the size and the quality of rations, the marches they have made, and the regiments they have fought against. All sense of personal spite is sunk in the immensity of the contest."[20] On the night before the battle of Stones River, the two armies were encamped only a few hundred yards apart separated by a narrow creek. The soldiers could see the glint of each other's campfires, smell the cooking bacon and bitter coffee, and hear snatches of conversation and laughter in the still winter air. As darkness fell, brass bands struck up patriotic tunes and the men on both sides sang along trying to drown out the sound of the enemy's singing, the Union boys belting out "Yankee Doodle" and the southerners "Dixie." Suddenly, one of the regimental bands started playing "Home Sweet Home." Then another followed, and another, until all the bands and all the singing soldiers on both sides of the stream sang in harmony.

One of the common enemies that both sides faced was the prospect of dying not a glorious battlefield death but from unpleasant diseases. Confederate General Richard S. Ewell's medical history exemplifies the personal medical challenges that were common to soldiers in both armies. Before the war he had suffered from recurrent bouts of malaria that he had apparently contracted during the Mexican War, and from a sore throat that must have been made worse by the prescribed remedy which involved swallowing a concoction of cayenne pepper and turpentine. While serving in the US army against Native Americans in Arizona before the Civil War he was repeatedly plagued by nausea, severe headaches and dyspepsia, a painful digestive problem that caused him to eat eccentric combinations of food, some of which, such as a wheat paste, can hardly have helped. After the Civil War began, his bad health continued. He was reported to be suffering from such a bad "nervous condition" that the only position in which he could sleep was curled up around a camp stool. In May, 1861, he was wounded in the shoulder, and could not ride for several days. A year later, he suffered from a severe headache and complained that his dyspepsia had never been so bad. In June, 1862, his horse was shot from under him and a bullet lodged in his foot. Shortly afterwards, along with most of his army, he contracted malaria during the battle of Chickahominy. On August 28, a minie ball shattered his knee cap, and the seemingly ubiquitous Dr Hunter McGuire amputated his leg. His recovery was set back when his crutches slipped on ice on Christmas Day, 1862, and another inch of bone was knocked off. His stump did not heal properly and the wooden leg attached to it was so badly made that he was plagued by continual boils and infections. On one occasion, he fell while trying to walk and it caused extensive bleeding. On June 14, 1863, he was hit in the chest by a spent bullet but suffered no more than a bruise. At Gettysburg his wooden leg was shot through with a bullet. During the winter of 1863–1864, he suffered from chills, fever and pain in his leg, and in January was badly bruised when his horse slipped from under him in the snow. In May, he contracted "something in the nature of scurvy" and suffered from acute diarrhea. During the siege of Petersburg, he fell from his horse again and was so badly bruised that his whole head and shoulders had to be swathed in bandages, leaving only small peep holes for his eyes and mouth. On April 6, 1865, Ewell was captured and while a prisoner of war complained of neuralgia and dyspepsia. Yet he was one of the lucky ones; he survived the war, dying of typhoid pneumonia in 1872.[21]

More than two-thirds of the soldiers on both sides who perished in the war died from disease rather than battle wounds. Of the 360,000 northerners who died in the war, only 110,000 were killed in battle. Among southerners 164,000 died from disease and 94,000 on the battlefield. "Sickness among the troops rapidly increasing," noted a physician with the Army of the Potomac during the Peninsular Campaign. "Remittent fever, diarrhea, and dysentery prevail."[22] The death rate from bowel infections—which the soldiers sometimes referred to as the "Kentucky Quick Step"—has been estimated at 2 percent of the entire Union army, and the number who were rendered unable to fight was vastly more than that.[23] The fecal stench around camps, noted one Union officer, was "inseparable from the army . . . it might properly be called the patriotic odor." Poor sanitation in camps was compounded by epidemics of childhood diseases such as measles, mumps and diphtheria. After "chronic diarrhea," measles was probably the second biggest killer in the war. Approximately 10,000 surgeons served in the Union army and about 4000 in the Confederate army, but a poor understanding of the bacterial origins of disease meant that their primary function was to dress wounds and amputate limbs. Chloroform was sometimes used as an anesthetic during amputations but supplies often ran out (General Ewell was lucky to get some), rendering the hacking off of limbs no more bearable than it had been in the Napoleonic wars. An incalculable number of soldiers died from infections because they were too scared to face the surgeon's saw.

ATTITUDES AND MOTIVATIONS

The large body of letters from Civil War soldiers which survive, often having been kept with reverence by a loved one at home and then passed down the generations, constitutes a distinctive genre. Typically, requests for news from home were accompanied by stories from the front, sometimes lighthearted, sometimes grim, a ritual invocation of the cause for which all this sacrifice was being made. Sometimes soldiers would explain their motivation to doubting family members, others sought reassurance that they had made the right choice. The word that appears most often in these reflective passages is "duty": duty to their country, to God, to their families, to their fallen comrades. Duty appears to have been a sustaining as well as an initial motivation. After more than two years of fighting, a captain in the 28th Mississippi Cavalry was convinced that war was an "unmixed evil [of] blood, butchery, death, desolation, robbery, rapine, selfishness, violence, wrong . . . palliated only when waged in self defense." He was "heartily sick of it," but "sustained along by a strong sense of duty."[24] For fathers and husbands in particular, the sense of being judged by future generations was a powerful one. Typical were the sentiments of an officer in a New York regiment who told his wife that their children would look back on the war "either with pride or shame" in their father. "I would rather my children would mourn a Father's death than his disgrace." Joshua Lawrence Chamberlain insisted on returning to the army even after being repeatedly wounded, and nearly losing his life on several occasions. "I am not scared or hurt enough yet to be willing to face the rear, when other men are marching to the front," he told his wife in February 1865. To fight so long as he was physically able was the only course "which honor and manliness prompt."[25]

Soldiers' conception of duty, valor and courage, were rooted in their society's understandings of masculinity. Soldiers always referred to themselves as "boys," whatever their age, but soldiering was also the classic coming of age experience. Soldiers' accounts of the war all contain the theme of transformation. "War is *hell* broke loose and benumbs all the tender feelings of men and makes of them *brutes*," recalled an Iowa soldier, Cyrus F. Boyd. On the one hand, soldiers had to learn to control their emotions while, on the other, preventing themselves from being desensitized and thus brutalized. "More men *die* of homesickness than all other diseases—and when a man gives up and lies down he is a *goner*," wrote Boyd. His prescription for getting through the conflict was for soldiers to become masters of themselves: "Keep the mind occupied with something new and keep *going all the time* except when asleep."[26] True manhood was not just about the willingness to be physically violent on the battlefield, but required morality and self-restraint. In using violence to punish rebellion, northerners regarded themselves as fathers chastising children: it was violent, but it was violence within a moral and civilizing context. Northern soldiers portrayed secession as emotional and treacherous—in other words childlike and feminine—and they believed the appropriate response was to be an adult: rational, loyal and masculine.[27] One Union soldier wrote after the battle of Shiloh, "we showed them on the 2nd day that northern obstinacy was more than a match for southern impetuosity."[28] Confederates were, if anything, even clearer in labeling Yankees as effeminate, pasty-faced clerks and hirelings, hiding behind their superior artillery, who could never prevail in a fair fight. Southerners saw themselves as engaged in the supremely moral task of defending their communities, their civilization, against the barbarism of the Yankee invaders. In other words, manliness, for Civil War Americans was about self-discipline and restraint, not a matter of sexual achievement or license. Drinking and whoring was seen as giving in to temptation in a way that was unmanly. The self-image of restrained, manly fighting, belied the reality of war. Violence was not inflicted reluctantly brother against brother but with accompanying apocalyptic visions. Soldiers wound themselves into mad furies in order to launch themselves on the enemy. Yet barbarism was always something the enemy engaged in.

If war could elevate, stimulate patriotism and serve as a fiery coming of age ritual, it also contained inherent dangers for the Victorian man. Acutely aware that every day they were treading a fine line between civilization and barbarism, civilian soldiers felt the need to demonstrate to the folks back home that war had not brutalized them. "I know the popular mind is that we become accustomed to the dangers of the field and as a consequence cease to be sensitive on that account," wrote Alvin C. Voris. But that is a delusion. We may meet these dangers more calmly, but we appreciate them more accurately than the [un]initiated."[29] Voris found the duties of an officer difficult to perform:

> A poor corporal came to me tonight and wanted leave to go home to see a sick wife. He expects she will die. I had to say to him no, having positive orders to permit none to go home unless to save life or prevent his permanent disability. One came to me and says his wife is about to go under the trial of maternity, that he had a promise from the recruiting officer that at the time he could go home, his wife in almost extreme fear begs him by letter, with tears down his cheek he comes to me, begs to be permitted to go but a few days, & shows me his letter. This is repeated over & over again, but the service will not permit even in small cases the absence of a soldier & I must say no.[30]

Anticipating the imagery of poppies in the wheat fields of the Somme, the juxtaposition of beauty and ugliness—of life in the midst of death—struck many Civil War soldiers as particularly poignant. The "magnolias in full bloom" in a field near Cold Harbor were a refreshing smell, reported Brewster, "after the continual stench of the dead bodies of men and horses which we have endured for the last 19 days."[31]

For many soldiers on both sides, the Civil War became a Holy crusade. The strains of war reinforced rather than undermined faith. Evangelical revivalism spread through the camps of both armies. The peaks of revivals were in the aftermath of defeats, beginning in the Army of Northern Virginia after Antietam. In the wake of Bragg's defeat at Chattanooga, a revival whipped through the camp of the Army of Tennessee. Samuel C. Clyde of the 2nd South Carolina Infantry reported a religious meeting which was "one of the most glorious revivals I ever witnessed. I came away after the benediction, leaving them still singing, shouting & praising God." This was far from untypical. Clyde continued:

> Very many of our brave defenders are enlisting under the 'blood stained banner of the Cross of our salvation.' The Christian soldier is praying, the ministers of God are laboring. In short, the followers of the Lord Jesus are engaged in a mighty struggle with Satan and his wicked legions, and I am happy to add, are victorious in every conflict.[32]

One historian has estimated that 200,000 Civil War soldiers may have been "born again" in these revival meetings.[33]

Confederate soldiers were encouraged to equate the cause of the Confederacy with the cause of Christ by the efforts of religious journals such as *The Army and Navy Messenger* and *The Soldier's Friend*, many of which began publication after 1863. "Whenever we become humble and acknowledge Him our deliverance is nigh," wrote a private in the 8th Texas Cavalry. "Until we do this and amend our wicked ways we may expect this war to continue and horrors will be added to horrors till the great end is achieved."[34] Northern soldiers, too, were encouraged to find scriptural justification for the Union cause, particularly over the matter of slavery. Frequent references to "our holy cause" in soldiers' letters are enough to indicate that for many, their faith in God was intertwined with their patriotic duty. Nothing illustrates this so well as the "Battle Hymn of the Republic," written by abolitionist Julia Ward Howe during a visit to a camp of Massachusetts soldiers in late 1861. It was published on the front cover of the March 1862 issue of *Atlantic Monthly*. Set to the tune of "John Brown's Body," Howe's lyrics connect the sacrifice of soldiers with the suffering of Christ: "as He died to make men holy, let us die to make men free/While God is marching on." The words bristle with the evangelicals' view that the

Union army was doing the lord's work in redeeming the nation of the sin of slavery. "I have read a fiery gospel writ in burnished rows of steel," runs the third verse. " 'As ye deal with my contemers, so with you my grace shall deal/Let the Hero, born of woman, crush the serpent with his heel.' "

For Southerners, a sense of personal duty reinforced their political commitment to liberty and self-government. To fail in their bid for independence would be to lose their honor. "Let [the war] be long or short meat or no meat shows or no shoes [we are] Resolved to fight it out," wrote a soldier in the 32nd Mississippi in early 1864. "If we give up now we will certainly be the most degraded people on earth."[35] A popular Confederate soldiers' song connected these personal and political themes:

> We fight for our homes, we fight for our wives,
> We fight for our children, their rights and their lives
> We fight for our lov'd ones, our country and its good,
> And we'll fight till we shed the last drop of our blood.[36]

Fear of personal dishonor helped to maintain discipline in armies made up of men with little or no prior military experience. But introspection and moments of honesty jostled with bravado. "I am scared almost to death every battle we have, but I don't think you need be afraid of my sneaking away unhurt," wrote Brewster.[37] Men who avoided military service were unmanly. "Any young man who is drafted now and forgets his manhood so far as to hire a substitute is'nt worthy the name of man and ought to be put in petticoats immediately," fumed Private Wilbur Fisk.[38] Local and family loyalties reinforced a patriotic commitment. One Union officer spoke to his men of the bonds of nationhood as an all-embracing feeling: "Dear are our parents, dear our children, our relatives, our friends; but our country, in itself embraces all these affections."[39] "Just Before the Battle Mother," a ballad published in 1862 by the prolific northern songwriter George F. Root, expressed the intimate role of home and hearth in the thoughts and motivations of soldiers. As Reid Mitchell explains, this song and others like it served not only "to express soldiers' deepest feelings— their longings for family and home—but also to instruct them as to what their feelings should be."[40] Other songs which dwelt on the theme of mothers, often mothers in mourning for their dead sons, included "Kiss Me before I Die, Mother!," "Mother, Oh! Sing Me to Rest,"

"Who Will Care for Mother Now?", "Keep Me Awake Mother!," "Rock me to Sleep, Mother" and "Dear Mother I've Come Home to Die." When northern soldiers spoke or sang about their families, or when they compared the Union to a family, as they often did, they were merely reflecting their own experience, in which national intuitions, and abstract concepts like nationhood, were mediated through local leaders and community values. Private Wilbur Fisk, on picket duty in Virginia, mused on these themes in one of his regular dispatches to his hometown newspaper:

> When we reflect that we are standing on the outer verge of all that is left of the American union, and nothing but darkness and rebellion is beyond, and that we are actually guarding our own homes and firesides from treason's usurpations, we feel a thrill of pride that we are permitted to bear a part in maintaining our beloved government.[41]

The family was at the center of mid-nineteenth-century Victorian culture. And, as Reid Mitchell has put it, "the Union was a man's family writ large."

For all the intimate connections that bound military units to their home communities, the gulf between the experiences of civilians and soldiers created tension. Soldiers complained of the lack of understanding of those left at home, and the impossibility of conveying in words the true nature of war. "It was a fearful, fearful sight," Charles H. Brewster wrote to his mother of the battlefield at Williamsburg, "but language fails me and I cannot attempt to describe the scene. If ever I come home I can perhaps tell you but I cannot write it." Later in the war he mentioned "lots of other things which I cannot write about that you cannot understand when I tell you," and, after complaining about an anti-Lincoln newspaper editorial that he had seen in a Massachusetts newspaper, he snapped that "a soldier has more misery in one day than occurs in a lifetime of a civilian ordinarily and their greatest comforts would be miseries to people at home."[42] In countless letters home, soldiers—even lifelong Democrats—"choked with rage" and frustration at home front dissenters. An Illinois Democrat exhorted his family to take strong measures: "Is there no grit left [in] the inhabitants or be they afraid to use their shotguns and riffles . . . [and] hang every Cussed one of the traitors as quick as you would kill a snake?"[43] Confederate soldiers, who may have been unaware of the hardships and deprivations their families were suffering, were no less angered by talk of peace.

The notion of manliness as self-mastery did not preclude emotionalism. "I cannot sing yet those songs such as, the vacant chair, the tears come," confessed an Illinois soldier to his wife. The tears, he explained, were evidence that he was true to his familial duties: "A man that cannot shed a tear when he thinks of those he left at home is no man."[44] On picket duty again, Wilbur Fisk unleashed a classic outpouring of Victorian sentimentality which captures very well the idea that manliness was defined by familial responsibility, loyalty and devotion to family and community, a capacity for moral feeling and, through all these things, a duty to country that was grounded in protection of home.

Through their writings, soldiers created a romantic image of heroism, based on triumph of courage over cowardice. They prided themselves on imposing order, purpose and meaning on the otherwise wanton, uncontrolled destructiveness of war. By facing up to their own fears, acknowledging them and never shirking their duty, soldiers presented themselves as having met the ultimate test of manhood. This ideal meant that the daily struggle with sickness and diarrhea was all the more humiliating. Soldiers wrote of the ignobility of dying in a field hospital of a bowel disease. Brewster described his feelings of frustration and humiliation at having to spend the battle of Fredericksburg in December 1862 five miles behind the lines because he was suffering from chronic diarrhea. "I lie here like a skulking coward and hear the din of battle but cannot get there it is too bad."[45]

The overtly ideological motivation of so many Civil War soldiers did not, of course, mean that they didn't fight for other reasons as well. The capacity of so many men to keep fighting in spite of the hardships and the prospect of death or injury can be explained by what military historians call "small unit cohesion"—a sometimes fatalistic pride in one's unit and a desire not to let down comrades. Some historians, notably Bell Wiley and Gerald Linderman, have emphasized the nonpolitical motivations of soldiers, and have doubted whether the political motivations that were in evidence at the start sustained men through four years of combat. Certainly, there were many soldiers in both armies who were cynical, or hostile, or at least became so when they understood how brutal and unromantic war could be. There is plenty of evidence that the conscripts, substitutes and bounty-men who entered the ranks of the federal armies in 1864 were very different in their attitudes than the original volunteers from 1861 and 1862. Yet taken as a whole, it is striking how constant soldiers remained to the ideals for which they had joined up. Given the option of returning home with honor after their three years of service was completed, more than half of the veterans chose to remain in service, which is surely testimony to their commitment to the cause. Terrified of the best regiments melting away just as the spring 1864 campaign begun, the War Department offered incentives for veterans to re-enlist for the duration, including a cash bounty of $400, a 35-day furlough and a "veteran volunteer" chevron to wear on their sleeves. But bribery would not have worked unless it had been reinforced by a powerful appeal to duty and patriotism. Many re-enlisted against the wishes of their families back home. One New York veteran rather tactlessly told his wife that while "I feel as keenly as any other the sacrifice made of home and those I love", such matters were "but dust in the balance for my Country's in the scale." Like so many other men in uniform on both sides, he went to invoke his reputation in the years to come: "My children will remember me for having been found among those who challenge treason and battle for the right."[46] An Ohio officer who also re-enlisted admitted that "there is nothing pleasant about soldiering," but grimly concluded that he could "endure its privations" because "there is a *big idea* which is at stake...the principles of Liberty, Justice, and of the Righteousness which exalteth a Nation."[47]

> The veil of night has now shrouded everything in gloom. No sound charms the ear, nor sight greets the eye—nothing but dull vacancy. The moments seem oppressively long, and the pickets wear long faces. Merriment seems sadly out of place, like laughter at a funeral. At such a time how natural for the mind to revert back to the pleasant homes we have left behind. We almost fancy we can see the family circle gathered round the fireside, and hear them speaking of the absent one, and wondering if he is picketing this cold night. It may be a weakness unbecoming to a soldier, and if so we will forfeit all claim to being strong, but in these moments of loneliness, in spite of us, thoughts of parents, brothers and sisters and kind friends at home, will throng upon our memory, and picture glowing anticipations of the time when the rebellion shall be crushed and we be permitted to return home and greet them face to face.[48]

Soliders in both armies believed, in the spirit of their common republican heritage, that they were struggling for freedom against tyranny.

Both drew comparisons between their present struggle and the Revolution. "By the sacrifice and blood of our fathers was the Republic founded," wrote a New York captain, "and by the treasure, faith, honor, and blood of their sons shall the same glorious flag forever wave over us."[49] The patriotic role of women was to inculcate in their children a love of country. Union soldier Henry H. Seys encouraged his wife to "teach our children that their duty to the land of their birth is next to their duty to their God. And that those who would desert *her* in the hour of danger, should be deserted by Him when *their* final calamity comes."[50]

The readiness of Americans on both sides to go to war is testimony to the nature of government in the mid-nineteenth century. Most Americans, North and South, felt a personal stake in the government. This was especially true for northerners, who did not have the direct incentive of fighting to defend their homes against invasion. Many Union soldiers articulated a strong sense of civic duty, rooted in republican ideas of the public good, as the explanation for why they fought. Every northern boy (and every southern boy as well) knew the story of his nation, the desire to protect freedom from tyranny, the dignity and patriotism of the god-like Washington, the heroic sacrifice of those who had lost their lives in the Revolution. Now the time had come to protect that nation—"all that I hold dear", as one Union soldier put it—from the corrupt designs of slaveholding aristocrats. National symbols like the star-spangled banner were quasi-religious objects of devotion. Southerners needed to be "shown a lesson", to be chastised by the manly patriotism of republican citizens of the Loyal States.

While there were certainly soldiers whose initial political commitment faded in the face of battle, a more common experience was for army life to politicize those who experienced it. Politics was everywhere in Civil War armies. Soldiers formed debating clubs, held mock elections, and above all avidly scrutinized newspapers for their political news and opinions. Political participation was an important manifestation of the status of the soldier as citizen. Many soldiers consciously regarded elections as solemn political festivals that affirmed republican government, a faith illustrated by the many occasions, recorded in soldiers' letters and diaries (and later in newspaper reports) in which voting took place even when it was clear that it could have no impact on who was elected. Prisoners of war held in Confederate jails rigged up polling booths on Election Day and solemnly cast their ballots.[51]

Political influence in the army flowed both down from the officers and also from one's peers. One Illinois regiment exercised its political muscle by resolving that all "C[ommanding] officers who do not endorse the president's proclamation of emancipation, and who will not to the utmost of their ability endorse and sustain the administration in its efforts to crush the rebellion, be politely requested to go home and let better men fill their place."[52] In the 1864 election, Republican-controlled state legislatures gave soldiers the right to vote from the battlefront, but Democratic states, correctly predicting a heavy soldier vote for Lincoln, did not. This meant that unless soldiers from Illinois, Indiana and New Jersey could get furloughs home, which few could, they were disenfranchised. Even that, however, did not stop them from participating in mock votes. After one such vote in an Illinois regiment, one strongly pro-Lincoln private recorded his candidate's comfortable victory and noted that "the regiment was largely Democratic when it left Illinois in February, 1862, [so] this vote showed that the political opinions of the rank and file had, in the meantime, undergone a decided change."[53] In the Union army as a whole, a huge majority of soldiers—perhaps 78 percent—cast their ballots for Lincoln. Peer pressure, and the expectations of officers, no doubt increased the tally, but there is no doubting the grassroots support for the president from the army. Since about 40 percent of the army came from Democratic families, Democratic neighborhoods back home, the vote for Lincoln is evidence of how far the war transcended prewar partisanship.

If the Union was the carrier of the values of the republic, "Father Abraham" seemed to many soldiers to personify the struggle. Regular appearances to inspect the troops, in which he would talk at length to private soldiers, and visits to hospitals to talk with the wounded made Lincoln a visible presence. "I had a good chance to see 'Uncle Abe,' " reported a Vermont soldier after the president's visit to the Army of the Potomac near Petersburg in March, 1865, "and I believe he is the homeliest man I have seen for three years. But I guess he is good natured, for he was a grinning all the time he was here."[54] Lincoln also regularly addressed groups of soldiers on their way to or from the front from an upstairs window of the White House and in addition he held perhaps 2000 or more private interviews with enlisted men who came to him with problems related to sickness, furloughs or pay.[55] News of these meetings spread rapidly through word of mouth and through letters to local newspapers. The president had the common touch, a remarkable ability to connect to people on an individual level, to make them feel that he understood and shared their problems and concerns. As Richard Carwardine has put it, Lincoln became a "virtual presence" within the Union army.[56] His extraordinary capacity to relate to ordinary people was a vital source of Lincoln's political authority within the Union army. No less important was his increasingly obvious physical deterioration under the strain of wartime command, an indication of shared suffering which reinforced his bond with the troops.

6   The Ordeal of the Confederate Republic

The Confederate States of America was created with remarkable speed. Within months of the secession of the Deep South, the new nation had not only a flag and a name, but a functioning government, its own currency, a Post Office and armies in the field. The constitutional convention that met in Montgomery, Alabama, in February 1861, completed its work rapidly, installed Jefferson Davis as provisional president, and began the all-important task of seeking international recognition. Four months later the new government was installed in Richmond, complete with a Confederate version of all the key elements of the federal government—a Congress, Supreme Court, State and War Departments, a Treasury, even a Confederate "White House." For four years a Confederate nation-state existed. In institutional terms, its deficiencies were immense—even if in some regards it achieved extraordinary feats of organization. By 1863 it had lost control of vast swathes of its territory to internal opposition as well as to Union troops; in 1865 it collapsed completely and its elected leaders became hunted outlaws. Yet in its short life, the Confederate States of America inspired fervent loyalty and immense pride. In the end, it was destroyed by war. It was not an intrinsically fragile entity, nor was it bound to fail, nor even did popular nationalism die when the state collapsed, although inevitably its meaning changed. An 1864 school textbook, *Geography for Beginners*, published in Richmond and written by the Rev. K. J. Stewart with the aim of inculcating national pride in the children of the South, concluded its section on the history of the Confederacy with this optimistic summary: "the people of the Southern States have fought their own way to political independence and the respect and amity of the great nations of the world."[1] That was how things were meant to turn out. Within a year after the book was published these words must have prompted an aching sense of loss in many southern readers.

BIRTH OF A NATION-STATE

Southerners shifted their allegiance from the old Union to the new Confederacy with ease. Even stalwart "conditional Unionists" like Alexander Stephens quickly embraced the Confederate cause once secession was an accomplished fact—in Stephens' case, so much so that he agreed to serve as vice president. The key to understanding this transformation is that the creation of a Confederate identity did not require southerners to repudiate the values and history of the American republic as they understood them. Indeed, southerners claimed that their new nation was the true embodiment—the apotheosis, in fact—of the American Revolution. In their own minds, the leaders of the Confederacy were not rebels or traitors but patriots. The immortal founding fathers, argued Confederates, would have acted no differently in the face of tyranny. At stake, they argued, was the protection not only of their honor, but, in the words of Confederate General Daniel Ruggles, no less than the great principle laid out by Jefferson in the Declaration of Independence: "that 'all governments derive their just powers from the consent of the governed.' "[2]

By presenting their Revolution of 1861 as a replay of 1776, the founders of the Confederacy sought to anchor their new republic on reassuringly conservative foundations. "*We* are not revolutionists," protested the influential southern editor J. D. B. De Bow. Indeed, agreed the "fire-eater" Robert Barnwell Rhett, it was the "Black Republicans" who were the "the practical revolutionists and hatchers of trouble."[3] Yankees, with their rabid, dangerous abolitionist zealotry had led a once-virtuous nation away from the path of righteousness. The four-year military struggle to create an independent South was a revolution to preserve an idealized past; one historian has aptly called it a "reactionary revolution."[4] For Rev. William Hall, one of many southern clergymen who published patriotic tracts justifying the Confederate cause, it was northerners who were the true revolutionaries and the Confederates who were merely trying to maintain free government that had been fought for by their common forefathers in the Revolution. "The epithet, *rebels*," Hall wrote, "so fiercely hurled upon us by the Northmen is sadly amusing when it is remembered, that we are simply contending for the inherent right of self-government, which was so nobly vindicated by their fathers and ours."[5]

Confederate nation-builders argued that the spirit of the South was generous and tolerant, as opposed to the mean, self-righteousness of the Yankees. At the same time, southerners were more civilized and cultured than the "trashy" Yankees who devoured pulp fiction and sensational newspapers. In 1862, General Grant issued an infamous order expelling Jews "as a class" from the area under Union control in Tennessee, Kentucky and Mississippi on the grounds that they were exploiting a flourishing black-market trade in Southern cotton. It was never implemented, and Lincoln later rescinded it, but it was noticed in the South. The Richmond *Daily Dispatch* dryly observed that it was "in keeping with the professed religious toleration of the Puritans" and pointed, by way of contrast, to Judah P. Benjamin, the Jewish Confederate Secretary of State, as evidence of the reality of southern liberal toleration.[6]

Confederates were quick to identify the old Union as corrupted by Yankees in much the same way as their colonial predecessors saw the British state as diseased and decadent. Along with the hypocrisy, fanaticism, materialism, and greed that southerners identified with Yankees, they blamed raucous partisanship for sapping the spirit of unity and selflessness from the republic. Consequently, the political culture of the Confederate republic was infused with a strong antiparty spirit.[7] Secession, argued a clergyman, Benjamin Palmer, had "separated us from a country that had become bloated in party corruption and was destined soon to fall into premature decay."[8] Significantly, in seeking to transcend the grubbiness of politics, southerners turned back to what they saw as the patriotic, antiparty ideals of the founders. The delegates to the southern constitutional convention demonstrated that their quarrel was not with the handiwork of the founding fathers by adopting a constitution which echoed the Federal Constitution in form and, in large part, repeated it word for word. There were some constitutional innovations: the executive power of the president was strengthened by giving the right to veto particular elements of a bill rather than either accepting or rejecting it in toto, which gave Jefferson Davis an active role in shaping legislation. The executive was also given more influence in the legislature by the provision that allowed members of the cabinet to speak in Congress. The presidential term was also extended to six years rather than four. In other respects, the southerners took the opportunity to enshrine a Jacksonian vision of limited central government. Citizenship was a matter for the states to decide, and, most strikingly, the states had the right to remove officials—such as judges—appointed by the Confederate government. The power of judicial review, which had been expanded in the United States by the long-serving Federalist

Chief Justice of the Supreme Court, John Marshall, was to be severely restricted in the new southern nation.[9] In these critical respects, the Confederates sought to turn back the clock to an idealized version of federalism. Nor were the Confederates shy of using the word "slavery" when they meant slavery, unlike in the Federal Constitution, which contained euphemisms. But protection of slavery was taken for granted rather than trumpeted loudly. The leaders of the new southern Confederacy knew from the outset that they would be vulnerable to the charge that they represented only the plantation elite, and so they were keen to cast their new government in a broader light.[10]

European liberal nationalists whose sympathies Southerners hoped to rouse had learned, not least from the creation of the United States in the eighteenth century, that constitutions were inextricably linked to the character and life of a nation-state. The battles fought out in 1848 and afterwards for liberty and the rule of law against arbitrary rule often boiled down to a demand for American-style constitutions. Unsurprisingly, then, Confederates assumed that their constitution was more than simply a convenient means of stipulating the powers of the various branches of government, it was the essential bedrock on which their national identity and their legitimacy as a nation would be based. It was as important to Confederates that their republic was constitutionally grounded and founded on the rule of law as it was to northerners that secession was defined as an anarchic challenge to constitutional government. That Confederate constitutionalism was so dependent on the Federal Constitution, and that southerners shared with Yankees the assumption that constitutional law was the basis for a well-ordered and free society was neither surprising nor an indication of a lack of commitment to separation. To southerners, such continuity conferred legitimacy on their nation as the purified version of the old, corrupted Union. And along with familiar structures of government, the Confederate States of America was born wrapped in the iconography of the old republic. Images of George Washington were used everywhere—on postage stamps, on the Great Seal of the Confederacy, and on Confederate currency. As the historian Anne Sarah Rubin has pointed out, Jefferson Davis "invoked the Founder's values and sought his blessing" when he chose Washington's birthday as the date for his official inauguration in 1862 and delivered his address beside a statue of the United States' first president.[11]

Jefferson Davis realized that one of his major tasks was to generate and sustain popular support for the Confederacy and the war effort and to this end he undertook grueling speaking tours, ceaselessly urging his fellow southerners to ever-greater sacrifice. There was an elitist, even Spartan theme to the way that Jefferson Davis defined the new republic. His consistent theme was that only united action could save the Confederacy from invasion. "Our safety—our very existence," he argued, "depends on the complete blending of the military strength of all the States into one united body, to be used anywhere and everywhere as the exigencies of the contest may require for the good of the *whole*."[12] This ideal of unity was ultimately unattainable, and the contrast between the ideal and the reality became ever more visible as the war entered its final year. At first, however, southerners appeared to embrace fully the rhetoric of duty and the moral value of suffering. The determination to prove themselves more virtuous, selfless and morally superior to their enemies proved tenacious, even when the news from the battlefield was unrelentingly bad. When the famous southern diarist Sarah Morgan was forced to leave Baton Rouge, she was proud to declare, "I have lost my home and all its dear contents for Southern Rights, have stood on its destroyed hearth stone and looked at the ruin of all I loved without a murmur, almost glad of the sacrifice, if it would contribute its might towards the salvation of the Confederacy."[13] The fatalism of this remark was one of the chief characteristics of Confederate nationalist rhetoric, encapsulated by General Lee in a famous letter to President Davis in the wake of the battle of Gettysburg in which he offered his resignation. "We must expect reverses, even defeats," wrote Lee. "They are sent to teach us wisdom and prudence, to call forth greater energies, and to prevent our falling into greater disasters. Our people have only to be true and united to bear manfully the misfortunes incident to war, and all will come right in the end."[14]

The demands for sacrifice and ceaseless loyalty pointed to a tension at the heart of the Confederate project: how much freedom should be sacrificed in pursuit of the ultimate goal of national salvation? The Confederate government attempted to centralize the war effort more quickly and in some respects more effectively than did the federal government in the North. Confederate leaders' rhetoric about the protection of liberty sat uneasily with conscription and the suspension of habeas corpus. Evidence of how far the Confederates were prepared to undermine their theoretical commitment to states' rights and individual autonomy was Congress's willingness to impose direct income and property taxes. In April 1863, in an attempt to stave off complete financial collapse, Congress levied a graduated income tax on all incomes over $15,000 a year, an 8 percent property tax and another 10 percent tax-in-kind on livestock and farm produce. In December, 1863, the final session of the first Confederate Congress extended the government's control over the labor force, giving the authorities in Richmond the right to reassign civilian workers. The government also claimed the right to direct and control blockade-runners by buying and commandeering ships and banning the importation of anything that was regarded as unnecessary to the war effort. In March 1863, Davis' plan to allow Confederate quartermasters to confiscate food and animals from the local population was passed by Congress, giving official sanction to what was already happening on the ground. Much of the state and Confederate legislation and the presidential proclamations dealing with such matters as restricting the use of corn to distil liquor were never fully implemented. Ultimately, the greatest irony of all was that the Confederate government interfered with the rights of slaveowners, and ultimately with the survival of slavery itself, far more than the federal government had ever done, or would ever have been likely to do in peacetime.

In Jefferson Davis, the Montgomery delegates hoped that they had found their Washington. Davis was immensely experienced compared to his counterpart Abraham Lincoln. A slaveowner, a vocal spokesman for southern rights who had nevertheless distanced himself from the most rabid fire-eaters, a former secretary of war with a West Point training and long experience in the US senate, he seemed perfectly qualified to lead the new republic through its birth pangs. Davis stood out in 1861 for his clear-sighted perception of the risks and sacrifices entailed in secession. In the course of the war, he endured the death of a child, the never-ending vitriol of his political opponents and debilitating illness which caused him a near-permanent headache and on several occasions forced him to retreat to his bed for weeks at a time.

Davis was hardworking, abstemious and correct to the point of being sanctimonious, and, like Lincoln, he became notorious for the liberality with which he issued pardons to condemned soldiers. But he was not a warm or charming man and unlike Lincoln he did not easily inspire loyalty. Perhaps Davis' principal weakness as a leader was his lack of judgment about people and the often astonishing insensitivity with which he handled them. A good example was his utter failure to deal effectively with a crisis of confidence in General Braxton Bragg's leadership among the senior officers of the Army of the

Tennessee following the battle of Chickamauga in September 1863. So bitter were the recriminations and infighting that Davis decided to resolve the matter in person. Having made the long and tedious journey from Richmond to the army's headquarters, Davis convened a meeting of all the senior officers. In Bragg's presence, one officer after another condemned the incompetence of their commanding officer and demanded his removal, but Davis remained loyal to his old friend and announced that despite what he had heard he still had his full confidence on Bragg. Although he toured the Confederacy exhorting the people to ever-greater patriotic sacrifices, he never found the words to encapsulate the Confederate cause in a positive way, resorting increasingly to attacks on Yankee tyranny and playing on fears of racial revolution. A man conscious of his status and with an unswerving belief in the rightness of his cause, Davis could be prickly and oversensitive. He made political enemies easily, although his exasperation at any sign of dissent and disunity meant also that he tolerated incompetent and disloyal cabinet colleagues longer than he should have done.[15] In spite of this, he demonstrated considerable political skill in handling major issues. His own firm conception of what was right was often interpreted as arrogance, but it gave him a single-mindedness that sometimes worked to his advantage. Davis managed the querulous Confederate Congress with skill. Only one of his vetoes was overridden and, as the war continued, his appeals for greater authority and ever more draconian military measures, were acceded to by Congress. Davis found a core group of supporters among those congressmen who represented districts that were occupied by the Union army (and in the case of the delegates from Missouri and Kentucky from states that had never seceded in the first place). These "outsiders", as they were known, were, unsurprisingly, much more enthusiastic about measures that increased central government control over manpower or the economy.[16]

The administrative record of the Confederate government was a mixed one. It was never going to be easy for the Confederacy to finance a long war, or to deal with the economic impact of the Federals' efforts to blockade their ports and thus cut off their cotton exports to Europe. But the breathtaking incompetence of Christopher C. Memminger, the South Carolinian who Davis appointed Secretary of the Treasury, was a serious self-inflicted wound. To the astonishment of many in the North, the new Confederate government failed to use arguably its most valuable bargaining chip—European demand for southern cotton. Had the

Confederate government bought up southern cotton supplies in 1861 it might have exploited the porous northern blockade and maintained exports to Europe, raising relatively cheap loans on the back of the cotton crop and giving Britain and France a financial stake in the success of the Confederate cause. In 1863, the Confederacy did manage to float a large loan with the help of French financier Emile Erlanger using the government's cotton stockpile as collateral. Perhaps, had this strategy been tried in 1861 much more money could have been raised. Memminger also crippled the Confederate cause by failing to prevent northern merchants withdrawing specie from southern bank accounts and for not removing the hard currency from the mint at New Orleans before it fell into federal hands in 1862.[17] There was much less scope for financing the Confederate war effort through taxation than there was in the North, but Memminger preferred in any case to rely on paper money. He issued more than one billion dollars worth of Confederate notes during the war. The irredeemable paper currency and rampant inflation sapped southern morale and undermined the credibility of the Confederate government.[18]

If the Confederate government's economic management illustrated how the central government could exacerbate the difficulties the nation was facing, it scored some remarkable successes in the vital task of creating an industrial base that would supply the army. The greatest disadvantage the Confederacy faced at the start of the war was probably its weak industrial capacity. The only foundry capable of producing weapons of war was the Tredegar Iron Works in Richmond. The soaring inflation and lack of private credit made it impossible for private entrepreneurs to fulfill the government's insatiable need for arms. Into the breach stepped the government in Richmond. Unlike in the North, where economic output was shifted onto a war footing because industry responded to government contracts, the Confederate government and state governments in the South ran war production directly. Under the direction of the energetic Josiah Gorgas, the head of the Confederate Ordinance Bureau, the government set about establishing foundries, chemical plants, powder mills and small-arms factories at Fayetteville, Charleston, Columbus, Macon, Selma, Atlanta and other places. Augusta, Georgia, was one of several southern cities that were transformed from a sleepy market town in 1860 to a bustling industrial center—the Powder Works there, reputedly the second largest such plant in the world, supplied the Confederate armies with gunpowder right through the war. Given such an unpromising starting point, the

Confederate effort to create war industries must stand as one of the South's greatest accomplishments.

CONFEDERATE NATIONALISM AND THE SOUTHERN PEOPLE

Southern nationalism has long been a subject of controversy among historians. Up to a point, the disagreements among scholars are terminological or conceptual rather than empirical. There were many southerners in the antebellum period who claimed a cultural or literary or even an ethnic distinctiveness for the South, comparing southerners' descent from good Scots and English stock to the polyglot North, for example, or arguing for a religious and cultural descent from cavaliers in the English Civil War. Certainly, on the eve of secession, southerners routinely talked of their distinct identity and values, defining themselves explicitly or implicitly in opposition to Yankees. This perception of difference was mirrored by northerners at the same moment, who exhibited exactly the same chauvinistic tendencies and it should not necessarily be described as nationalist. What defined Confederate nationalists was not the view that southern society was distinctive and superior—although they almost invariably did argue that—but their loyalty to the project, the potential or, most potently, the reality of the Confederate state. It follows that Confederate nationalism cannot really be said to have existed on a large scale before the creation of the Confederate nation-state in 1861, although there were certainly those, like Edmund Ruffin, who had always dreamed of a separate South. When military defeat effectively crushed the possibility of an independent South for all but the most romantic dreamers, Confederate nationalism lingered as a residual loyalty to the memory of the Confederate state.

Like so many other people in the mid-nineteenth century, southerners associated freedom and independence with nationhood. In the end, Confederate nationalism proved to be only one of a series of strategies that could be used to defend southern institutions and the southern racial order. The eventual failure of the nation-state they created does not diminish the depths of the popular commitment to it. There is another parallel here with the American Revolution, which also began as a political conflict over individual liberties and political control. Confederate nationalism was the product of secession and war, just as American nationalism was the product of secession and war with the

British Empire, even though in both cases a sense of being in some respects a distinctive society preceded the split. The Confederacy had no less a claim to be a distinctive nation worth dying for than did the nascent United States. In both cases, local communities were the primary focus of identity. In both cases it was the need to protect liberty from encroachment by a tyrannical power that drove men, sometimes reluctantly at first, to support a revolution against the central power. In both cases the rebel flag was a way of defying a hated government that suddenly seemed alien to their local interests. Nationalism is no less compelling on an individual or collective level for being founded on such negative impulses.

The Confederate nation-building project was confronted with practical obstacles that similar efforts to sustain popular commitment to the war in the North never had to face. No printing presses were manufactured in the South and the few paper mills were concentrated in Tennessee and New Orleans and other areas that were vulnerable to Union occupation. Even well-established southern journals like the *Southern Literary Messenger* and *De Bow's Review* found it increasingly difficult to publish, in part because of the difficulty of distribution, but mainly because their supplies of paper dried up. The result was that, compared to the mountains of pamphlets and broadsides produced in the North, Confederate wartime propaganda was extremely thin on the ground. To some extent, music stepped into this breach. The absence of a national anthem meant that at Jefferson Davis' inauguration as provisional president the guests sang the *Marseillaise*. Something more specifically in tune with the southern rebellion, and less tarnished with sans-cullottism, was clearly needed, and Confederate soldiers found it in an unlikely place: a Yankee black-face minstrel called Dan Emmett who had been peddling a catchy new "walk-around" song containing the lines "In Dixie Land I'll took my stand/To lib and die in Dixie."[19] Sometimes, Confederate soldiers would take smuggled copies of sheet music for songs composed by northerners and change the words.

Since they lacked the resources to generate national loyalty in a top–down manner, the strength of popular loyalty to the Confederate state is all the more remarkable. Confederate identity was certainly shaped by public printed material such as schoolbooks, newspapers and journals, as well as by music and material culture, but it was the shared experience of war and sacrifice, mediated through thousands of private letters and diaries and sustained in private conversation, where the strength of Confederate nationalism is most evident. The letters of Confederate soldiers and civilians makes clear that for many, perhaps most, southerners whose literary record remains with us referred frequently to the Confederacy as "our nation" or "our country." A young Virginia woman fervently expressed the wish in her diary that every traitor to the Confederate cause could be executed. They are "more dangerous by far than those with whom we are at war. . . . Let every man help to protect his County, & not rend and lacerate her by internal discords."[20] The symbols of nationalism, the flag and the faith in Lee's army, remained strong until the very end. And even defeat did not rob most southerners of their conviction that southern independence was a cause that had been noble and worthwhile. Southern nationalism was more powerful than the more vaguely articulated national allegiance of American rebels in the war of independence of the 1770s that was such an important source of inspiration. Typical were the words of Confederate soldier, Daniel Pope:

> When we consider the great duty we owe our country in the struggle for independence, I cannot be but content with my fate, although it be, indeed, a cruel one . . . If it should be my misfortune to fall in the glorious struggle, I hope that I shall go believing that I have contributed my mite and that you and my little boy will be entitled to the great boon of freedom.[21]

Similar sentiments were recorded by W. W. Heartsill, a private fighting in Braxton Bragg's army at Chickamauga in September 1863: "Up men of the South and strike for God, and our native land, may the God of Justice hover o're our battle flag and may our Independence be dated from the beginning of the coming contest."[22]

Women played a critical role in the creation of a Confederate patriotic identity. In public, they encouraged men to remember that they could defend their families and community only by defending southern liberties. Across the South, rituals involving the presentation and raising of a southern flag, usually sewn by the women of the community, were a visible symbol of the intimate connection between the domestic realm and the larger struggle. Flag-making and raising was a way for women to endorse the independence struggle while remaining within their prescribed gender role. Public duty was indistinguishable from private duty, and in the face of such a crisis, any hesitancy on the part of the men of the South was unthinkable. "Your mothers, wives, & sisters all bid you go, trusting to the God of Liberty & your own brave deeds to bring you off conquerors in the conflict," urged one delegation of women at a flag-presenting ceremony in North Carolina.[23] Such public endorsement of volunteering cannot always have obscured private anxieties. "The Howell Guards left on the mid-day train," reported Susan Bradford Eppes from Tallahassee in northern Florida.

> A crowd had gathered around the depot to see them off. Mothers, wives, sisters, sweethearts and friends—all were there. Standing on the platform and looking around I marveled at what I saw. Women with bright, smiling faces, looking tenderly on the soldiers, who were ready to depart. Saying fond, loving words of advice and of hope: pressing the beloved grey-clad figure in a parting embrace; kissing the dear lips, maybe for the last time, and yet those brave women smiled. As soon as the train pulled out and the soldier boys could not see, the scene changed. Sobs and tears, wild outbursts of grief on every side, and yet, this had been suppressed lest it grieve those brave hearts, who were going forth to battle for home and country.[24]

The letters and diaries of Confederate women are filled with testimony to the complexities of the emotional context in which men went to war. Mary Chesnut was amazed when an acquaintance told her in March 1861 that she hoped her husband would go to war and be shot. "Don't you know he beats her?" confided a friend. So "I have seen a man 'who lifts his hand against a woman in aught save kindness'," Mrs Chesnut reflected.[25] In public, however, women were portrayed, in the tradition of republican motherhood, as the moral and Christian beings responsible for inculcating patriotism. Newspapers, songs and printed images praised women's willingness to sacrifice their husbands and sons for the cause and for their unstinting, selfless work making bandages, nursing the wounded, sewing uniforms, forming aid societies, and memorializing the dead.

Christianity was integral to the process of creating a Confederate identity. Efforts to create a civil religion for the new nation were signaled from the outset by the Confederate constitution which invoked "the favor and guidance of Almighty God," something which the Federal Constitution, written at the high tide of Enlightenment rationalism, notably did not do. Southerners duly took pride in the notion that theirs was a truly Christian nation, the instruments of a Divine plan for the world. Indeed, the role of the Protestant clergy in the South elevated the conflict with the Yankees into a holy war. Meeting in Savannah not long after the attack on Fort Sumter, the Southern Baptist Convention agreed that God was on the side of the Confederacy. Deliberately conflating the Confederate cause with the will of God, President Davis proclaimed days of fasting and prayer at pivotal moments in the war. Southerners would prevail, Davis explained, because they maintained a "firm reliance on that Divine Power which covers with its protection the just cause, and we will continue to struggle for our inherent right to freedom, independence, and self-government."[26] Clergymen used fast-day sermons to inveigh against sin, and warn that God was testing the resilience of the nation through the trial of war. Redemption lay through further sacrifice. Southern clergymen had no difficulty in fitting a war in defense of hearth and home into the Christian Just War tradition. The southern battle flag, based on the St Andrew's Cross, rapidly surpassed the official national flag, the derivative stars and bars. The blood of dead soldiers fused with the Christian symbolism to sanctify the flag in the imagination of southerners.[27]

Southerners turned to their faith in God's favor to keep up their morale. A Christian faith helped many Confederate women to bear the sacrifices of war, and, through the revivals in army camps, bolstered the courage and resilience of many soldiers as well. Southerners' belief that they were a chosen people, doing the work of the Lord, gave a higher purpose to their struggles, and reinforced their sense of themselves as purifiers of a republic that had become soaked in sin. The example of Christ's suffering on the cross was, to judge from the frequency of its ritual invocation in private letters as well as in sermons, a source of great sustenance during the dark days of the war. Confederates often observed that their soldiers were more devout than the Yankees. Stonewall Jackson, a devout Presbyterian, particularly embodied the Christian martial virtues that the South needed. After his death at Chancellorsville, Jackson became the ultimate martyr. That God had given the South such a "perfect Christian hero," one Presbyterian minister told his congregation, was surely proof that He had "designs of mercy for us" and was "preparing for us a glorious deliverance." By seeking the grace of God and emulating Jackson's faith, the South as a whole would be redeemed.[28] Faith in an interventionist Old Testament deity was so widespread that it was commonplace for southerners to interpret the outcomes of battles in terms of God's judgment on the righteousness of the southern people. Military reversals, explained preachers, were sent by God either as a test of the people's faith or as a chastisement for their sins. As events were to prove, southerners' faith that national salvation rested in the hands of the Lord could prove a double-edged sword when the tide of war ran strongly against them.

THE STRAINS OF WAR AND THE LIMITS OF LOYALTY

The centrality of women to the creation of Confederate identity was, in the end, to prove a mixed blessing. The women of the South were lauded for their role in keeping up the morale of the troops, but, by 1864, the correspondence between the home front and battlefield made clear that the dynamic often worked the other way around. "The chief source of depression, when any exists, among the troops," reported one Confederate soldier in the autumn of 1863, "is the intelligence of faintheartedness, and in some sections base 'caving-in' that reach them from home."[29] Beneath the rhetoric, men in the army often felt themselves to be sustaining the morale of the women at home. The ideal of southern womanhood was one that was impossible to live up to. Like the ideals of virtuous self-sacrifice that were intrinsic to the identity of this warbound nation, the fine sounding words were tested to the limit and beyond by the physical and emotional hardships that southerners had to endure. The strains in southern society became particularly visible in the final months of the war. It is notoriously difficult to measure morale among populations in anything other than an impressionistic way, but the evidence from letters and diaries clearly suggests a gradual loss of faith in the likelihood of eventual Confederate success.

One of the most helpful barometers of morale are the rates of volunteering and the rates of desertion from the army, a factor that, especially in the case of the South, was driven in most cases by pressure from home at least as much as a desire not to be in the frontline any longer. By these measures, the ability of southerners to continue the fight for independence was waning by the beginning of 1864 when it became harder and harder to find men to replace those who had died, were not fit for duty or who were absent from their commands without leave.[30] By 1864, the occupation of large parts of the Confederacy by the Union army, and the accompanying confiscation and destruction of property, was a severe test for the Confederacy, not least because of the pressure of refugees. One Mississippi woman witnessing the arrival of more refugees fleeing the advancing Yankees, complained that "there was nothing to eat for them that was already here, and these that came bring nothing with them they will be sure to starve."[31] Tensions were reported between refugees and their hosts, leading to fears that the unrelenting hardships and sacrifices of war were not creating a more virtuous citizenry, as they had predicted at the outset, but were instead demoralizing the southern spirit. People were horrified by evidence that southern society was becoming brutalized by the horrors of war, becoming indifferent to death, less loyal to their family, less hospitable to their neighbors. Mary Chesnut was astonished at how easy it was for her to block out the sounds of gunfire from a nearby battle while she read a George Eliot novel. Was she "the same poor soul who fell on her knees and prayed and wept and fainted as the first guns boomed from Fort Sumter," she wondered.[32]

The scale of the economic crisis facing the southern people was quite beyond anything they had imagined when the war began. The paper money issued by the Confederate Treasury was worthless almost as soon as it was printed. In December 1863, John B. Jones, a war department clerk in Richmond, reported in his diary that it took 28 Confederate paper dollars to buy one prewar gold dollar.[33] A more senior war department official, Robert Kean, reported in 1863 that his salary of $3000 went "about as far as $300 would do in ordinary time in purchasing all the articles of household necessity." Kean's income was among the highest and the most reliable anywhere in the Confederacy, yet his family, he complained, were "reduced to two meals a day, . . . and they are of the most plain and economical scale."[34] Overall, prices multiplied 27 times in the South during the war. Inflation on this scale was useful to the government, insofar as it effectively transferred wealth from ordinary people to the Treasury. But it prompted food riots in the streets of Richmond and other southern cities by 1863, exacerbated by the overcrowding from displaced refugees. The most serious public disorder was in Richmond on April 2, 1863. A crowd shouting "bread or blood" roamed the streets smashing shop windows and looting food where they could find it. Jefferson Davis himself appeared to try to calm the crowd but had nothing to offer them other than appeals to patriotism. In the end the crowd dispersed only when threatened by a militia unit.[35]

One of the many paradoxical outcomes of secession was that the great economic strength of the South—its cotton production—was slashed in the name of patriotism. The staple crops of the South, cotton and tobacco, were no use for food. In the first two years of the war, patriotic appeals backed up in some places by vigilance committees and, from 1862, by punitive state legislation restricting cotton acreage, prevailed upon cotton producers to switch to corn. From 4.5 million bales of cotton in 1860, the size of the cotton crop fell to just one million in 1862 and a mere 300,000 in 1864.[36] This was partly due to the destruction that came in the wake of the invading Union army, but mainly due to a concerted effort to gear southern agriculture to the needs of war. Like so many other aspects of the Confederate experience, a startlingly successful combination of voluntary effort and central direction ultimately proved insufficient. Food shortages, especially in the towns, became ever more acute despite the shift in agricultural production. The labor shortage on small farms because of the numbers of men in the army, and the fall in the productivity of slaves did not help, but ultimately it was the inadequacy of the southern transport infrastructure and the priority given to feeding the army that meant that the urban populations suffered. A shortage of salt meant also that meat could not be kept for long. The South was still a rural, localistic place, ill-equipped to deal with the demands of a vast army of consumers who were not producing their own food. And all these handicaps were immensely complicated by the invasion of the Union army and the destruction in its wake. The privations of soldiers and civilians were made harder to bear by the perception and the reality that there was a class of men who were making a handsome profit from the war. One visitor to Richmond was shocked by the evidence that while some were going hungry—not to mention dying on the battlefields—others, "a class that like obscene birds and beasts have grown fat on the war," apparently living as if there were no war on.[37]

In the face of the threat of starvation and mounting social tensions, state governments began a program of poor relief, the scale of which was unprecedented in American history. Half of the entire state budget of Georgia in 1863 went on poor relief, despite the massive military spending. Ashe County, North Carolina, for example, was allocated $22,500 in the winter of 1863 by the state legislature for the relief of soldiers' families. According to one estimate 37 percent of families in Alabama were in receipt of poor relief by 1864. States passed stay laws preventing private collection of debt. Communities levied extra taxation and took out bank loans to provide help to families of soldiers.

On top of these immense economic pressures, southern civilians were subjected to an increasingly demanding state. Confederate civilians were almost as likely to lose their property to the demands of the Confederate army as to the enemy. Not only did southern generals rely on the local population for supplies, they also proved themselves quite prepared to burn supplies rather than let them fall into the hands of the Yankees. The earliest example of this was the burning of Hampton, Virginia, in 1861 by Confederate General John Magruder's cavalry, who feared that it would fall into the hands of Union troops who were pushing out from their enclave around Fortress Monroe on the James River. The impressment of supplies, property and slaves by the Confederate army led to serious deprivation and intense political opposition. Governor Watts of Alabama warned that "if we fail to achieve our independence in this contest, the failure will arise from breaking down the spirits of the people by acts of tyranny by our own officers."[38] Governor Vance of North Carolina complained about the attitude and behavior of Confederate cavalrymen who were wintering their horses in the mountains and demanding corn and forage for their horses. They were making themselves a "terror to the whole population", he protested, and given the poor harvest and the general state of deprivation of the local people, the actions of the army were offensive. "When the question of starvation is narrowed down to women & children on the one hand and some worthless Cavalry horses on the other, I can have no difficulty in making the choice."[39]

Conscription had an especially harsh impact. Facing the prospect of the 12-month volunteers returning home and depleting the armies en masse, and with the Union's spring offensive already underway, the Confederate Congress passed, by a margin of two-to-one, a compulsory conscription act on 16 April, 1862. In reality, the Confederacy lacked the apparatus to enforce universal conscription effectively, but the legislation sent a powerful signal. It stimulated enlistments everywhere in the South, and compelled men who would otherwise have returned home to help on the family farm to stay in uniform. "There seems to be a general impression amongst the men that they will volunteer rather than be subjected to a draught," reported a North Carolinian.[40] The 1862 Conscription Act was incomparably more draconian than anything that the old US federal government had done, and it came a full year before the Union resorted to something similar. It aroused serious political opposition. By June, 1863, William W. Holden, the editor of the Raleigh, North Carolina, *Standard*, had begun advocating a negotiated peace. For him, the means being used to wage war were undermining the ends for which it was being fought.[41] A war that had been launched to protect the communities of the South from the menace of black Republicanism had spawned a draconian conscription, the impressments of food and other property, the impoverishment of the people and an outbreak of violence and lawlessness. In the wake of the defeat at Gettysburg in July 1863 public meetings were held across the South demanding, in the words of one such meeting in North Carolina, "a speedy, honourable and permanent peace."[42] The peace meetings were opposed by Governor Vance. Clearly, by the end of 1863, large numbers of southerners were deeply disillusioned by the war. It is more difficult to know how many translated their despondency into active disloyalty to the Confederate cause. The 1863 elections results suggest widespread disengagement and apathy but not widespread opposition to the Confederate state. In August 1863, at least one enrollment officer complained in his official report on his attempts to enforce the draft in South Carolina that "it is no longer a reproach to be known as a deserter."[43] In North Carolina, peace advocate Holden was trounced at the polls by sitting Governor Vance. The result seemed to indicate that however alienated by the repressive acts of the Confederate government and despairing at the sacrifices and hardship of the war, the voters of North Carolina were not prepared to stomach the capitulation that Holden's negotiated peace strategy seemed to imply. The 1863 congressional elections demonstrated the unpopularity of the Davis administration. None of the new members from North Carolina, for example, had originally been in favor of secession, and one representative from northern Alabama was so plainly in favor of an immediate peace that Congress refused to seat him. In the febrile, strongly antiparty culture of Confederate politics, opposition to the administration tended to be conflated with opposition to the Confederate project as a whole; it would be a mistake for historians to fall into the same trap.

In the heartland of southern rights, South Carolina Governor Francis W. Pickens, who was implementing a statewide draft of his own, fought to exempt South Carolinians from the Confederate draft. Georgia Governor Joseph E. Brown protested that the act was a "bold and dangerous usurpation by Congress of the reserved rights of the States." To fellow Georgian, Vice President Alexander H. Stephens, Brown explained that "I entered into this revolution to contribute my humble mite to sustain the rights of the states and prevent the consolidation of Government, and I am a rebel till this object is accomplished, no matter who may be in power."[44] Brown exploited the provision of the conscription act which exempted state officials by distributing thousands of unpaid official positions to constituents who pleaded that their families needed them at home. The exemption from the draft of owners, agents or overseers on plantations with at least 20 slaves kindled a latent class tension in southern white society. Despite Brown's opposition, Davis defended the right of the Confederacy to conscript in the Georgia state courts, and won.

As the war dragged on, opposition politicians increasingly appealed to traditional defenses of individual, community and state liberty, while Jefferson Davis continued to stress the importance of unity and class harmony. Davis' opponents warned the people not to surrender their rights to a potentially tyrannical central government.[45] But Governor Vance steadfastly maintained his loyalty to the cause even while articulating the concerns of his constituents about policies like conscription. Other governors played a similar role of mediating the relationship between the government in Richmond and ordinary people, but all remained loyal. Texas governor Pendleton Murrah attacked the Davis administration repeatedly over such issues as conscription and the regulation of the cotton market, but he always did so on the grounds that such policies undermined the Confederate cause. Even Georgia's Joseph E. Brown, who railed against Jefferson Davis, and fiercely fought to protect his authority within his state, in the end knew that his political position depended on proving himself more patriotic to the Southern cause. When his state was invaded by Sherman's "vandal hordes," Brown ordered a levée en masse to meet the foe, warning Georgians that the "destiny of our posterity for ages to come may hang upon the results of the next few days. He who remains at his home now will soon occupy it as a slave, or be driven from it."[46]

Of course there were parts of the South where the reach of the Confederate nation-state never fully penetrated. In some parts of northern Alabama, eastern Tennessee, southwestern Virginia and western North Carolina, the Confederate state never effectively established control and an alternative southern Unionist identity took root. Active disloyalty to the Confederate cause was geographically concentrated in nonslaveholding areas. Clandestine peace societies such as the Heroes of America recruited mainly from nonslaveholders.[47] In the hilly Virginia counties in the Appalachians, bordering Kentucky, North Carolina and Tennessee, the Heroes of America plotted to emulate the Unionists of West Virginia and create a breakaway "Free State of Southwest Virginia"[48] Elsewhere in the poor, nonslaveholding, upcountry South, the initial enthusiasm to join a fight and whip some Yankees soon began to fade when the reality of a long war and the absence of menfolk began to bite. As early as the summer of 1862, social order was threatening to break down completely in some communities. Self-appointed "regulators" or "committees of public safety" terrorized neighborhoods, sometimes in the name of enforcing "loyalty." Especially from 1863 onward, bands of deserters from East Tennessee and western North Carolina roamed the Appalachian mountains. North Carolina Governor Zebulon B. Vance warned the Confederate secretary of war of "disaffected desperados of the worst character, who joining with deserters from our army, form very formidable bands of outlaws, who hide in the fastness, waylay the passes, rob, steal and destroy at leisure."[49]

War-weary southerners increasingly began to place their families' immediate needs above their loyalty to the army. By the summer of 1864, argues the military historian J. Tracy Power, "countless" soldiers in the Army of Northern Virginia had begun to "base their relationship to the army almost entirely on their physical wants and needs, and to abandon it when they believed that those wants and needs outweighed any other considerations."[50] The dream of securing the independence of the South was dying, and by the end of 1864 many southerners realized it, however hard they tried to keep their spirits up. Soldiers received emotional letters from their families detailing the suffering at home. It is important to remember, though, that when soldiers chose their duty to their families over their duty to the Confederacy it did not necessarily represent a rejection of the idea of independence, but a heart-wrenching choice between two loyalties that had once seemed mutually reinforcing but were now, it appeared, incompatible. These were agonizing choices, not least because veteran soldiers were deeply aware of the bond that they shared and which, despite the suffering and privations on the homefront, separated them from civilians. Even a loyal sergeant, who remained in the Army of Northern Virginia to the end, saw the writing on the wall by January 1865: "The facilities of the Yankees for carry[ing] on the war is so much better than ours," wrote R. P. Scarbrough, "that I cannot for my life see how we can hold out with them much Longer. They already have an army much larger than ours . . . while our army is decreasing faster than we can recruit in spite of all we can do."[51] Desertion was a symptom of defeat rather than its cause. It was not until the final dark winter of 1864–1865 that desertion rates in the Confederate army began to exceed that in the Union forces. Draconian measures to prevent desertion were still attempted by Confederate officers, but by the end of January, 1865, General Lee reported that "hundreds" of men were deserting each night his army. "I don't know what can be done to put a stop to it."[52] Soldiers usually deserted the Confederate army in order to protect their homes from an invading enemy—a factor that did not apply to the North—and which did not necessarily indicate a lack of commitment to the Confederate cause. The vast majority of southerners clung tenaciously to their faith in the Confederacy even as the harsh reality of their situation sank in. Very few war-weary southerners actively wanted the Union cause to prevail, however much they yearned for peace. As Sarah Anne Rubin has put it, "if Confederate nationalism was too weak to exert a hold over its people, they would not have worried so much about remaining true to their new nation and their new identities."[53]

There is overwhelming evidence that class tensions were exacerbated by the war. When the sacrifices required for victory became too great, the mass of nonslaveholding whites inevitably put their families and communities ahead of the slaveowners' republic. Yet, to argue that southern society was divided is one thing; to argue that this indicates structural or ideological weaknesses that account for southern defeat is quite another. Few of the manifestations of social unrest—even the bread riots that struck Confederate towns and cities in 1863 and 1864—had a discernible impact on the South's capacity to fight. Only in the final months of the Confederacy did social disorder, banditry, and desertion damage the cause. Notwithstanding the variation from place to place and through time, the big picture painted by the surviving evidence from white southerners is a remarkably uniform allegiance to the Southern republic. Clearly for many southerners, physical privation and loss merely reinforced rather than undermined loyalty to the Confederate cause. The principal impact of emancipation and the use of black troops was similarly to intensify southern resistance. When Union soldiers came near, rumors spread of black soldiers gang-raping southern women and inciting slaves to do the same.[54]

Even in the face of massive military reversals, there is abundant evidence of the capacity of the South to resist. Like other societies with their backs to the wall, the Confederate South rallied in the face of adversity. "The yankee flag waved from the Capitol—Our degradation was bitter," lamented a young woman in Milledgeville, Georgia, after federal troops occupied her city in November 1864, "but we knew it could not be long, and we never desponded, our trust was still strong. . . . How they can hope to subjugate the South. The people are firmer than ever before."[55]

A fully rounded view of the Confederate South must balance an analysis of the centrifugal forces unleashed by the strains of war with the continuing bonds that generated extraordinary sacrifices even in the winter of 1864–1865 when the military outlook was grim. As great a unifying force as any was the popular identification with the Army of Northern Virginia. Robert E. Lee transcended even the symbolic importance of General Washington in the war of independence. Lee's character—his quiet faith, his dignified bearing, his sense of duty—was important, but what made Lee an object of popular devotion was quite simply his brilliance at winning battles, again and again. One of the many reasons why the eastern theater mattered so much more than the west was that the Confederate armies in Virginia led by Lee were so much more successful than those in the west led by the likes of Johnston and Bragg. By whipping Yankees, Lee vindicated southern manhood. Catherine Ann Devereux Edmondston of North Carolina was not unusual in describing Lee as "the idol, the point of trust, of confidence & repose of thousands! How nobly has he won the confidence, the admiration of the nation."[56] So long as General Lee was in the field, it seemed impossible that the South could be defeated. The dependence of southern morale on the success of Lee's Army of Northern Virginia explains the ability of the South to sustain extraordinary levels of popular commitment. It also explains why when Lee finally did surrender—at Appomattox Court House, Virginia, on April 9, 1865—it signaled the definitive defeat for the South, even though other Confederate armies remained in the field.

SLAVERY AND THE CONFEDERATE CAUSE

The class tensions in southern society that were heightened by the pressures of war were inextricably related to the immensely privileged position enjoyed by the 10 percent of southerners who owned slaves. It is revealing that despite its centrality to the coming of the war, slavery was not a rallying cry which could unite the South, still less secure the Confederates that foreign recognition that they so craved. Images and memories of the Revolutionary war were a less divisive means of securing the loyalty of nonslaveholders. But, if most Confederates saw their republic as a continuation of the American Revolution, some bluntly argued that it was the means of correcting some of the errors that those Lockean founding fathers had made. George Fitzhugh, one of the most prominent southern polemicists, worried that experience had shown that liberty was descending into licentiousness. The Confederate revolution, wrote Fitzhugh, was "rolling back the excesses" of the American Revolution.[57] A similar argument was made in an astonishingly frank speech by Alexander H. Stephens in 1861. While praising much of the legacy of 1776 and 1787, Stephens explained that southerners had now learned the limits of Jefferson's egalitarianism:

> The prevailing ideas entertained by [Jefferson] and most of the leading statesmen at the time of the formation of the Old Constitution were, that the enslavement of the African was in violation of the laws of nature; that it was wrong in principle, socially, morally, and politically. It was an evil they knew not well how to deal with; but the general opinion of the men of that day was, that, somehow or other, in the order of Providence, the institution would be evanescent and pass away . . . Those ideas, however, were fundamentally wrong. They rested on the assumption of the equality of races. This was an error. It was a sandy foundation, and the idea of a Government built upon it—when the "storm came and the wind blew, it fell." Our new Government is founded upon exactly the opposite ideas; its foundations are laid, its cornerstone rests, upon the great truth that the negro is not equal to the white man; that slavery, subordination to the superior race, is his natural and moral condition. This, our new Government, is the first, in the history of the world based on upon this great physical, philosophical, and moral truth . . . "[58]

However hard they tried, Confederates could not escape the fact that the fate of their experiment in independent nationhood was bound up with slavery. As Stephens had not been afraid to acknowledge, the protection of slavery was the major factor propelling southerners into creating their new nation, and even if it was not the sustaining motivation, it created distinctive vulnerabilities which in the end could undermine the entire nationalist project.

As the Union army advanced, slaveowners in vulnerable areas "refugeed" their slaves to safer areas. Thousands of slaves were sent to Texas, as Union forces advanced north from New Orleans and south along the Mississippi. Some slaves who had previously remained loyal ran away at the threat of being deported from their homes. And the arrival of more and more refugees in zones not directly touched by the conflict threatened to destabilize slavery there, as well as providing an unavoidable reminder of the remorseless contraction of the Confederacy and prompting fears of insurrection as the slave population mounted. Masters began to bribe their slaves to remain faithful, promising them a share of the crop.[59] In some places, such as the South Carolina Sea Islands it was the owners who ran away, abandoning their plantations as the Union navy took control. In 1863, slaves of Davis Bend, the home plantation of the Confederate president, were suddenly left in de facto control of the plantation when their white overseers fled as the Union army came closer. Slaves who took control of plantations practiced subsistence agriculture.

The desire of slaves to be free was felt well beyond the fifth of slaves who ran away. On some plantations, with the loss of the most productive slaves to impressments and flight and with the loss of animals to the army as well, it sometimes became impossible to feed those who remained. As able-bodied white men left the plantations to fight, the old level of control over slaves was hard to maintain. One Louisiana planter complained that his slaves were "insolent and idle." They were "working not more than half a day, yet [were] demanding full rations."[60] Other masters reported that their slaves were challenging the authority of the overseers, and even in some cases demanding wages. As Peter Kolchin has put it, they were "refusing to act like slaves."[61]

For the slaveholders, who had always boasted of the loyalty and even the love of their slave "family", the mass desertions struck at the foundations of their world view, and the result was traumatic. Even if the majority of slaves did not run away, masters were suddenly, and with good reason, profoundly uncertain about the loyalty of those who remained. The apparent arbitrariness of slaves' behavior was particularly disconcerting. Especially favored slaves, such as house servants, mammies and drivers might leave without a word, while those with reputation as "bad niggers" remained. Many whites observed with bewilderment that the slaves of benevolent masters were as likely to desert as those of harsh owners. As Eugene Genovese has written, it was especially difficult for masters to come to terms with the idea that "their slaves might have developed their own standards of accepted behavior and evolved their own concepts of freedom." Mary Jones of Georgia became "thoroughly disgusted with the whole race."[62] Even had slavery survived the war, relations between master and slave would have been utterly transformed. The lies that white southerners told themselves about their peculiar institution had been brutally exposed.

It is possible to exaggerate the internal collapse of southern society. There was no mass slave revolt. Most of the South, after all, was not directly touched by the war, and there the system of slavery did not collapse entirely. But the added psychological pressure on whites as the Yankee troops came closer of knowing that they were vulnerable to their slave populations was tangible. When rumors spread of a slave rebellion to take place at Christmas, 1864, in Richmond County, North Carolina, one terrified lady penned a letter to the governor:

> The country is in a great confusion at this time and not without a cause. The Negroes are making every effort in their power to murder the people & their intention is to carry it out Christmas! Their plans are to kill all of the white men & old white women & Negro women and have all the young white Ladys for their companions. Some of them has even gone so far as to tell which Lady he is going to take for his Wife. . . . There is not half enough of men in the country to protect it. . . . Do you suppose that we Ladys will be willing to submit to Negro husbands after giving up our Brothers that has been slain on the memorable battle field? & see our old gray headed Fathers murdered by the notorious Negroes. Now cant you suggest some plan by which thus can be broken up?

The solution she urged upon the governor was startling: "I think as all the white men have been taken if it will be well enough to fill the ranks with the africans."[63]

The ultimate test of whether the South was committed to independence was whether they were prepared to free their slaves in order to achieve it. In the last months of the war, the Confederate Congress considered a proposal to purchase 40,000 slaves for immediate enlistment in the Confederate army with the promise of emancipation as a reward. Patrick Cleburne, an Irish-born corps commander in the Army of Tennessee, who revealingly was not a slaveholder himself, had first argued for some form of Confederate emancipation as early as January 1864. "As between the loss of independence and the loss of slavery, we assume that every patriot will freely give up the latter—give up the negro slave rather than become a slave himself."[64] This was a misjudgment. Cleburne's proposals were regarded with horror. But less than a year later, with the Confederacy facing final defeat, Davis and his supporters had come to the conclusion that they had nothing to lose by harnessing the military power of the slaves themselves. The letter from the woman of Richmond County, North Carolina, reveals one motivating factor. If the security of slavery could not be guaranteed on the home front, perhaps enlistment was an alternative way of controlling blacks. At the very least it would remove them from southern white womanhood. The emancipation plan grew out of this pragmatic recognition that arming slaves would go some way toward neutralizing the damage done to the Confederate cause by freed slaves fighting for the enemy. The response of Confederate soldiers mirrored the divisions among southern politicians. The son of a prominent South Carolina planter complained that arming slaves was to "throw away what we have toiled so hard to maintain." There is evidence that the Negro Soldier bill increased desertion from the Confederate armies. One North Carolinian complained to his mother that "I did not volunteer to my services to fight for a free negroes country but to fight for a free white mans country & I do not think I love my country well enough to fight with black soldiers." Others pragmatically reasoned that between emancipation and subjugation, the South now had to choose, in the words of the son of a wealthy Georgia planter, the "lesser of two evils." As a Tennessee officer reasoned, "we can certainly live without negroes better than with Yankees and without negroes both."[65]

Even as the last of all last resorts, emancipation seemed to many of the leaders of the rebellion to be unthinkable. Howell Cobb, the Georgia Congressman and General, told Davis that "the day you make soldiers of [slaves] is the beginning of the end of the revolution. If slaves will make good soldiers our whole theory of slavery is wrong." Virginia Governor William Smith bluntly responded that without slavery the South would "no longer have motive to continue the struggle."[66] Even the supporters of the plan did not abandon crucial tenets of the pro-slavery ideology.[67] The proposal initially went nowhere. But after General Lee publicly endorsed the plan in February, 1865, the Congress, by slim margins in both houses, relented. Emancipation would certainly occur if the South lost, Lee argued in January 1865, so "a well-digested plan of gradual and general emancipation" would ensure that the benefits of slave soldiers accrued to the Confederacy rather than their enemies. After the war, he claimed that he had told President Jefferson Davis "often and early in the war that the slaves should be emancipated, that it was the only way to remove a weakness at home and to get sympathy abroad, and to divide our enemies, but Davis would not hear of it."[68] The first black Confederate companies were enlisted at the end of March,

1865, just days before the final Confederate surrender. Confederate "emancipation" did not indicate that southerners had abandoned their efforts to maintain white supremacy and a docile black labor force. They still sought those things by different means: freedom for blacks would give them the right to marry, to learn to read and even to own property—all things denied slaves—but it would not imply any political rights. And crucially, restrictive labor laws would compel blacks to labor on plantations as they had before. As Bruce Levine has put it, "in this revised Confederate vision of the South's future, blacks would no longer be slaves, but they would be free only in the narrowest possible sense of that word."[69] When the war was lost, these were some of the strategies that at one time or another white southerners would adopt in their efforts to hold onto what vestiges they could of their plantation world and their racial supremacy.

In overwhelming numbers, southerners embraced their cause, believed in its ultimate success until remarkably near the end and were prepared to suffer horrendous privations, poverty and death on a scale that matches anything in the western military tradition. In defense of their homes, southerners showed themselves capable of astonishing sacrifice. Sherman's march to the sea was briefly held up on November 22, 1864, by a division of the Georgia militia that was made up largely of old men and young boys. Six hundred of the Georgians were killed. "The devils seem to have a determination that cannot but be admired," conceded General Sherman. "No amount of poverty or adversity seems to shake their faith—niggers gone—wealth and luxury gone, money worthless, starvation in view within a period of two or three years, are causes enough to make the bravest tremble, yet I see no sign of let up— some few deserters—plenty tired of war, but the masses determined to fight it out."[70]

7 The Last Best Hope of Earth: The War for the Union

"It is not so much the capacity to win battles" that gives victory to a people, mused Alvin C. Voris of the 67th Ohio Infantry, but "the ability to bear grief." As Voris knew, northern manpower and material superiority were not enough to guarantee victory. Against a determined foe the North would need all its reserves of determination. "The South," thought Voris, "have made up their minds to bear with fortitude what the North never will bear unless a question of national existence is forced upon them, an issue this war has not even as yet intimated."[1] Political leaders in both North and South warned that defeat would mean the end of republican government, but for northerners such claims were necessarily more abstract. Northerners' homes, families, and way of life were not usually threatened by the southern rebels in the literal sense that was true for southerners. The challenge of defining the meaning of the sacrifice was in some respects a greater one for Lincoln than for Davis, and the resulting strains on northern society were at times severe. Voris was not alone, even if he was somewhat alarmist, in fearing "the total breaking up of [Northern] society and government before we get out of the war."[2] The critical question northerners confronted was how great a price they were prepared to pay for victory.

ORGANIZING NORTHERN SOCIETY FOR WAR

Before the war, increasing numbers of northerners had come to define the values of their republic in opposition to the slaveholding South. The attack on Sumter was so galvanizing because it was seen as the culmination of a long campaign by southern "aristocrats" to take control not only of the South but of the nation as a whole. It was a direct assault on law and order, on democratic processes, and thus on the people themselves. "Secession," as Lincoln succinctly put it, "is the essence of anarchy."[3] The Union cause, then, represented order against chaos and democracy against tyranny. In a profound sense it was seen as a test of the capacity of Americans to stand up for free government. As battle lines were being drawn, Lincoln sought to identify the Union cause with the survival of individual liberty, economic opportunity and democratic institutions. "This is essentially a People's contest," he explained in his message to Congress in December 1861.

> On the side of the Union, it is a struggle for maintaining in the world, that form, and substance of government, whose leading object is, to elevate the condition of men—to lift artificial weights from all shoulders—to clear the paths of laudable pursuit for all— to afford all, an unfettered start, and a fair chance, in the race of life.[4]

Lincoln was the most important spokesman for this distinctive American conception of democracy which linked political to economic opportunity, but his words echoed those of countless newspaper editors across the North. One Cincinnati editor explained the crisis to his readers as the battle between, on the one hand, "an established and beneficent government, resting on the democratic principle of the will of the majority" and, on the other, "a disorganized usurpation, resting on the ambition of a political faction, and deriving no authority whatever from the people."[5] The idea that the American Union was unique in human history and divinely blessed was at the core of American identity. Self-government was not just an abstract concept; it was a living reality, an experience and a practice as well as a faith. The phrase "free institutions," constantly reiterated by the Civil War generation, was a catch-all that encompassed not just government, but the whole system of voluntary associations, schools, small farms and workshops—everything, in other words, that made American society, in the generally accepted formulation, a society of freedom and opportunity. Southerners shared these values as well, and for them secession was self-government in action. Most Northerners took a profoundly different view for two reasons. First, they denied the legitimacy of Southern self-government because the demands of slavery had created an oligarchy that had rotted away the values of republicanism and enslaved the average white southerner in a fundamentally hierarchical system. Second, they had elevated the Union into the carrier of the basic values of the republic. For Lincoln—and many other Northerners as well—if the Union was destroyed, freedom, self-government, the "last, best hope of earth", would go down with it.

A war to preserve the nation from the actions of a minority was always likely to increase the popular support for a stronger national government. This was a prospect which exposed the conflicting interests of different groups in northern society. A war that posed great dangers to the political agendas of some groups played into the hands of others. While most Democrats feared that Republicans would use their sudden political dominance to create the kind of consolidated government that Federalists and Whigs had always favored, a group of patrician New Yorkers saw the war as the opportunity they had long been waiting for to tackle what they saw as fundamental weaknesses in American society. Men like the banker George Templeton Strong, the architect of Central Park, Frederick Law Olmsted, and the Unitarian minister Henry W. Bellows had long been anxious about the unruly, raucous excess of democracy and the cultural and political impact of the vast numbers of uneducated, often Catholic foreigners into their city. The problem with the antebellum republic, according to this wealthy Whiggish elite, was that it lacked discipline and social order. Bellows declared that the purpose of the war was to "save order and civilization" against "any faction, conspiracy, rabble, or political party that strives, in illegal and treasonable ways, to break up the government."[6] They hoped that the republic that emerged from what they saw as the "birth pangs of the nation" would be more centralized, more orderly, more culturally homogenous, and with a loyal, patriotic populace. This vision was intrinsically anti-partisan, and was shot through with nativism and anti-Catholic prejudice. Critically, by defining citizenship as loyalty to the national idea rather than by membership of the white race, it provided the basis for a more racially inclusive civic nationalism.

Fearing that the war could not be won unless a new sense of patriotism was instilled in the people, they set about creating organizations that would combat threats to social order at home as well as on the battlefield. An early example was the Union Defense Committee, which was established by leading New York City businessmen, half of whom were Democrats, half Republicans.[7] The committee was in effect a quasi-governmental body, playing an important role in organizing New York's response to the war. Its self-created responsibilities overlapped with the efforts made by the state government to recruit and supply regiments. Even a member of the committee, Charles Russell, acknowledged that it was "extraordinary that a committee of citizens, not holding office, . . . should have taken in hand such important public measures."[8] Henry W. Bellows was the driving force behind an even more ambitious, national organization called the United States Sanitary Commission. The Sanitary Commission both responded to and helped to inculcate the idea of women's disinterested, selfless patriotism. In his memoirs, General Grant recalled how the women of Galena, Illinois, where Grant was living when war broke out, sought his advice as a former soldier on the details of a US infantry uniform, and then made the uniforms for the first company of volunteers.[9] Local, voluntary action remained at the core of the northern war effort, but the Sanitary Commission was designed to coordinate the plethora of local women's organizations that manufactured bandages and other necessary supplies for the army. More generally, Bellows wanted to create an efficient national system that would be based on rational principles and would ensure the highest standards of cleanliness and medical care in military hospitals. There was no equivalent network in the South. The highest profile activity of the Sanitary Commission was to organize huge fairs in the big cities, which were intended to stimulate patriotism and raise money for the war effort. Women, children and families came to be dazzled by circus performers, sang patriotic songs, ate picnics and hog roasts, and heard speeches from politicians, churchmen and other local worthies. The fairs illustrated that even the Sanitary Commission had to work within the structures and habits of local communities.

Women increasingly took on public roles in the wartime North, as public speakers, authors of patriotic pamphlets and in the workplace. But overwhelmingly, their role was as symbols of voluntary self-sacrifice. "I hope you will be cheerful," Colonel Alvin C. Voris wrote to his wife in Akron in a letter that perfectly illustrates the dominant view. "Remember that you and a great many others who are making equally great sacrifices, are doing a duty that every patriot wife & mother owes to the law that gives them protection."[10] The voluntary war work of women was lauded at the time and in the immediate aftermath of the war, but the choices women made to work, or not to work, for the Commission were seen as political statements. It ensured that national issues intruded into local communities.[11] Unmarried and in her forties when war broke out, Elizabeth A. Livermore of Milford, New Hampshire, was an archetypical stalwart of the local branch of the Sanitary Commission. Her work for the commission—coordinating Milford's contributions of pickled fruit, cider and knitted socks—was to her frustration, her only political outlet. Barred because of her gender from more overtly political paths, her work for the Sanitary Commission was a weapon she could wield in the "earnest and decisive" crusade against rebels in the South and their northern sympathizers.[12]

Even in an organization like the Sanitary Commission which depended on women's work, women were not in leadership roles, and condescending male attitudes remained. If Bellows and his colleagues intended the Sanitary Commission to be an agent of centralization and nationalism, its effects were ambivalent. Led by patrician men whose main aim was to create an efficient system of supply for the army, the Sanitary Commission sometimes antagonized some of the women it depended on for its supplies. Its complacent assumption that female patriotic toil should be unpaid was ill-matched to the reality of the lives of many propertyless northern women who struggled to make ends meet. The number of women earning wages increased by 40 percent in wartime. This was no revolution: women were concentrated mainly in textile and shoe manufacturing where they had always been. A few worked in munitions. But the increased presence of women in industrial occupation did not outlast the war. Women did make long-term gains in the teaching and nursing professions, both predominately male before the war and seen afterwards as areas where feminine virtues could be exhibited, and women also entered the civil service in clerical roles way for the first time.

The strength of the tradition of voluntary civic activism coupled with traditional American antistatism did not prevent the dramatic growth of government during the war. The logistical challenge facing the federal government may not have been as extreme as that confronting the fledgling Confederate state, but it was still an immense task. In 1861, only a few hundred federal civil servants were employed outside the Post Office Department or the Customs Houses. Lacking any clear precedents, and with little idea at first of the scale of the task ahead, politicians adopted a pragmatic approach, feeling their way toward an extraordinary, if short-lived, expansion in the scale and scope of government, one that was to transform the imagined and real place of the federal government in the lives of ordinary citizens.

The War Department was by far the most important arm of the expanding federal government. Led, from 1862 onward, by Edwin M. Stanton, an energetic and incorruptible former Democrat from Ohio, the War Department supervised the creation of a vast military machine, spread over an area of thousands of miles. Inevitably, there were some serious glitches, but the big picture is one of remarkable efficiency. Union troops, especially in Virginia, were generally well-fed and well-clothed, especially in comparison with the rebels. Much of the credit for this logistical operation must go to the Quartermaster General Montgomery Meigs and General Henry W. Halleck, who had a prag-matic and hardheaded approach to the use of private companies. Meigs and Halleck worked tirelessly to coordinate the often chaotic efforts of state governors.

On rare occasions, the government moved to take direct control of private companies. The government owned and ran a few war-related enterprises. In addition to the arsenal at Springfield which produced rifles, the government set up clothing factories in Cincinnati and Philadelphia to make army uniforms, and established meat-packing houses in Tennessee and Kentucky to supply the armies with food. In the occupied South, the government took control of the railroads. But even in that instance their approach was to create a public corporation, the United States Military Railroads (USMRR), which drew on the expertise of civilian railroad engineers and managers. By the end of the war, the USMRR was operating over 2000 miles of track, making it the largest railway company in the world. More commonly, the government relied on a close partnership with private railroad companies, many of which made huge profits out of the war as a result of charging the government to transport troops and supplies. The relationship between the government and business elites intensified during the war. Charges of profiteering were widespread: John D. Rockefeller, J. P. Morgan and Andrew Carnegie all made their first fortunes in war-related industries during these years, corruption scandals surrounding the issuing of government contracts contributed to the sacking of the first Secretary of War, Simon Cameron, in January 1862. He was exiled for a brief period to Russia as the American minister to St Petersburg, where Lincoln clearly felt he could do less damage.

The two priorities confronting northern political leaders were raising money and mobilizing men. In July 1862, Congress passed the Militia Act which authorized the president to call out the state militias for nine months (as opposed to the previous limit of three months). This act was a step down the road to general conscription, and it followed the general trend of enhancing the power of the federal government and the executive branch in particular. But compared to the general conscription that had already been implemented in the South, the most striking thing about the 1862 Militia act was its conservatism. Republican Senator Henry Wilson had originally proposed to grant the president power to make indefinite call-ups, but opposition from conservative Republicans as well as Democrats to the idea that a man may be bound to military service for life forced a compromise. The responsibility for recruitment remained with the states.

A more serious problem was raising money. The cost of waging the war came close to two million dollars a day, which meant that the government was spending as much in a month as it had in a year before the war. Especially in comparison to his Confederate counterpart Christopher Memminger, Secretary of the Treasury Salmon P. Chase proved himself to be flexible and imaginative in dealing with the unprecedented problem of how to finance a war on this scale. Since the era of Jackson, the federal government had dealt only in specie rather than in bank notes. In the antebellum period, government spending accounted for no more than 2 percent of the gross national product, and government raised money mainly though tariffs and land sales rather than direct taxation. An old Jacksonian Democrat "hard money" man, Chase's first strategy for financing the war was to borrow money through the sale of bonds, but because he insisted on maintaining the practice that all payment must be made in specie, the entire financial system was forced to the brink of collapse. On December 30, 1861, the banks suspended specie payment. The only solution was the introduction of government-backed paper money. On February 25, 1862, Congress passed the Legal Tender Act, which authorized the Treasury to issue $150 million in paper notes which were not backed by specie but were made legal tender by legislative fiat. Because of the color of the ink used, these notes became known as Greenbacks. The effect of Greenbacks was to double the amount of money in circulation which created inflation, although not on anything like the scale suffered in the South. Throughout the rest of the war, the price of gold would reflect investors' confidence that the government was capable of one day redeeming its paper money. That in turn reflected confidence in the military fortunes of war. George Templeton Strong recorded the price of gold in his diary as a running commentary on the state of the Union cause.

Chase and the Republican majority in Congress proved far more willing to tax than their Confederate counterparts, although the much greater income levels in the North made this a far more useful option for them. The first direct federal income tax in US history was the most startling innovation. It was eventually extended to cover all incomes over $600, which meant that the majority of wage earners were included. With the Internal Revenue Act of 1862, Republicans in Congress voted for an inheritance tax, and stamp duty on most legal documents. The latter was especially controversial given the role of Stamp Duty in sparking the American Revolution. The Treasury naturally expanded its manpower to collect all these new taxes. Income taxes spread the burden more widely than would the alternative of property taxes, which would have fallen disproportionately on land-rich westerners. A leading Republican Congressman, James G. Blaine, later described these wartime measures, with some exaggeration, as "one of the most searching, thorough, comprehensive systems of taxation ever devised by any Government."[13] In truth, even with these innovations, taxation could only cover around a fifth of the cost of the war. Some of the rest was raised through direct bond sales to the public, which were organized by the financier Jay Cooke. The government borrowed the rest from private banks. Bond sales cemented the relationship between the national government and financial elites, giving the wealthy a stake in the outcome of the war and a privileged role in the process of nation-building.

After the war, Greenbacks remained controversial and income taxes were abolished for a generation or more. But in fundamental respects, wartime finance had a lasting nationalizing impact. Republican congressmen would have been astonished by the suggestion from some historians that they had legislated for the benefit of big business or that they had merely pieced together domestic legislation to meet the exigencies of war. They wanted to create a new nation based on an economic ideal that promised everyone the opportunity to advance while fueling growth. Republicans had not had a majority in either the House or the Senate after the 1860 elections, but the withdrawal of almost all the members from seceded states (Senator Andrew Johnson of Tennessee was a notable exception who stayed behind) gave them an unprecedented and unexpected majority. Unencumbered, for the first time, by a large block of congressmen from slave states, Republicans created an economic program that put into effect their free labor ideology. Tariffs were raised in response to the long-standing demands of Republicans in the eastern states that their manufacturing industry be given more protection from cheap imports. Congress also provided public subsidies and oversight to enable private companies to realize at last the dream of building a transatlantic railroad across the northern route from Chicago first championed by Stephen Douglas. Republican congressmen's desire to regulate and standardize was best illustrated by the banking legislation passed in 1863 and 1864 which created a national system of chartered banks. The old system had been so deregulated that before the war federal and state governments had not even claimed a monopoly on minting gold and silver coins, never mind printing paper notes. The reforming 37th and 38th Congresses also introduced national bank notes, which could only be issued by chartered national banks. In theory at least, national bank notes, unlike Greenbacks, were redeemable in specie, although the banks in practice did not resume specie payments for the duration of the war.

PARTISANSHIP, DEMOCRACY AND THE LIMITS OF DISSENT

In the first months of the war, Democrats as well as Republicans agreed to suspend party conflict. Many northerners, like southerners, retained a republican suspicion of the "wire-pullers," political fixers and the excessive partisan "hullabaloo" of election campaigns. Many in the North shared the *New York Times*' view, expressed in July 1861, that partisanship had brought "the nation to this state of Armageddon."[14] Popular songs celebrated the ideal of unity in wartime with lines like "No party nor clan shall divide us/the *Union* we'll place above all" or "All ties of your party now sever/And flock 'round your Standard so true."[15] Newspapers warned that it was unpatriotic to "plot for partisan ends," and denounced the "the licentiousness of modern partisan politics," as "an evil to be deeply deplored by every lover of his country."[16] But the unanimity was fragile. In the months after the Emancipation Proclamation was issued a massive opposition movement gathered pace. Concentrated in the Border States, and the southernmost counties of Ohio, Illinois and Indiana, areas largely populated by southern migrants with commercial and familial ties to neighboring slave states, opposition to the war was inevitably channeled through the local Democratic newspapers and articulated by local party leaders.[17] A former governor of Illinois declared that "with the objectives announced in this [emancipation] proclamation as the avowed purpose of the war, the South cannot and ought not to be subdued."[18] In the Border States in particular divided loyalties, the threat of Confederate invasion and continuing guerrilla warfare created a turbulent political world from which the Democrats profited. Some Democratic newspapers openly encouraged desertion from the army. All but 35 men in the 128th Illinois deserted when they heard about the Emancipation Proclamation, and many other regiments from southern Ohio, Illinois and Indiana suffered serious desertion or insubordination, including from officers.[19]

In the mid-term congressional elections which took place in the two months following Lincoln's controversial Preliminary Emancipation Proclamation in September 1862, Democrats made significant gains, although not enough to take back control of either the House or Senate. The state legislatures in Illinois and Indiana, however, which had had narrow Republican majorities, were taken over by pro-peace Democrats. Both legislatures promptly passed resolutions calling for an armistice and a peace conference, and tried to cut funding for state troops and even to recall them from the front. Peace commissioners appointed by these northern state legislatures appeared in Richmond, bolstering the confidence of southerners. John B. Jones of the Confederate War Department concluded in January 1863 that

> all over the North, and especially in the Northwest, the people are clamoring for peace, and denouncing the Lincoln Emancipation Proclamation. I have no doubt, if this war continues throughout the year we shall have the spectacle of more Northern men fighting against the United States Government than slaves fighting against the South.[20]

Governor Richard Yates of Illinois dealt with this threat by adjourning the legislature. His counterpart in Indiana, Oliver P. Morton, adopted a more dramatic strategy. Since the state constitution required two-thirds of the state legislators to be present in order to be quorate, the minority of Republican members simply absconded. Governor Morton ruled the state without a legislature for two years in contravention of the state constitution. Without a legislature present he could not raise any revenue from taxes, but he filled the gap with bank loans, voluntary grants from Unionist counties, and a subsidy from the federal government.

By the end of 1862 a majority of northerners appeared to lie somewhere on the spectrum between fulsome support for emancipation and "hard war" on the one hand and outright opposition to all military action on the other. When the Union army suffered serious setbacks, as in the disaster at Fredericksburg in December 1862, the Democratic message that the war was being mismanaged by abolitionist fanatics received a wider hearing. Democratic opponents of emancipation echoed General McClellan's Harrison's Landing letter in arguing that emancipation would destroy any lingering pro-Union sentiment in the South, as well as jeopardizing support for the war in the Border States. They also charged that it amounted to forcible seizure of property without due cause and was therefore a tyrannical, unconstitutional usurpation of power. Most of all, opponents of emancipation reacted to, and exploited, deep-seated racial anxieties among northern whites. Democrats insisted

that "God made the White Man superior to the Black, and no legislation will undo or change the decrees of Heaven."[21] Using arguments
that would develop in intensity over the following two years, antieman-
cipation campaigners played on fears about the prospect of "tides of
Negroes" coming north, competing for jobs and status and threatening
the social order. Politicians and editors predicted that 300,000 freedmen
would "invade" Ohio alone, competing with white labor, filling up
the poor houses and jails, and generally degrading society. Big cities
and other parts of the country with obvious class distinctions provided
the most fertile ground for Democratic "race baiting." In New York,
Democrats described the Preliminary Emancipation Proclamation as a
measure for the "butchery of women and children, for scenes of lust and
rapine, and of arson and murder."[22] Even supporters of the President's
Proclamation acknowledged the deep racial anxieties in northern white
society by trying to make the case that emancipation would be more
likely to lead to the migration of blacks down south rather than the
other way around. In an echo of the old colonization arguments, one
Unionist editor told Secretary of the Treasury Salmon P. Chase that the
best strategy was to declare that blacks "don't want to come north and
we don't want them unless their coming will promote the conclusion
of the war. Our newspapers ought to advocate this view persistently,
and demonstrate that even our free colored population would go south
if they were secure from sale into slavery."[23]

Emancipation crystallized a much broader set of fears that many
northerners harbored about whether it was possible to fight an increasingly bitter and long war without sacrificing the very freedoms for
which the war was supposedly being fought. For decades Democrats
had warned of the encroachment of national power, the ever-present
threat to liberty from elitist Whigs and Republicans who wanted to
monopolize economic and political power and meddle in people's lives.
Democrats fumed that the administration represented the "persecuting,
intolerant, hateful and malignant . . . Puritan spirit of New England."[24]
Most of his fellow Democrats, explained James Maitland of Ohio,
"think that many of the acts of Old Abe's Administration does more
for disunion, than any thing done on the part of the democrats, and
they call upon the Authorities to modify and repeal some of the most
obnoxious of them".[25] The two issues that Maitland highlighted as
points of disagreement with the administration were the idea that "the
present war could never be stopped until slavery was entirely eradicated," and "arbitrary arrests."[26] Indeed, Democratic speakers habitually

tied together the Preliminary Emancipation Proclamation with the president's announcement two days later that he was suspending the writ of habeas corpus throughout the North.

Arbitrary arrests were a shock to many northerners. Only days after his first call for troops, Lincoln suspended habeas corpus in Maryland and simply ignored the subsequent decision of the Supreme Court which declared his action illegal. Most controversially, Lincoln appointed military commanders to control military "departments" that included not only areas of the occupied South and the frontline Border States, but parts of the North as well. In these areas, civilians were tried in military courts, again despite the ex post facto judgment of the Supreme Court. Secretary of State Seward was alleged to have boasted with a characteristic flourish that he had a "little bell" which he could ring if he wanted any critic of the government locked up. Not long afterwards, Lincoln transferred responsibility for internal security from the Department of State to the War Department, but Seward's remark played into the hands of the administration's critics. The Lincoln administration was hardly tyrannical, as its opponents claimed, but Lincoln demonstrated again and again his willingness to push the Constitution to its limits, and beyond, in order to do whatever he thought necessary to save the Union. In this, as in so many other respects, he was the supreme pragmatist. "I felt that measures, otherwise unconstitutional, might become lawful," Lincoln argued, "by becoming indispensable to the preservation of the constitution, through the preservation of the nation."[27]

The man who most came to symbolize partisan opposition to the war was Clement L. Vallandigham of Ohio, who predicted that the "sober second thought" would calm the "surging sea of madness" and prevent "thirty million butchering each other."[28] At 2 a.m. on May 5, 1863, a company of Union soldiers broke into his home in Dayton and arrested him.[29] The decision to arrest him, for breach of a military order forbidding treasonous talk, had been made by General Ambrose E. Burnside, who, after the bloody debacle at Fredericksburg, had been demoted to the command of the Department of the Ohio in the hope that he could do less harm there. Vallandigham was deliberately courting arrest and martyrdom in order to dramatize his case that the war had eroded the liberties of the American people, and, thanks to Burnside's overreaction, he succeeded. Later in the year, the maverick politician was nominated by the Democrats of Ohio for the governorship. In the Border States, constant clashes between the military and the civilian authorities generated more opposition and prompted the active intervention of provost marshals and troops in the electoral process.

Loyalty Oaths were required of voters in slave states, adding to the discretionary power of local military authorities to obstruct voters. To administration supporters the new "ironclad" oath introduced in March 1863, which required past as well as future fidelity to the Union, was an essential weapon in the fight against secessionism and anarchy. To many conservatives, however, they were yet more evidence of the destruction of the old constitutional order and its replacement by despotism. "Never since God made this world has any party been so infamously treated as has the Democratic party since the war began," complained one Democrat. "Though you give your flesh and blood to put down the rebellion, if you do not favor abolition you are denounced as a rebel sympathizer."[30] Democratic Senator James A. Bayard of Delaware was so angered by having to take a loyalty oath that he resigned his senate seat warning that oaths were "demoralizing acts of tyranny . . . The first weapons young oppression learns to handle; weapons the more odious since, though barbed and poisoned, neither strength nor courage is necessary to wield them."[31] His fears were compounded by the tendency of local military commanders to adapt oaths to suit their own purposes. Officers at the polls in Cardsville, Kentucky, in 1862 reportedly required those wanting to vote to first swear to "support the policy of the present federal administration."[32]

George R. Browder, a Methodist minister who spent the whole war declaring himself to be "neutral," described the moral contortions prompted by the military-imposed loyalty oaths on his small town in Kentucky in 1863:

> There is much excitement in the country & hundreds are flocking in to take the oath of allegiance—grumbling as they go & yet swearing that they "do it of their own free will, without any mental reservation whatever." I do not see how I can conscientiously swear that I do "of my own free will" what if left to myself I should not do—& yet I must or be banished from my home & my property confiscated. Ought a Christian man to swear against his conscience to avoid suffering any more than to obtain any desired good? Is the duress sufficient to force a man so to swear or is the injunction of scripture "submit to the powers that be" a law of conscience requiring obedience to the civil or military power right or wrong! I confess that I am in some trouble about it & do not know what to do, but suppose I must submit to what I cannot avoid considering that the action is not mine—just as if I should compel my son or servant to break the Sabbath, against his will. I should be the Sabbath breaker & not he.[33]

Rev. Browder was caught in this situation because the meaning of loyalty was in flux. Northern Democrats campaigned on the slogan "the Constitution as it is; the Union as it was," which implied loyalty to a vanished antebellum constitutional order. It was unclear what such loyalty to the old antebellum republic could mean in practice, since day by day the transformations wrought by the war was making a return to the old status quo antebellum ever more impossible.

If rural southern counties in the Border States and the Midwest were one source of increasingly vociferous opposition to the Lincoln administration, another was found in the industrial cities of the northeast. Tensions were fueled by a combination of resentment at the draft, republican fears of a centralizing government, the hardships created by inflation, the alienation of some ethnic communities from what they saw as a rich man's war, and the heavy-handed tactics of employers and local elites. War issues and economic grievances became intertwined. Military force was used against striking workers on a number of occasions, notably at the Parrott armaments factory in Cold Spring, New York, and in the coal fields of western Pennsylvania. Strike leaders were imprisoned without trial. Employers wrapped their burgeoning power in the bunting of patriotism and tarred opponents with treason, condemning strikers as unpatriotic and portraying union organization as a sinister threat to the nation. Ironically, given Karl Marx's address to Lincoln in 1864 which described him as a "single-minded son of the working class" leading a struggle that would initiate a new era of ascendancy for the proletariat, workers found that the ideological as well as the physical power of the Civil War state was used against strikers.[34] Some sectors of the economy suffered in the war years. Even the shoe and boot manufacturers of Massachusetts had to cut output by 30 percent: war contracts did not make up for the loss of southern markets. One of the few occasions when the federal government exercised its right to take control of a private railroad company was in July 1864, when striking workers on the Philadelphia and Reading railroad threatened to cut off the supply of coal to Philadelphia. The most dramatic incidence of violent discontent took place in New York City in July 1863. In three days of some of the worst rioting in American history, thousands of workers, most of them poor Irish immigrants, rampaged through the city in a howl of rage against attempts to implement the draft. They targeted the visible property of the rich, the offices of Republican newspapers the *Times* and the *Tribune*. They also launched indiscriminate attacks on the black population of the city, lynching them, and burning a black orphan asylum. The rioters' targets reflected their perception that the Republican Party's war for the Union and emancipation was destroying the old egalitarian white man's republic. The total death toll is unknown, but may have been as many as a thousand. Order was restored by troops who marched north after the battle of Gettysburg.

In retrospect, the New York City draft riots were a watershed in the North's Civil War. In mainstream magazines like *Harpers'*, images of white men rioting to avoid fighting for the Union in New York were deliberately contrasted with black Union soldiers launching a heroic failed assault on Fort Wagner near Charleston. The old race-based conception of citizenship, to which many northerners still clung, had never faced such a severe challenge.

One response of Lincoln supporters to this internal dissent was to launch a massive propaganda campaign. In 1863, some of the men who ran the Sanitary Commission also formed the Loyal Publication Society which printed and disseminated hundreds of thousands of pamphlets designed to shore up the wavering loyalty of the masses. In a similar vein, the New England Loyal Publication Society, based in Boston, copied pro-Lincoln editorials and sent them to the editors of small town newspapers, many of whom reproduced them. Characteristic of the output of the Loyal Publication Society was Francis Lieber's *No Party Now But All For Our Country*, which put the case that the war was "no question of politics, but one of patriotism" and argued that he who failed to support the government was a "traitor to his country."[35] The organizers of the publication societies wanted to reinvent a new, more virile national culture, to bind society together against the threat of class tensions and partisan division. As Sven Beckert has recently argued, the Civil War hastened the formation of an upper-class identity. Elite clubs were formed in 1863 in Boston, New York and Philadelphia with the explicit purpose of fostering a "true American aristocracy." The great achievement of the clubs was, as Philadelphian Edwin P. Whipple later noted, "to make patriotism fashionable. Its political power consisted . . . in informing the rich and fashionable that they would lose caste if they became Copperheads."[36] Henry Bellows took these ideas further by declaring in his sermon, *Unconditional Loyalty*, that "the head of a nation is a sacred person." By protesting about the unconstitutionality of the government's action, critics threatened to "loosen every link in that chain of law and order which binds society together."[37] This amounted to an organic conception of nationhood that was more akin to the way in which nationhood was invoked in the Old World than it was to traditional American ideas.

For the members of these new associations, the draft riots served as frightening evidence of why they needed to exercise cultural and political authority, especially over Catholic Irish immigrants who, not at all to the surprise of nativists who for years had warned of the dire consequences of Irish immigration, had seemingly proven their disloyalty and their lack of manly virtue. Paradoxical as it may seem, anti-Catholicism, elitism and a commitment to black equality were mutually reinforcing. Few people illustrate this better than Thomas Wentworth Higginson, a Unitarian minister and antislavery campaigner from Boston who had been a member of the "Secret Six" who funded John Brown's raid on Harpers Ferry. In November 1862, Higginson was appointed the colonel of the first federally authorized black regiment, the First South Carolina Volunteers, which was made up of former slaves. In the introduction to a compilation of biographies of Harvard alumni killed in the war, Higginson asserted that "if there is any one inference to be fairly drawn from these memoirs, as a whole, it is this: that there is no class of men in this republic from whom the response of patriotism comes more promptly and more surely than from its most highly educated class."[38]

While wealthy elites were putting their prestige, time and money behind the Union cause, mass membership Union Leagues were formed across the North to generate loyalty on an avowedly nonpartisan basis. Leagues not only organized public displays of patriotic support, but also served a more clandestine purpose, identifying and intimidating those who they considered disloyal. The Republicans, charged one Democratic newspaper, were trying to "indoctrinate the people with the Austrian idea that the administration is the government."[39] Administration supporters were not completely paranoid when they warned of the existence of secret societies that provided active support for the enemy. Clandestine organizations like the "Sons of Liberty" emerged in 1863 and 1864, especially in the "butternut" counties of the Midwest. The allegation that parts of the North were honeycombed with rebel sympathizers and that they were infiltrating the Democratic Party at the highest level fitted into a conspiratorial rhetorical tradition. After all, Republicans had been warnings of conspiracies to destroy free institutions since the Kansas Nebraska Act.

In a sense, Civil War politics in the North was an ongoing debate about a problem that had plagued the American republic ever since its founding: how was it possible to maintain the balance between a government that was strong enough to resist challenges to its existence but not so strong that it destroyed freedom? One answer was provided by dissenting Democrats and draft rioters who saw the war as the destroyer of fundamental individual liberties. An alternative answer was provided by the Union Leagues and the Loyal Publication Societies. For them, the solution was a more virtuous, self-controlled citizenry, one that placed patriotism above "narrow" partisanship.

The Leagues and the Publication Societies were the means by which the Republican party's conception of the war was disseminated. For this was a Republican war: run by Republicans and defined by them too. Democrats were locked out of meaningful power and they spent the war flailing in increasingly shrill opposition: sometimes, as with Vallandigham, to the war on any terms; more often to the way the war was being fought; and, in all cases, to emancipation. Stirring up racist fears, and denigrating the effectiveness of the military strategy, Democrats became increasingly alienated as it became more and more clear that the war did not, *could not*, restore the old Union as it had been, but was instead creating a new nation, one which would include what had once seemed the impossible radical dream of emancipation. By 1863, the label "Republican" was falling out of use in election campaigns and Republicans were running instead as "Unionists", a label that fitted their self-projection as the embodiment of patriotism. The Union Leagues became not only a tremendously effective organization for the dissemination of the Republicans' (or Unionists') vision of the war, but also a means of delegitimizing their Democratic opponents. Local Union Leagues drew up lists of men whose loyalty they deemed suspect, often because they were outspoken critics of the Lincoln administration's policies on emancipation and conscription.

Without Abraham Lincoln, northerners would still have fought for the Union, still would have defined the war as a struggle for the survival of free government. Countless thousands of pamphlets and editorials bolstered popular commitment. But Lincoln had an extraordinary capacity for expressing ideas in compelling, memorable prose; so much so that he imposed his vision of the war far more effectively than—to cite the most relevant comparison—Jefferson Davis was able to do in the South. Lincoln projected his message through effective use of the press. He wrote carefully worded public letters and made numerous short speeches to delegations of soldiers who "serenaded" him outside the White House, relying on the press to report his words. He also relied on sympathetic newspaper editors to print reports of meetings Lincoln had had in which he made sure he expressed himself clearly but in an accessible and colloquial style. The most famous of Lincoln's speeches was a two-minute address to dedicate the military cemetery at Gettysburg in November 1863. Lincoln was not the main speaker—he wound up the proceedings after a two-hour oration from Edward Everett—but it was Lincoln's words that are remembered. "Four score and seven years ago," he began, "our fathers brought forth on this continent a new nation, conceived in liberty and dedicated to the proposition that all men are created equal." The effect of this opening sentence was to date the origins of the republic to the Declaration of Independence of 1776 with its grand preamble authored by Jefferson and appealing to universal ideal of equality rather than the workmanlike Federal Constitution of 1787. Lincoln was implying that the Constitution merely gave form to the nation and that the nation mattered not as an end in itself but as an embodiment of the idea of equality and liberty. Echoing in secular language the Christian idea of a trial of faith, Lincoln went on to claim that the Civil War was a test of "whether that nation or any nation so conceived and so dedicated can long endure." In little more than 200 words, he went on to explain why the struggle and the sacrifice had a dignity and a purpose of universal and transcendent significance:

> We are met on a great battlefield of that war. We have come to dedicate a portion of that field as a final resting-place for those who here gave their lives that that nation might live. It is altogether fitting and proper that we should do this. But in a larger sense, we cannot dedicate, we cannot consecrate, we cannot hallow this ground. The brave men, living and dead who struggled here have consecrated it far above our poor power to add or detract. The world will little note nor long remember what we say here, but it can never forget what they did here. It is for us the living rather to be dedicated here to the unfinished work which they who fought here have thus far so nobly advanced. It is rather for us to be here dedicated to the great task remaining before us—that from these honored dead we take increased devotion to that cause for which they gave the last full measure of devotion—that we here highly resolve that these dead shall not have died in vain, that this nation under God shall have a new birth of freedom, and that government of the people, by the people, for the people shall not perish from the earth.[40]

Lincoln's eloquence was noted at the time, but the reputation of his Gettysburg Address has grown over the years, as Americans have sought to find an uplifting meaning in the slaughter of the war.

RECONSTRUCTION AND UNION POLITICS

By the time that Lincoln delivered his address at Gettysburg, the Union army already occupied large swathes of Confederate territory. Northern politicians had to confront the issue of what was to be done once the battles had been won. Civil wars are often especially vicious since, by definition, they raise issues of sovereignty that are difficult if not impossible to compromise. As Lincoln succinctly put it, "they cannot voluntarily reaccept the Union; we cannot voluntarily yield it."[41] The way in which each side represented the other reflected the distinctive tensions of a civil war. On the one hand, even in the midst of the conflict, the language of "erring sisters" did not entirely disappear. On the other hand, though, unlike in most foreign wars, the North refused to recognize the legitimacy of the Confederacy. Like the American War of Independence, which had many of the characteristics of a civil war, one side denied the right of the other to exist and would not recognize its legal existence. In such circumstances negotiation was almost impossible. Yet civil wars also contain countervailing pressures that mitigate the drive toward an ever more absolute conflict. The northern faith in southern unionism was one such factor. Even more important was Lincoln's preoccupation with the need for an eventual Reconstruction of the Union and his consequent desire to win "hearts and minds" in the South. As the war continued, the president gradually realized that the Union army had to be an agent of destruction in order to create the conditions for future stability, but he never gave up on his hope that the worst ravages of anarchy and guerrilla war could be avoided, and he anxiously grasped at any hope, however slim, that Unionist white southerners could provide the basis for a postwar recovery.

The issue of Reconstruction went to the heart of how the war was understood. The limited war approach exemplified by McClellan implied that when the rebellion was shown to lack military staying power, southern Unionism would reassert itself. Even in 1864 McClellan and most of his fellow Democrats continued to see the war as a sort of giant police action, a show of force before which the rebel leaders and their state governments would eventually yield, and would thereafter return, chastened, to their old status. For increasing numbers of northerners, however, the war would not be won unless the South was remade in a northern image.

In 1864, Reconstruction was the source of conflict between Lincoln and Republicans in Congress. The tension had roots in the unaccustomed lead role that the White House was assuming in wartime. Congressmen were instinctively suspicious of the power and authority that his role as commander in chief gave the president in wartime. Much of the activity of Republican congressmen was aimed at increasing their influence over war policy. But there was an underlying political disagreement as well. Lincoln saw Reconstruction policy in highly pragmatic terms as a political weapon to end the rebellion, whereas congressmen, looking to the future, were concerned to secure the "fruits of victory." The division between Lincoln and congressional Republicans was not clear-cut or fixed. As events moved, so did positions on both sides. Earnest debate raged in the northern press and in the halls of Congress about the constitutional position of rebel states. If secession was constitutionally impossible, as everyone in the North agreed it was, did that mean that when the rebel forces were defeated, states would by default be restored to their old relationship with the Union, including the right to send representatives to the US Congress and participate in elections? Or, as radical Republicans argued, had the rebel states renounced their rights by seceding? This controversial "state suicide" theory was based on the principle that the states were legal actors that could be held responsible for rebellion in the same way as could individuals. To many congressional Republicans, emancipation was just the beginning of the reconstitution of southern society, which they believed could only be achieved using the authority of the national government. At the start of the war a small number of northerners were interested in the principle of equal rights—or at least substantially expanded rights—for blacks, but circumstances allowed that minority to push forward their agenda. The example of black troops fighting for the Union played a critical role in softening the racism of many northerners.

Most Republicans believed that the northern free labor economy— small-scale capitalism based on the ideas of individualism, meritocracy and self-discipline—should be the model for the nation as a whole. In 1863, the War Department created a Bureau for Freedman's affairs, an agency with a sweeping brief to create a free labor society out of the wake of slavery, a startling indication of the centralizing tendency of the war. In addition to these political goals, there was a basic revulsion shared by most northerners at the prospect of rebels returning to Washington as congressmen as if nothing had happened. As the most

forthright radical congressman, Thaddeus Stevens, put it, in a characteristically graphic way, "I do not wish to sit side by side with men
whose garments smell of the blood of my kindred."

Lincoln formulated his approach to the occupied South on the basis
that it was individual southerners who were to blame, and that loyalism
could be encouraged wherever it existed. Ideally, Lincoln wanted to
encourage southern whites to come to terms with the end of slavery
and the end of the rebellion, and to create loyal governments of their
own. He was completely pragmatic about this. The war was fought
over the supposed impossibility of secession, yet when the mountainous
western counties of Virginia (an area with few slaves and strong ties
to the free states) formed an ad hoc government, declared that they
had seceded from Virginia and applied for admission as a state of
the Union, Lincoln was enthusiastic in his support. He was generally
content to allow local military commanders to make practical judgments
about such critical matters as the status of freed slaves. In some parts
of the occupied South, radical antislavery military commanders used
this leeway to redistribute abandoned lands. A very different approach
was taken in occupied Louisiana, where General Nathaniel P. Banks,
the federal military commander, instituted a system of forced labor at
wages fixed by the government for former slaves who would not, or
could not, join the Union army. Concerned not to alienate unnecessarily
any white Unionists who could form the nucleus of a loyal government in Louisiana, Lincoln accepted this "apprenticeship" system, but
it attracted much criticism in the North. The "hard war" strategy did not
necessarily have any implications for the future status of freedmen, or
more generally for the process of restoration. This was made abundantly
obvious by General Sherman, who had embraced emancipation only
in the narrowest sense as a military tool.[42] The terms of surrender he
offered Joseph E. Johnston were so generous that they were repudiated
by Grant.

In December 1863 Lincoln issued a proclamation requiring 10 percent
of the voters of rebel states to take an oath of future loyalty to the
Union before new state governments and constitutional conventions
would be recognized. At the time, this approach did not attract much
opposition from congressional Republicans, but by the spring of 1864,
when new loyal governments had been set up under this scheme in
Louisiana, Tennessee and Arkansas, the president was being assailed
for his leniency. Notably absent from the "Ten Percent Plan" were any
guarantees about the political rights of freedmen. The prospect of the

old southern planter class resuming their former places in southern state capitals appalled many Republicans. The president's policy represented a "dangerous conservatism," charged one.[43] In June, 1864, the Union Party national convention in Baltimore not only renominated Lincoln for a second term, but also refused to seat delegations from Arkansas and Louisiana. This was a clear sign that the dispute over Reconstruction was fast becoming the central issue of northern politics. In the final days before Congress dispersed for the summer, it passed a bill sponsored by Senator Ben Wade of Ohio and Representative Henry Winter Davis of Maryland which would have wrecked Lincoln's Reconstruction policy by undermining the new governments in Louisiana and Arkansas. The congressional bill demanded that 50 percent—rather than 10 percent—of voters take an "ironclad" oath, promising not just future loyalty but that they had never given aid or comfort to the rebels. Furthermore, all persons who had held high civil or military positions in the Confederacy were to be disfranchised and disqualified from holding office. Lincoln pocket-vetoed the bill—meaning that he refused to sign it and allowed it to expire—prompting a very public protest from Wade and Davis. This nasty spat over Reconstruction revealed not only profoundly different approaches to the defeated white south, even within the Republican Party, but also widespread concern in Congress about the expansion of presidential power that had taken place since the war began. Wade and Davis' public attack bound together disparate anxieties not all of which were consistent. They accused Lincoln of attempting to create puppet governments in the South which were "mere creatures of his will," while also warning that the "ten percent plan" governments would allow rebels to return an "enemy of the government" to Washington.[44]

Secretary of the Treasury Salmon P. Chase was the leading cabinet advocate for the moral case that freed slaves were entitled to all the rights of American citizens, including, most controversially, the right to vote. To argue, as Chase and his congressional allies like James S. Ashley, Charles Sumner, Thaddeus Stevens and Ben Wade did, that loyalty to the national government rather than skin color should determine whether a man was entitled to a vote was truly revolutionary. Lincoln's own views on black suffrage have been the subject of much speculation. He did not live long enough to have to commit himself on the critical question of whether the right to vote was so important that it would have to be secured by the federal government. We do not know how his ideas might have evolved after the war had he lived, but the evidence suggests that he was not prepared to impose black voting as a precondition of Reconstruction. In an oft-quoted letter to Michael Hahn, the Governor of Louisiana elected by the small number of whites who had taken an oath of loyalty, Lincoln gently raised the issue without forcing the point. "I barely suggest for your private consideration," he wrote, "whether some of the colored people may not be let in—as for instance, the very intelligent, and especially those who fought gallantly in our ranks. They would probably help, in some trying time to come, to keep the jewel of liberty within the family of freedom. But this is only a suggestion, not to the public, but to you alone."[45] For Lincoln, black suffrage does not appear to have been matter of principle, but he recognized the justice of rewarding black soldiers, and was evidently sympathetic to the argument, being made vociferously by radicals, that voting rights would help secure the new post-slavery dispensation.

Lincoln had to tread a very difficult line between, on the one hand, the demands of radicals that he be much less lenient in his approach to white southerners, and, on the other, the perception, stoked by several influential newspapers, that the administration's emancipation policy was needlessly prolonging the war. In late July and August 1864, while northerners tried to come to terms with the unprecedented death toll of Grant's Virginia campaign, Confederate emissaries arrived at Niagara in Canada and made public calls for negotiations to end the war. The editor of the *New York Tribune*, Horace Greeley—a man who never knowingly saw a bandwagon without jumping on it—made a dramatic plea to the president. In the name of "our bleeding, bankrupt, almost dying country," he begged the president to "invite proposals for Peace forthwith" so as to avoid "new rivers of human blood."[46] Lincoln understood very well that the only reason the southerners raised the issue of negotiations was to encourage the peace party in the North. There was no basis for compromise in the summer of 1864 any more than there had been in the summer of 1861. Davis was committed to independence, the one thing that the vast majority of northerners were still committed to preventing. The complicating issue, though, was slavery. In response to Greeley, Lincoln reluctantly issued a letter setting out his terms for peace. Since he did not acknowledge the legitimacy of the Confederate commissioners and did not want to engage in formal negotiations, he addressed the letter "to whom it may concern." In it, the president reiterated that the only basis for peace was the "restoration of the Union" and the "abandonment of slavery." This second clause created a firestorm of opposition even from moderate Republicans who feared that Lincoln had played into the hands of his political opponents by allowing them to claim that only the emancipation policy prevented the South from coming to terms. George Templeton Strong thought that Lincoln's "blunder" in his letter "to whom it may concern" may cost him his reelection: "By declaring that abandonment of slavery is a fundamental article in any negotiation for peace and settlement, he has given the disaffected and discontented a weapon that doubles their power of mischief." In a similar vein, Henry Raymond, the editor of the *New York Times*, and leading figure in the National Union Party warned the president that because he had made emancipation a precondition for peace, "the suspicion is widely diffused that we can have peace with Union if we would."[47] When the war began, Lincoln had been prepared to countermand the orders of military commanders on the ground in order to preserve slavery because he believed that that was the best way of preserving the Union. From 1863 onward, he argued that the same ultimate goal of preserving the Union justified his emancipation policy. Lincoln was utterly consistent in arguing that only by harnessing the physical power of slaves could the South be defeated. To those who opposed the enlistment of black troops, Lincoln replied that if the North were to "abandon all the posts now possessed by black men [and] surrender all these advantages to the enemy . . . we would be compelled to abandon the war in three weeks."[48]

Along with the depression that followed the Emancipation Proclamation and the defeat at Fredericksburg, this mid-August crisis was the most serious wobble in northern commitment to prosecuting the war until the South was defeated. As Raymond and Strong realized, it increased the likelihood that the Democratic candidate—none other than George B. McClellan—would defeat Lincoln in the November election.

THE 1864 ELECTION

At the start of September, two factors combined to boost Lincoln's chances. The first was the fall of Atlanta, which transformed the mood in the North and induced another bout of optimism that the war was soon coming to an end. The second factor was the political miscalculation of the Democrats. By nominating McClellan, Democrats offered a Union general who claimed to be a fervent Unionist but who represented—thanks in large part to the public circulation of his 1862 Harrison's Landing letter—a very different conception of the meaning of the war, and especially of the function of emancipation. But McClellan's candidacy was hobbled from the start by the party's platform, which, reflecting the increasingly prominent role of copperheads in the Democratic Party, committed a McClellan administration to an immediate armistice and described the four-year "experiment" of war as a "failure." To the immense relief of Lincoln and his supporters, the effect of this was to polarize the campaign around the basic issue of whether the war should be fought until the South submitted. With optimism surging about the prospect of military victory, and with Union soldiers supporting Lincoln by lopsided margins, it was relatively easy for Lincoln's supporters to imply that support for McClellan was tantamount to treason and to make the election a test of loyalty to the national cause. "For four summers the loyal North has been firing *bullets* at the rebellion," ran a typical editorial, "The time has now come to fire *ballots*."[49] The Washington correspondent of the *New York Times*, William Swinton, claimed in a widely circulated pamphlet that the Democratic Party had the "entire sympathy and moral support" of the leaders of the rebellion.[50] Unionists stirred up fears about internal security. Newspapers and campaign tracts exploited a high-profile treason trial in Indiana of five men allegedly members of the Sons of Liberty. At about the same time, the Judge-Advocate General Joseph Holt published a report on treasonous secret societies, the general thrust of which was made clear by the opening sentence: "Judea produced but one Judas Iscariot, but there has arisen together in our land an entire brood of such traitors."[51]

Union Party campaign literature represented their candidates as "stout-hearted inflexible men," who transcended "mere politics"; they were "fresh from the loins of the people" and thus not "tainted by party intrigue."[52] War Democrats were featured prominently at Union campaign meetings in order to encourage the impression that Lincoln's reelection was not dependent on the old Republican vote. Pamphlets with titles like *Country Before Party: The Voice of the Loyal Democrats* argued that "the self-styled 'Regular Democracy' has become thoroughly Vallandighamised" and now "stands in an attitude of virtual hostility to the country."[53] Opposition to Lincoln, argued Unionists, was evidence of narrow-minded partisanship, a lack of patriotism, or a failure to take manly responsibility for the future of republican government. "If the voters stoop so low" as to elect McClellan, wrote one Unionist pamphleteer, they will have proved their "incapacity to govern themselves."[54] The claim of the 1864 Union Party to represent more than the old Republican Party was given substance by the presence of Andrew Johnson of Tennessee on the ticket as Lincoln's running mate.

Johnson, a nonslaveholding southern Unionists and the only senator or congressman from a seceding state who had remained in his place in Washington in 1861, had been a brutally effective military governor of Union-occupied Tennessee since 1863. He was also a lifelong Jacksonian Democrat. Radical Republicans were delighted by Johnson's determination to use emancipation as a weapon to destroy secession. Only later when the unimaginable had happened and the Tennessean became president did they discover to their apparent shock that support for wartime emancipation did not necessarily imply support for any level of racial equality.

The role of clergymen in the Union Party campaign in 1864 revealed how far northerners had come in their attitude to the moral significance of the conflict. For Yankee evangelical Protestants, the 1864 election would pave the way for national redemption. Remarkably few churchmen raised moral qualms about the war, or even the brutality and scale of the killing, although a few felt uneasy about fighting on the Sabbath. Instead, drawing on a long tradition dating back to the Puritan founders, wartime ministers sought to interpret the war in the light of God's plans for the American republic. If it was a chastisement for national sins, it also was an opportunity for national redemption and purification. Secular nationalist ideas about the discipline and sacrifice of war marking the "coming of age" of the American republic were reinforced by the religious notion of "our soil made sacred by such a baptism of fraternal blood."[55] The Methodist Bishop Matthew Simpson spoke for many when he expressed confidence that "if the world is to be raised to its proper place, I would say it with all reverence, God cannot do without America."[56] The nation, once redeemed, would be "henceforth the crowning national work of the Almighty, the wonder of the world."[57]

There is some truth to the suggestion made by some historians that the Republican (or Union) Party downplayed their support for emancipation in the election campaign.[58] The "letter to whom it may concern" affair revealed the fragility of northern popular commitment to emancipation, and Lincoln supporters took heed. Plenty of Union Party campaign literature pandered to northern racism, and little of it explicitly addressed the issue of political equality for blacks. Emancipation was separated from broader questions to do with Reconstruction. Yet somehow everyone knew that the fate of slavery was at the center of the campaign. In several prints and cartoons, the goddess Liberty was pictured together with Lincoln and a copy of the Emancipation Proclamation. Unionists thus built a campaign that implicitly transformed emancipation into an aspect of nation-building: slavery must die not so much because slavery was wrong—for many northerners, including Lincoln, that had not previously been a sufficient reason for abolition—but because it threatened the life of the nation. John Murray Forbes, a wealthy Boston conservative, confessed that he was "more antislavery because slavery is anti-republican, anti-peace, anti-material progress, anti-civilization than upon the higher and purer ground that it is wicked and unjust to the slave. I have no special love for the African, anymore than for the low-class Irish."[59]

When the ballots were counted, Lincoln gained 55 percent of the popular vote. This was a convincing, but hardly overwhelming endorsement. The strength of the Democratic vote, even in the face of a Union campaign that branded a vote for McClellan tantamount to support the rebels, was a measure of the discontent among northerners about the transformations that the war had wrought. But for many of those who voted for Lincoln in 1864, emancipation sanctified their sacrifice. "May your life be spared," a Congregationalist minister wrote to Lincoln after his reelection, "to finish up the great work of freedom which God in his good providence has re-committed to your hands."[60]

8 The Magic Word, "Freedom"

THE ROAD TO APPOMATTOX

By the beginning of 1865, the capacity of the Confederates to resist was so weakened that, for once, northern predictions that the end was in sight were not exaggerated. Although many of them were barefoot and on quarter rations, the Army of Tennessee that Hood had inherited from Johnston in July 1864 had fought its way back to Nashville, where it was crushed on December 15 and forced to flee back into Mississippi. Of the 60,000 men of the Army of Tennessee who had faced Sherman the previous spring, death, injury and desertion meant that only 15,000 remained by January 1865. Hood resigned his command in despair. His army had effectively ceased to exist. On January 8, a combined Union military and naval operation captured Fort Fisher, which protected the Confederacy's last remaining major port at Wilmington, North Carolina. Three weeks later, Sherman was on the move again, marching his army on a second, and logistically far more challenging, march. This time, his troops tramped north through the Carolinas, crossing apparently unbridgeable rivers in the midst of a rain-soaked winter. The pillaging and destruction of private property was even greater in South Carolina than in Georgia. "Here is where treason began," reasoned one private, "and, by God, here is where it shall end!"[1] On February 18, the Confederacy experienced a symbolic death rattle when Charleston, birthplace of secession, was surrendered to the (white) colonel of a black regiment.

As Sherman's men cut a swathe through the heart of the Confederacy, a heartrending train of freed slaves trailed in their wake. Leaving their plantations often with nothing more than the clothes they wore, tens of thousands of men, women and children placed their faith in Sherman's army of deliverance. On January 12, 1865, Sherman met with Secretary of War Stanton and a delegation of freedmen to determine how the federal authorities should deal with the refugees. The outcome was

Sherman's Special Field Order number 15, which allocated land in the offshore Sea Islands to families of freed slaves in parcels of 40 acres a piece, and also offered the freedmen the use of worn-out army mules to work the land. By June, 40,000 freedmen were settled on more than 400,000 acres of land.

Still, the Confederates fought on. Lee, more than ever the last, best hope of the southern cause, was finally made general-in-chief of all Confederate armies on February 6, 1865, and one of his first acts was to restore Joseph E. Johnston to command and urge him to halt Sherman's seemingly inexorable march northward. Not that Johnston had much to command any more. Mustering about 22,000 ragged and tired men Johnston made one token assault on Sherman's army and then retreated into the hills in the hope of joining with Lee's Army of Northern Virginia. Lee, too, had concluded that slipping away from Grant and joining forces with Johnston was his only option. After one final fling at the Union trenches outside Petersburg on March 25, the once invincible Army of Northern Virginia retreated from one line of trenches to the next and escaped west across the Appomattox River. In their wake, they abandoned Richmond, setting fire to the city after Confederate government officials loaded the treasury and archives into railroad cars and fled west. At long last, the Confederate capital, which northern newspapers had expected to take nearly four years previously, was in Union hands. "Babylon is fallen and we are going to occupy the land," exulted a Vermont soldier.[2] The following day, April 4, 1865, President Lincoln visited the ruined city, protected by a detachment of black cavalry. Black people thronged the street cheering him. "I know I am free," shouted one, "for I have seen Father Abraham."[3]

Over the following four days, the ragged and half-starved remnants of the Army of Northern Virginia, now grossly outnumbered by the Army of the Potomac, were chased west of Richmond into the remote far southwest corner of Virginia. On April 8, Sheridan's cavalry overtook Lee's army and captured two trainloads of desperately needed rations at Appomattox station. The following morning, Lee ordered one final effort to break through the ring of federal troops that now surrounded him. When that failed, he realized he and his men had finally come to the end of the road.

During the night of April 8–9, Lee and Grant exchanged letters agreeing terms of surrender. Grant was generous. Artillery and ammunition was to be surrendered, but officers were allowed to keep their side arms, and those who had them were allowed to keep their horses.

The entire army was "paroled," which meant, in Grant's words, that "each officer and man will be allowed to return to his home, not to be disturbed by United States authority" so long as they obeyed the laws and did not take up arms again. Grant and Lee met in the drawing room of a private home in the village of Appomattox Court House on the morning of April 9. Lee arrived first. He had put on his full dress uniform for the occasion, whereas Grant, whose baggage wagon had not kept up with the army, hurried to the meeting in his usual front-line battle dress and muddy boots. For a few minutes the two generals exchanged pleasantries. Grant asked Lee if he remembered that they had met once before, during the Mexican War. Lee said he did, and they spoke of mutual friends for a few moments. Then Lee brought them to the business at hand. Grant wrote out the surrender terms and Lee signed them. The two generals shook hands. Grant later wrote that he felt "sad and depressed" at that moment, at the downfall of a "foe who had fought so long and so valiantly, and had suffered so much for a cause, though that cause was, I believe, one of the worst for which a people ever fought."[4] As Grant and Lee talked, President Davis, ignorant about what was happening at Appomattox and with his government on the run, dispatched a letter to Lee with news of fresh supplies and reinforcements. The letter never arrived.[5]

There was one conceivable alternative to surrender: Lee could have scattered his army into small bands and send them into the hills as guerrillas. One of Lee's artillery officers suggested this move on the morning of April 9. But Lee refused to countenance such a plan. Guerrillas, he warned, would simply become bands of marauders who would legitimize the Union army expanding their war against the infrastructure and civilians of the South. This final decision was entirely in line with Lee's conception of the war from the start. If the civilian authority of the independent Confederate Republic could no longer be sustained, then the military contest was over. In any case, the mountainous areas where Confederate partisans would have to seek shelter were precisely those areas of the Confederacy which had been least dedicated to the cause, while the plantation-rich lowland areas where support was strongest were also most vulnerable to Sherman-style sweeps by the Union army. Even so, Lee warned Grant the day after the surrender terms had been agreed that the South was "a big country" and the US army might have to "march over it three or four times before the war entirely ended."[6]

General Lee underestimated his own role in sustaining southern morale. When news spread of the surrender at Appomattox, southern morale finally collapsed. " 'It is useless to struggle longer,' seems to be the common cry," reported Eliza Andrews from Macon, Georgia. "The poor wounded men go hobbling about the streets with despair on their faces. There is a new pathos in a crutch or an empty sleeve, now, that we know it was all for nothing."[7] In Tallahassee, Susan Bradford Eppes was desolate:

> General Lee has surrendered the Army of Northern Virginia. Oh I wish we were all dead! It is as if the very earth had crumbled beneath our feet. In our minds all is chaos and confusion and yet, outwardly, there is no difference. The skies are just as blue, the flowers just as bright, the mocking-birds are flitting in and out teaching their young ones how to fly and tonight they will be singing just as gaily as if this crushing sorrow had not come to us.[8]

Eliza Andrews was incensed to see companies of Union soldiers, including black troops, marching past her home in May 1865. "Their hateful old striped rag was floating in triumph over their heads," she fumed. At the start of the war, she confessed, she had felt it "a pity to break up a great nation about a parcel of African savages, if we had known any other way to protect our rights," but now, "since the Yankees have treated us so abominably, burning and plundering our country and bringing a gang of negro soldiers here to insult us, I don't see how anybody can tolerate the sight of their odious old flag again."[9]

Most Americans shared the assumption that the surrender of Lee's army effectively signaled the end of the war. On the fourth anniversary of the firing on Fort Sumter, black and white abolitionists, freed slaves, some of them in Union army uniform, held a formal ceremony in Charleston to raise the Stars and Stripes and over the following weeks the remaining ragged Confederate armies were cornered. "I hev conkludid that the dam fulishness uv tryin to lick shurmin Had better be stoped," wrote a private in the remnants of Johnston's army on April 13. "We hav bin getting nuttin but hell & lots uv it ever sinse we saw the dam yankys & I am tirde uv it."[10] On April 26, General Johnston surrendered to General Sherman near Durham, North Carolina. On May 4, General Richard Taylor (son of President Zachary Taylor) surrendered at Citronelle, Alabama. On June 2, in Texas, General Edmund Kirby Smith surrendered the last regular Confederate forces. After four years and two months of warfare, secession had been crushed. This was not just a defeat of their four-year experiment in independence, but of freedom and republican government as the Confederacy had understood it. Thus, on seeing Yankee troops in the City Hall of her hometown, Judith McGuire wrote despairingly in her diary of the building that since her childhood she had regarded with "respect and reverence" because it was the place from which the Constitution and the laws had been expounded." For Confederates, military defeat meant the Constitution and the laws, which they had revered for 70 years were "trampled under foot."[11]

WHY THE SOUTH LOST THE WAR

To the makers of the myth of the Lost Cause in the late nineteenth century, the South fought a heroic struggle against overwhelming odds. General Lee set the tone for this interpretation with his message to his men after the surrender at Appomattox: "After four years of arduous service, marked by unsurpassed courage and fortitude," he told them, "the Army of Northern Virginia has been compelled to yield to over-whelming numbers and resources."[12] If Lee was right, historians need not look south of the Mason–Dixon line to explain the war's outcome. Shelby Foote, the author of one of the most enduringly popular histories of the war, echoed Lee's view in a 1991 television documentary:

> I think the North fought that war with one hand behind its back. I think that if there had been more southern victories, and a lot more, the North simply would have brought that other arm out from behind its back. I don't think the South ever had a chance to win that war.[13]

It was certainly the case that, by the end of 1864, the North had found ways of making its industrial and manpower superiority count on the battlefield. Grant and Sherman had large, well-fed and well-equipped armies at their disposal. The northern economy was more efficient than ever at churning out arms and military supplies. The extent of the greater resources available to the Union is indicated by the fact that, thanks in large part to the increasing mechanization of farming, the North doubled its exports of wheat, corn and pork to Europe during the war, despite the demands of the Union army and the loss of agricultural manpower.[14] Large parts of the South, in contrast, had been devastated, crops and buildings burned, plantations left in disarray, and armies depleted by unimaginable losses. Technological and industrial superiority also gave some clear military advantages to the Union. This was especially true of the naval war. The South was never able effectively to contest the Union blockade. Steam-powered Union gunboats also had a huge advantage in river-based warfare, able to move fast enough to have a good chance of evading Confederate batteries. Meanwhile, railroads helped the North to supply its armies, although they were often a slower and less reliable way of moving troops than old-fashioned marching. It is true that the Confederates also used railroads effectively when they could and that in addition they benefited from interior lines, meaning that southern troops had shorter distances to travel moving from one front to another. But this advantage was steadily eroded as the Union armies advanced and took control of more and more southern railroads. At the end of October 1863, Lincoln was able to move 20,000 men by rail from the Army of Potomac in Virginia to reinforce Chattanooga in only a few days.

In the end, the South was battered into submission. Union officer Charles S. Wainwright noted after Appomattox that for three years the Army of Northern Virginia had "withstood every effort of the Army of the Potomac; now at the commencement of the fourth, it is obliged to succumb without even one pitched battle." The rebellion, he concluded, "has been worn out rather than suppressed."[15] The Lost Cause myth of gallant southern armies crushed by an industrial behemoth does have some basis of truth, therefore, but only when applied to the last few months of the war when the Army of the Potomac outnumbered Lee's Army of Northern Virginia by more than three to one.

The answer to the question of why the South lost the Civil War therefore changes depending on from what point in the war the assessment is made. If by the end of 1864 final defeat was only a matter of time, whereas the picture earlier in the war looked very different. The Confederates could have won against superior odds because, much like the American Revolutionaries, they had compensating advantages: a resilient population, talented military leaders, the advantage of fighting a defensive war in country they knew, and, above all, a cause for which the vast majority of white southerners were prepared to make great sacrifices. At the start of the war, few foreign observers thought that the North could conquer and occupy such a large area against determined opposition. The logistical and military challenges seemed too great. Thomas Jefferson's grandson, George W. Randolph, who was later to become one of no fewer than six successive Confederate Secretaries of War, expressed a common view in the South when he predicted in

1861 that "the Yankees may overrun our frontier states and plunder our coast, but, as for conquering us, the thing is an impossibility. . . . History offers no instance of a people as numerous as we are, inhabiting a country so extensive as ours, being subjected if true to ourselves."[16]

If Randolph was right, then the causes of Confederate defeat were internal rather than external. To some historians, the culprit was misguided military tactics. From the start, this argument runs, the South should have been prepared to retreat into the southern interior, exposing the Union army's major weakness which was its need to maintain supply lines. By conserving manpower and forcing the North to make costly offensive assaults, the South could have neutralized all the North's advantages. Up to a point, this was the kind of war that Lee was forced to fight in the summer of 1864 and, as the northern public's response to the carnage at Cold Harbor, Spotsylvania and the Wilderness demonstrated, it was certainly an effective way of wearing down northern commitment. The problem with this argument is that a truly defensive strategy was simply not a politically viable option. Southern public opinion demanded aggressive defense of the South. Similarly, while Jefferson Davis' determination to maintain territorial integrity so far as possible placed enormous burdens on Confederate armies, any other course would have been politically impossible. The possession of territory was the principal marker of the state of the war. Had the South allowed the North to take large swathes of territory without a fight it would have created the perception of northern victory that might have created its own momentum. The most basic demand that the southern people placed on their government was security from invasion and Davis would have been unwise to have disregarded that feeling. Furthermore, as Sherman's marches demonstrated, there was nothing more wounding to the pride and morale of the southern people than Yankee armies devastating their country like a biblical plague of locusts. In any case, offensive tactics could be an effective means of defense, as Lee proved conclusively at Chancellorsville. And had the battles of Antietam or Gettysburg gone the other way—as they might conceivably have done—then no one now would criticize Lee for trying to take the war to the enemy.

Some historians have criticized Lee's focus on the Virginia theater, accusing him of allowing his loyalty to his home state to cloud his judgment about the broader strategic picture. It is true that Lee's energies—as well as the attention of the press and public in both North and South—focused on the East, and he almost always resisted suggestions from Davis that troops be moved from the Army of Northern Virginia to other fronts. The Confederacy was not blessed with talented military leaders in the West, but even had Lee himself taken command of the Army of Tennessee, it is not clear how such a shift of focus would have helped the South's only meaningful strategic objective—wearing down the northern will to continue the fight. If Richmond had fallen to McClellan in the spring of 1862, as it could have done, the Confederacy might have survived, but it would have received a blow to morale from which it would have found it hard to recover. Moreover, the capacity of Lee's army to threaten Washington was one of his most valuable cards, and no Union setbacks in the West had anything like the same depressing effect on northern morale as the Army of the Potomac's defeats at Fredericksburg or Chancellorsville. As Gary Gallagher has put it, "the Confederacy could lose the war either in the West or in the East, but it could win the war only in the East."[17]

An alternative set of "internal" explanations for southern defeat focus on the supposed political divisions and institutional weaknesses that beset the Confederacy. According to this view, the Confederacy was hoist by its own petard: its devotion to decentralized government, endless checks on executive power, and obsession with individual liberty undermined its unity and capacity to fight. Jefferson Davis acidly told a political opponent in 1864, "if the Confederacy falls, there should be written on its tombstone, 'Died of a theory.' "[18] The theory he had in mind was states' rights. Perhaps, therefore, in David Donald's striking phrase, the South "died of democracy." Certainly, Davis battled with sometimes blinkered parochialism from state governors, but for all the bluster it is difficult to pinpoint how these political arguments affected the military capacity of the South. A related theory holds that the South suffered in comparison to the North because it did not have a functioning two-party system[19] Lincoln certainly benefited from having an organized network of party loyalists who used patriotic rhetoric to corral men to the polls in support of the administration. Jefferson Davis, who had to rely on general appeals to patriotic virtue rather than the tools of patronage to compel loyalty, could certainly have done with some Confederate equivalent of the grassroots Union leagues. But the notion that the opposition in the North was kept in manageable bounds because it was secured within a two-party system would have amazed anyone at the time. Although it is true that in certain respects Jefferson Davis's nonpartisan approach may well have resulted in weaker appointments, for example to his cabinet, than Lincoln made, it is now clear that in many other respects he was far from the hapless figure that he was once regarded as being. Indeed it can be argued that in terms of the coordination of manpower and resources, the efficiency of the Confederate government, even without a party system, exceeded that of the Lincoln administration, at least in the early stages of the war.

Another possible explanation for the outcome of the war is the differing abilities of Lincoln and Davis. Lincoln was not only a far more gifted communicator, he was also more psychologically astute, and infinitely better at getting the best out of subordinates. Compare, for example, Lincoln's brisk but effective letter warning Hooker to "beware of rashness, but with energy, and sleepless vigilance, go forward, and give us victories" to the cold 10,000-word legal brief that Davis penned to Johnston after Bull Run explaining why, even though the battle had been won, Johnston's strategy had been wrong. The difficulty Lincoln had finding a successful general in the Virginia theater was paralleled by Davis's problems with his generals in the west. Both men were hampered by political pressure to appoint or to retain "political generals." But Lincoln was better at putting aside his personal frustrations and animosities. Lincoln was a political genius with an unparalleled capacity for communication. His sparse, elegantly constructed prose spoke to northerners as no other politician could. Yet even Lincoln was not indispensable to the northern commitment to the Union, nor can Davis, for all his deficiencies, fairly be held responsible for whatever went wrong. Neither leader was ultimately so important.

More fruitfully, historians in recent decades have focused on the fault lines in southern society. A lack of southern commitment to the cause has become a familiar theme. The South, it is argued, was never a proper nation. The southern people were sustained in the fight only by their Christian faith and their desire to defend their racial order. When the tides of war turned against them they began to doubt God's favor, and when it became clear that the independent Confederacy could not protect their slaves from Yankee invaders, their confidence in the cause collapsed. More specifically, women, it has been argued, undermined the Confederate war effort by protesting against the sacrifices they were making, and encouraging the desertion of their sons and husbands. The foremost exponent of this view, Drew Gilpin Faust has speculated that the "alienation of southern women from the war effort" may well have caused the South to lose the war.[20] Women certainly played a critical role in encouraging desertion, especially in the final months of the war, but in many cases women not only encouraged enlistment of their menfolk in the first place, but sustained them in the army through words and deeds until the war was over. In southern communities that were occupied by the enemy, women frequently took the lead role in campaigns of subversion and resistance—not just by emptying chamber pots over the heads of Union soliders in occupied New Orleans but also in thousands of less memorable, but more effective ways. In some instances, women even attempted to regularize their military service. In December 1864, 28 women from Harrisonburg, Virginia, in the Shenandoah Valley, sick of the depredations of Philip H. Sheridan's men, petitioned the Confederate Secretary of War, James A. Seddon, to allow them to "raise a full regiment of ladies—between the ages of 16 and 40—armed and equipped to perform regular service." The women pledged that they were prepared to "leave our hearthstones—to endure any sacrifice—any privation for the ultimate success of our Holy Cause."[21]

Of course there were divisions and tensions within southern society. And in some key respects—such as a monetary policy that fueled inflation, or a conscription policy that was perceived as protecting wealthy slaveowners—the Confederate government exacerbated rather than alleviated suffering on the home front. War, especially a war that engages all available men of military age and exposes the civilian population to deprivation, invasion, destruction of property and occupation by a hostile army, can be expected to place a society under severe strain. In the case of the South in the Civil War, only in the final months, when Union military superiority became invincible did a failure of morale tangibly affect the ability of Confederate armies to resist. As late as August 1864, Union Colonel Alvin C. Voris was convinced that "the South are far from being reduced, either by famine, stress of war or broken finances." They had demonstrated a "zeal and fortitude that challenges my admiration and certainly worthy of a better cause."[22] The big picture is that southern divisions were overshadowed by the remarkable durability of the white South's commitment to the cause in the face of sacrifices that were immensely greater than anything the North had to deal with. About 38 percent of southern men died in battle or of disease compared with only one in six of northerners who fought. Furthermore, the South lost two-thirds of its assessed wealth—much of that total in slave property—and the war killed 40 percent of its livestock and devastated much of its countryside. Southern will collapsed only when the writing was already on the wall for the Confederacy. Only pressure from the Yankee invaders destroyed the South. Not until

April 18, 1865, did Eliza Andrews finally concede in her diary that "the spell of invincibility has left us and gone over to the heavy battalions of the enemy."[23] The loss of will thesis, in other words, appears to confuse cause and effect.

The problem with all these internal explanations for Confederate defeat are that they are all susceptible to what James McPherson has called the "fallacy of reversibility." In other words, for every southern weakness and apparent failure of will, a problem of at least equal seriousness can be found in the North. If Richmond and other southern towns saw bread riots, they were not on the same scale of destructiveness as the draft riots in New York, Boston and other northern towns. If southern society exhibited class and geographical divisions, so too did the North. Even the alleged lack of a coherent southern nationalism had its counterpart in the Union's struggle to define and explain the meaning of the war. Desertion devastated the Confederate army in the final months of the war, but the Union army was beset by the same problem. Perhaps as many as 85,000 Americans fled to Canada to escape the draft, more than a third of the veteran volunteers left the Union army at the expiration of their three-year terms in the spring of 1864, and the draftees and substitutes who came into the army to replace them were notorious skedaddlers.

The only potential southern weakness that did not apply to the North was slavery (at least not once the Border States were secured for the Union and the process of emancipation got underway there). Slaves who fought for the Union army confronted the leaders of the Confederacy with the falsehood on which their rebellion rested. In other, even more fundamental ways, slavery hampered the ability of the South to pursue the policies that might have maximized its chances against the enemy. One of the reasons why Davis had to try to hold all Confederate territory, for example, was because slavery was a vulnerable institution that had to be protected, and slaveowners wielded a political influence vastly disproportionate to their numerical strength in the South. It is true that slavery enabled a far greater mobilization of white men into the army than would otherwise have been the case, and slaves were never the internal "fifth columnists" that some abolitionists predicted—and some historians wish to have been the case. Yet, there is much evidence that slaves became harder to manage once the war began, and there was a massive escalation of tool breaking, arson, petty resistance of all kinds, and desertion. And in areas of the South that were touched by the war, slavery collapsed completely. It is difficult to avoid the conclusion that the presence of slaves made southern society more vulnerable, even if, without the incursions of the Union army and the collapsing capacity of the Confederacy to resist, slavery would probably not in itself have defeated the South.

Some historians have speculated that tensions and even a suppressed "guilt" about slavery hampered the Confederate war effort. Some have even argued that southerners' commitment to slavery was "essentially ephemeral." After the Emancipation Proclamation aligned the government of the United States with that of Britain and France in opposing slavery, southerners, these historians argue, were "unable to bear the weight of world moral disapproval."[24] Charles G. Sellers thought the problem lay in the awareness of southerners that they were fighting to defend an institution that was regarded as immoral by the rest of the world. Slavery, he concludes, "simply could not be blended with liberalism and Christianity."[25] Kenneth M. Stampp has gone even further, arguing that "a large number of white Southerners, however much they tried, could not persuade themselves that slavery was a positive good, defensible on Christian and ethical principles." These arguments overstate the case. Thousands of sermons delivered on every Sabbath and day of prayer and fasting in the Confederacy testify to the ability of southerners to reconcile slavery with their faith in liberty, and even with capitalism and progress. It is true that some southerners cursed slavery for bringing death and destruction upon them, and there are fleeting revelations that the end of slavery was sometimes a relief as well as a shock. "We felt lighter some how than usual," reported George Browder, a Kentucky planter and Methodist minister who awoke one morning in early 1865 to find that "his negroes" had deserted. He and his family "felt poorer, but freer, more dependent, yet more self-reliant."[26] Such comments bolster Bell Wiley's contention that "uneasiness about slavery gnawed at numerous Southern consciences," although it should be added that Reverend Browder's sense of a burden having been lifted did not prevent him from keenly seeking the recapture of his slaves and regretting the passage of the Thirteenth Amendment.[27] Almost all white southerners, even those who had never owned slaves, even those whose diaries and letters reveal moments of insight and empathy with the plight of black people, remained stubbornly wedded to slavery and regarded its passing with regret and anxiety for the future. Stampp's notion that the "moral burden of slavery" was so severe that large numbers of white Southerners "unconsciously felt that they had less to gain by winning than by losing" is simply not supported by the large body of evidence left by white southerners.[28]

As Jefferson Davis saw it, the South had two routes to victory. The first was to secure foreign recognition and the second to win enough military successes to persuade the North to stop fighting. The dog that didn't bark in the American Civil War was foreign intervention. Much has been written about the possibility of British and French recognition of the Confederacy, but in truth neither government came close to making such a move. Apart from the *Trent* crisis—a self-inflicted diplomatic imbroglio from which the Union managed to extract itself—the moment when the Confederacy probably came closest to securing foreign recognition was in the late summer of 1862 before the advancing tide of Confederate success was halted at Antietam and the Emancipation Proclamation increased popular support for the Union in Britain. The French government of Napoleon III in particular was extremely sympathetic to the South. In 1863, the French government backed the overthrow of the Mexican government and installed a minor Hapsburg prince, Maximillian, as Emperor. Even this flagrant breach of the Monroe Doctrine, which in theory threatened war with the United States, did not induce Napoleon III to agree to an alliance with the Confederates, although emissaries in Paris persistently tried to arrange one. Given the massive financial investment by European powers, particularly Britain, in the United States, it is unclear what the British would have had to gain from intervening in a war unless it was certain that the Confederacy would win anyway. So while Davis always understood that foreign intervention and military victory leading to the collapse of northern will were interdependent, what he did not, at least at first, understand was that in reality the direction of causation was one-way. In other words, military victory of a kind that made the North concede might well have led to foreign recognition, but there was no realistic prospect of foreign recognition happening first.

If the deus ex machina of foreign intervention was never likely, and if the South fought as hard as it could given the inevitable strains of a slave society at war, that leaves northern commitment to the war as the outstanding variable. So long as the North remained determined to crush the rebellion by force, it was always likely that their superiority in manpower and resources would tell in the end. The North was never subjected to anything like the level of social and economic disruption that affected the South. Yet, northerners may well have deserted Lincoln's administration in 1864 as a result of death rates in Grant's spring campaign that, while horrific, were less than the South had been enduring for at least two years. Given the deep conflicts within northern society over ends and means and the resistance to the transformations that the war wrought, northern commitment was never entirely secure. Throughout the war, the driving purpose of southern military strategy was to undermine northern commitment. In a letter to his wife in 1863, Lee outlined his plans. "If we can baffle them in their various designs this year & our people are true to our cause," he wrote,

> I think our success will be certain.... If we are successful this year, next fall there will be a great change in public opinion at the North. The Republicans will be destroyed & I think the friends of peace will become so strong as that the next administration will in on that basis. We have only therefore to resist manfully."[29]

As Lee knew, northern commitment to military subjugation of the Confederacy was inseparable from the political ascendancy of the Republican (or Union) Party. Significant Democratic victories in elections, especially in the 1864 presidential contest, would have transformed the war, and almost certainly to the benefit of the South. Democrats benefited from war weariness, they advocated armistices and bitterly opposed emancipation and the use of black troops. Lincoln's single-minded focus on a military solution to the crisis and his conviction that emancipation was a weapon to destroy secession, created huge divisions in the North which Confederates, naturally enough, sought to exploit. Arguably, then, the fate of the Confederacy was determined as much by northern ballots as bullets.

But if in one sense, northern public opinion and the electoral fortunes of the Republican Party were the factors that determined the fate of the Confederacy, the public mood was ultimately determined by military success or failure. Herman Hattaway and Archer Jones have argued that public opinion fundamentally and persistently misread the strategic significance of battles. Civil War Americans, according to Hattaway and Jones, were fixated on the outdated and irrelevant issue of which side was forced to retreat after a battle. Battles in and of themselves resolved little, they assert; what mattered to the military outcome was the proportional losses that each side suffered.[30] Battles that appeared to be Confederate victories—such as the two battles of Bull Run and Chancellorsville—in fact did more damage to the South than the North because the Confederates lost a higher proportion of their men. This grim analysis may be correct as far as the fighting capacity of each side is concerned. Lee won so often against larger forces that he perhaps failed to appreciate the ultimate importance of numbers until it was too late. But the whole point of Lee's strategy was that, recognizing that the North had more men and more industrial capacity, he wanted to hit them where they were most vulnerable—popular commitment to the cause, without which the war would not continue. Ultimately, the South lost because they did not win enough battles at the crucial moments before the northern war machine became unstoppable. Only decisive southern victories—measured by the public's standards of who held the field and who retreated—would have convinced the North that the war could not be won, or that the price of victory was too high.

Northern spirits sank low in the winter of 1862–1863, with the defeats at Fredericksburg and Chancellorsville the critical factors. The mood in the North was jubilant at the news of Gettysburg and the capture of Vicksburg but a year later, in the summer of 1864, it had soured and sunk to new depths after the bleeding of the Army of the Potomac at Wilderness, Spotsylvania and Cold Harbor. The fall of Atlanta transformed the mood again. There was nothing inevitable about the outcome of these battles. McClellan's defeat in his spring advance on Richmond in 1862 was not inevitable, and nor was Lee's dispiriting defeat at Gettysburg. We need to be careful not to confuse war weariness with a willingness to give in. From at least 1862 onward most northerners and most southerners wanted peace. The question was, "on what terms?" While only a small minority of southerners were prepared to return to the Union as the price for peace, only a minority of northerners were prepared to accept southern independence, however great the price. This was especially true of Union troops who, after all, bore the brunt of the sacrifices. After six weeks of constant engagement with the rebels southeast of Richmond, Colonel Alvin C. Voris of Ohio expressed the combination of weariness and determination that radiated from countless similar letters. "I see so much of horror and suffering in the army that I sometimes wish for peace at almost any terms," he admitted,

> I know this war *would* never have been had the people anticipated half the evils it has already entailed. But being in it, when I think earnestly, I of course insist that we must punish the enemy till we crush out all opposition to the just requirements of the Government. We have expended too much to quietly yield now. But I do wish I could see a speedy resolution of this question. I want to get home.[31]

At about the time that Voris was writing these words, Horace Greeley was imploring Lincoln to explore a negotiated settlement, albeit on the basis of the illusion that the Confederates would voluntarily return to the Union after having fought tenaciously for more than three years for their independence. Voris balanced exhaustion with the escalating human cost of the war with his determination to finish the job. His spirits were low, but he never reached the stage of disillusionment. But it is perfectly conceivable that war weariness may have led, had McClellan won the 1864 election for example, to a stampede for an armistice which in turn would have given the Confederacy the time they desperately needed to rebuild their shattered country. The North could very well have lost the war, but only if it had defeated itself.

THE NATION "REDEEMED"

In the end, despite social unrest, shrill partisan opposition and through numerous severe crises of morale, the North did stay the course. The leadership of Abraham Lincoln and the Republican-controlled Congress played a large role, but so too did the thousands of editors, ministers and ordinary northerners who came to an understanding of the Union cause as, in Lincoln's memorable phrase, "the last best hope of earth." It was a cause worth fighting for, they believed, because their sense of nationhood was founded on a blend of sacred and secular ideas according to which the Union was the guarantor of political liberty and economic opportunity, the triumph of which mattered to the whole "family of man." To a remarkable extent the Lincolnian notion that the war with the southern slaveocrats was a part of the global struggle between freedom and autocracy seeped into northern discourse. From the outset, Lincoln understood that winning the war meant mobilizing public opinion as well as arms and men. That the North remained committed to the military struggle despite the strength and unity of their opponents is testimony to the effectiveness of this political and ideological mobilization.

Nothing in the experience of nineteenth-century Americans had prepared them for the brutal and protracted nature of the Civil War. Yet in the midst of bewildering, sometimes anarchic brutality and confusion, most men and women tried to cling to ideas of decency and familiar notions of good behavior. They desperately wanted to see continuity amid the change. And, despite the horrendous human suffering, the American Civil War did not, for northerners, disrupt the fundamental institutions and operations of the state. Northerners went to war in 1861 to preserve their system of self-government and, as the final end to the conflict seemed to draw near, they celebrated the "amazing strength and no less amazing steadfastness of [their] democratic institutions."[32] Even amid this celebration of continuity, preservation and survival, however, all knew that the nation that emerged from four years of war was not the old republic of 1860. Northerners who marched into battle in 1861 to preserve their old Union did not succeed any more than did the southerners who struggled to preserve their way of life. The old white antebellum republic was as much a casualty of the Civil War as the dream of a slaveholding republic in the South. An article in the April, 1865, edition of *Atlantic Monthly* reminded readers that "our war... [was fought] for the preservation of our national power and greatness" rather than "distinctly and avowedly for the extinction of slavery." Nevertheless, looking back at the close of the war, the author saw clearly the inseparability of emancipation and national preservation. "A higher reason," he felt, had been moving the public will "in a game where the stake was the life not merely of their country, but of a principle whose rescue was to make America in very deed a New World, the cradle of a fairer manhood."[33]

In his Second Inaugural Address in March, 1865, Lincoln also dwelt on the relationship between the preservation of the Union and the end of slavery. His speech is chiefly remembered for its closing lines:

> With malice toward none; with charity for all; with firmness in the right, as God gives us to see the right, let us strive on to finish the work we are in; to bind up the nation's wounds; to care for him who shall have borne the battle, and for his widow, and his orphan—to do all which may achieve and cherish a just, and a lasting peace, among ourselves, and with all nations.

The main body of the brief speech, though, was the product of deep reflection by the president about God's will, and the relationship between the preservation of the Union and the emancipation of the slaves. He speculated that the nation was being punished by an Old Testament God for the sin of slavery: "He gives to both North and South, this terrible war, as the woe due to those by whom the offence came."[34] At his moment of triumph, Lincoln abjured triumphalism. Battered down as he was by the physical strain of office, Lincoln's determination was undiminished—"let us strive on to finish the work we are in," he urged. But most clearly in this speech he revealed his profound awareness of the frailty of mankind. We must show "firmness in the right," but know that it is only "insofar as God gives us to see the right."[35] Lincoln was not a humble man in the true sense of that word—he sought power and rarely doubted his own ability—but he understood the value of humility in the face of the subtlety of human motivation and the complexity of the world. His greatness lay in his ability to balance doubt with action, to act on the basis of conviction while not succumbing to the sin of hubris.

Little more than a month later, Lincoln was dead. On the afternoon of April 14, Good Friday, the president met with his cabinet for what proved to be the final occasion. He was in unusually good spirits, telling them about a dream he had had that he believed augured good fortune. That evening, he and his wife Mary were due to attend a performance of a popular British comedy, *Our American Cousins*, starring Laura Keene at Ford's Theatre, just a few blocks from the White House. It was a special benefit performance to raise money for the care of disabled Union soldiers. When, a few minutes after the play had begun, the Lincolns appeared in their box overlooking stage left, the packed auditorium erupted in applause and the actors halted in mid-sentence to join in the applause as the band struck up an impromptu rendition of "Hail to the Chief." Lincoln smiled and bowed to the audience.

Secretary of War Edwin Stanton had long been concerned about the president's personal safety, and with good reason: the previous August, Lincoln was shot at while riding to his summer retreat, the Soldier's Home, just outside Washington. Lincoln brushed off the incident. Now, the president who had walked unharmed in the streets of the Confederate capital only days beforehand was to be slain almost on his doorstep, amid his friends and supporters, at the very hour of his victory. The assassin was John Wilkes Booth, a moderately well known tragedian who lived perpetually in the shadow of his more famous father and brother, and had become consumed with a passion to strut upon the stage in a role that no one could ignore: that of avenging angel. Deranged by a craving for personal immortality and a zeal for the Confederate cause, he recruited a peculiar cast of misfits and hatched a vainglorious plot, originally to kidnap Lincoln and deliver him bound and gagged at

Jefferson Davis' feet, but then, after the fall of the Richmond government, to kill him instead. A fellow conspirator stabbed Secretary of State Seward at his home at about the time that the president arrived at the theater, but Seward survived. A plan to kill Vice President Johnson came to nothing when the would-be assassin went on a drinking binge instead. Booth, of course, had reserved the lead role for himself. Since he was well known to the staff of the theater, he was able to enter by the stage door and, choosing to strike at a quiet moment in the play, he slipped into the box behind the presidential party and fired a bullet into the back of Lincoln's head at close range. Then he leapt from the box onto the stage, spoiling the effect by breaking his shin as he landed. Before the shocked auditorium grasped what they had just witnessed, Booth, in a typically over-the-top dramatic gesture shouted "Sic simper tyrannis," hobbled into the wings, and made his escape on a waiting horse.

Lincoln did not die instantly. He was carried across the road to a room in a boarding house where he lingered until the early hours of the next morning, never regaining consciousness. With Mary convulsed with grief in a neighboring room, and news of the assassination spreading rapidly by telegraph, Lincoln's cabinet colleagues rushed to the boarding house. They were gathered round the bedside when the president drew his last breath at 7.22 a.m. on Saturday, April 15. Tears streaming down his cheeks, Edwin Stanton broke the silence with the words, "now he belongs to the ages."

The congregation of the Baptist church in Hudson, Wisconsin, were singing an Easter Hymn when someone arrived with the news that Lincoln was dead. The minister was so overcome that he asked to be excused from preaching. After a short prayer, the congregation filed outside in deep shock.[36] In Vermont, the wife of the governor wrote simply, "the bells are tolling which so lately rang in joy."[37] Public mourning was extravagant. "The church was draped in black," reported Catherine E. Parker from Burlington, Vermont. "The Rep[ublic's] flag was festooned twice—the center being fastened with black bands—to the middle of the two central pillars behind the pulpit—festooned either way—to the gallery. It was kept in place by bands of black wound around it. The organ was trimmed with two festoons of black. It looked finely but very mournfully."[38] Lincoln's death allowed northerners to weep for all their dead. The slogans sewn on flags and black banners, "The memory of the just is blessed," ensured that Lincoln stood in for many other private losses.

UNFINISHED BUSINESS

Several days later, John Wilkes Booth was shot dead by Union troops in a burning hay barn in Maryland while attempting to escape. A military court eventually convicted eight people as coconspirators. Four of them hanged and there were calls for punitive measures to be taken against the South. But most northerners had no such thoughts of revenge. As so often happens in such moments of collective shock, people searched for a great cause to match the enormity of the deed. Surely the death of a now-revered president could not have been caused by frustrated minor actor; had Booth been acting on the orders of Jefferson Davis? In the orgy of emotion that followed Lincoln's killing, some even pointed the finger at Vice President Andrew Johnson—a southerner, after all— and the most obvious beneficiary of the crime, who, bleary-eyed from too much drink and bewildered by the turn of events, was hurriedly sworn into office. Even as northern clergymen rhetorically transformed the gifted but very human Lincoln into a martyred patriotic saint, the slain president's call for "charity towards all" was temporarily forgotten amid the calls for punitive measures to be taken against the South. The extraordinary thing was not that northerners responded with such anger at first, but how quickly a more sober perspective returned. Union army veterans were especially likely to favor a liberal policy toward the ordinary people of the South. Even a radical antislavery man like Alvin Voris advocated a "generous clemency to the great body of the people of the revolting states."[39] Jefferson Davis was arrested fleeing through Georgia (he was alleged to have been disguised as a woman, a possibly apocryphal detail that served to further humiliate him in the eyes of the delighted northern newspaper editors who peddled the story). He was imprisoned for two years, during which time he wrote his memoirs. General Lee faced no criminal charges. For the rest of his life he remained the apotheosis of southern virtues: gallant, gentlemanly, heroic. The only Confederate to be executed for his part in the rebellion was Henry Wirz, the commandant of the Andersonville Prisoner of War camp in Georgia where as many as 13,000 men had died of disease and starvation. Under Lieber's new code, Wirz was singled out for violating the rules of war.

Lincoln's death at the moment of the Union's military triumph meant that he never had to commit himself to a plan for winning the peace. The South was defeated, resigned to the end of southern independence, but still determined to resist Yankee interference with their way of life. Emancipation—which would be made legal and permanent by the final ratification of the Thirteenth Amendment in December 1865—mandated some sort of change to southern society, but how radical that change would be and what freedom would actually mean for blacks were still uncertain. Northerners had shown themselves committed to the preservation of the Union by military means, and a majority of them had embraced emancipation as a means to that end and as a positive transformation in itself. Some radicals in the Republican Party were equally determined that with the Confederacy destroyed, the rebel states should now be reshaped in the image of the North, with freed black laborers the backbone of a new free labor loyal South and assured of political equality, including the franchise.

If that was what Reconstruction was to mean it would require the North to remain as focused and committed to that goal as they had been on the defeat of secession. "In my view, the war has just begun," argued the veteran abolitionist Wendell Phillips. "You do not annihilate [slavery] when you decree its death. You only annihilate it when you fill its place with another."[40] That meant the full weight of the federal government must be used to counterbalance the resurgent power of southern white elites who would try to restore as much as they could of their prewar world. In the summer of 1865, southerners tried to do just that by passing restrictive "black codes" that virtually restored slavery in all but name. Ex-Confederates found an unexpected ally in the White House. President Andrew Johnson of Tennessee promiscuously issued amnesties to those high-ranking Confederate civilian and military figures who had been barred from holding office under Lincoln's 1863 Proclamation of Amnesty and Reconstruction, and he countermanded Sherman's redistribution of land to freedmen, returning the land to its owners.

Congressional Republicans fought back, implementing a sweeping Reconstruction plan over Johnson's vetoes, and, from 1869, with the support of Ulysses S. Grant, who exchanged his brilliantly successful military career for a much less distinguished career as president. In the course of three remarkable years, between 1866 and 1869, Congress denied the former Confederate states representation in Congress, while they passed the Fourteenth and Fifteenth Amendments which guaranteed the equality before the law of all citizens of the United States, and—overturning the *Dred Scott* decision—they assured citizenship to all who were born in the United States, with no exceptions whatsoever on the basis of race or anything else. Black men were enfranchised, and with the support of small numbers of US troops and the extensive use of loyalty oaths to disenfranchise some white voters, every southern state was ruled for several years by Republican governments that included prominent black figures. Astonishingly, within three years, southern blacks had gone from being slaves to being equal citizens, holding office. Not until 1980 were there again as many black officeholders in the United States as there were in 1869. All this amounted to a radical remaking of the legal basis and the political meaning of American citizenship. The antebellum white man's republic had, in theory, been overturned. Along with it, the presumption that republican freedom was based on the ownership of productive property had fallen too. However radical they were in granting political rights to black men, Congress did not interfere with property rights. There was to be no land redistribution in the postwar South. Sherman's offer of 40 acres and a mule was never repeated. From now on freedom was defined as access to political rights rather than as economic independence.

Not all white southerners resisted all aspects of Reconstruction. J. D. B. DeBow revived his journal and argued that the only future for the South lay in emulating northern industry. A few prominent Confederates, including former Georgia Governor Joseph E. Brown, joined the Republican Party. But the majority of white southerners fought back, at the ballot box where they could, using force where necessary. Confederate cavalry commander General Nathan Bedford Forrest was a leading figure in the creation of the Ku Klux Klan, the first and most famous of several clandestine organizations that used violence and intimidation to coerce white voters to support Democratic "white line" candidates and, so far as they could, kept blacks away from the polls altogether. By the late 1870s, the revived Democratic Party was back in control of every state government in the South, a position they held, with barely an exception, for a century. The overthrow of these Republican Reconstruction state governments was described by those doing the overthrowing as the "redemption" of the South. No stronger word was available in their vocabulary. Driving blacks and their white allies from power was celebrated as a biblical deliverance from a Yankee assault far more brutal than anything Sherman had done to them. In the 1890s, southern state governments began formally implementing segregation ("Jim Crow" laws) and disenfranchising blacks through legislative as well as extra-legal means. In 1896, the Supreme Court gave its blessing to racial segregation. Some Republicans continued to pay lip service to enforcing the Fourteenth Amendment as late as the 1890s and even into the twentieth century, but by then they had largely given up seeking votes in the South. In 1935, the black intellectual and civil rights activist W. E. B. Du Bois brilliantly summed up Reconstruction in a single sentence: "The slave went free; stood a brief moment in the sun; then moved back again toward slavery."

The failure of Reconstruction was due to many factors. Between 1872 and 1877 white southerners waged what amounted to a second Civil War, a guerrilla campaign which united the Christian white people in the South at least as effectively as anything they managed in wartime. But the seeds of the failure of congressional Reconstruction were present at the outset: northern whites, who, through their control of the federal government had the power to effect change in the defeated South, were not, as a whole, sufficiently committed to black equality. Northerners were prepared to pay the price for saving the Union, but not for securing the rights of blacks. In the run-up to the fall elections in 1875, Mississippi Governor Adelbert Ames, a New England "carpetbagger" who had been a Union general, appealed to President Grant for military assistance to combat the rising tide of violence by white terrorists who attacked Republican Party campaign rallies and murdered black office-holders. Grant refused help, explaining that the northern public were "tired out with these annual autumnal outbreaks in the South." Grant and his advisors were not going to risk alienating prospective Republican voters in Ohio by inviting criticism that they were using military force to interfere in the internal affairs of the South.

Northern reluctance to keep southern whites under the cosh reflected a growing convergence of northern and southern interpretations of the war under the spell of a romantic cult of reunion. Patriotic literature celebrated the heroism on both sides, with Lincoln and Lee elevated into the pantheon of national gods. Union and Confederate veterans met at joint encampments, and reminisced about their shared experiences. The 1898 war against Spain was the symbolic moment of togetherness in which white northerners and white southerners fought together under the same flag. The fact that the initial fighting was done in Cuba, an island that antebellum southerners had long hoped to bring into the Union, was fitting. The cult of reunion was essentially an agreement by two parties in the Civil War—white northerners and white southerners—to exclude the third party, black people, from the post-war settlement. In 1913, on the 50th anniversary of Gettysburg there was a great reunion of surviving veterans of both sides on the battlefield—organizers called it a "peace Jubilee." The centerpiece of the festivities was the reenactment of Pickett's Charge by the elderly old men, most still wearing their faded old blue and gray uniforms. When the southerners reached the (specially rebuilt) stone wall before which so many men had been killed, the veterans shook hands, threw their hats in the air and cheered. And then, some with tears in their eyes, Union and Confederate joined in the singing of "God Bless America." After the reenactment, there was a short address by the president. Woodrow Wilson's Gettysburg Address strained to look at the future not the past. It was an "impertinence" to "discourse upon how the battle went, how it ended, or even what it signified." The quarrel was forgotten, Wilson insisted, "except that we shall not forget the splendid valor, the manly devotion of the men then arrayed against one another, now grasping hands and smiling into each other's eyes."[41]

Southerners had lost their bid for independence, and they had lost slavery. The Civil War had radically altered the distribution of power in the nation. White Southerners had been, per capita, almost twice as rich as northerners in 1860, if the capital invested in slaves is counted. By 1870, northerners were 44 percent wealthier than southern whites, who had also lost relative wealth to southern blacks. In 1860 the South's share of national wealth had been 30 percent. In 1870 it was 12 percent. Southerners had dominated national politics in the 70 years before the Civil War. In the 100 years that followed, Southerners reclaimed their seniority in the Senate but they were a perpetual minority in the House and only two presidents from the old Confederacy—Woodrow Wilson and, in 1964, Lyndon Johnson—were elected. Even so, the defeat of the radical attempt at Reconstruction was an important victory for the white South. Judged on the basis of their ability to regulate their own affairs, especially in the field of race relations, southerners had lost the war, but—as the events at Gettysburg in 1913 revealed—they appeared to have won the peace.

But not forever. In 1963, a hundred years after the Emancipation Proclamation was issued, Martin Luther King stood on the steps of the Lincoln Memorial and invoked the war's legacy of racial justice. He began his famous "I Have a Dream" speech with a deliberate echo of the Gettysburg address: "Five score years ago, a great American, in whose symbolic shadow we stand today, signed the Emancipation Proclamation . . . But one hundred years later, the Negro still is not free." Meanwhile, among professional historians, and in school classrooms and textbooks, the centrality of race in American politics since the 1960s has returned slavery and emancipation to the center of the Civil War story. The war has become the means of reconciling the apparent anomaly of slavery in a land of freedom.

In 1863 a young Pennsylvania soldier named Caldwell worried that fighting for mere political unity would appear selfish, and would not be understood by the world at large. The addition of "the magic word freedom," he thought, would raise the cause to an altogether different and higher level.[42] As Caldwell realized, the ending of slavery saved Americans from the otherwise uncomfortable implications of a nationalist war. Lincoln's words, most notably in his Gettysburg Address, bestowed a grandeur and moral purpose on the war. And to a remarkable extent, it is Lincoln's vision of the war that continues to exert a popular hold. It is his conception of a new birth of freedom, a rebaptism of the republic in the spirit of the founders, which Americans have embraced. As Edward L. Ayers has argued, there are dangers to this approach. It implies that progress is inevitable in American history, that wars have progressive purposes; even that wartime emancipation absolves the United States of the stain of slavery and racial injustice.[43]

The Civil War continues to exert an extraordinary fascination for Americans because it is a drama from which two satisfactory conclusions can apparently be drawn: national unification and integrity will always win through in the end; and the promise of America is one that is inclusive of all its people. Subsequent generations have found it as hard as the Americans who actually lived through the war to resist imposing a sort of providential meaning on the events of 1861–1865. The Civil War not only has provided patriotic tales of valor and heroism, but has also given the United States a second creation myth, a way of defining itself that reinforces its most positive aspects. The story of the war is molded into the most satisfying of all narrative genres: a "fiery trial" with a redemptive ending. The truth is more complicated and more intriguing. Only by recovering the chaos and contradictions of the war, the multiple meanings of victory and defeat, can we come to a true understanding of America's greatest crisis.

Notes

PREFACE

1. Quotes from Thomas Bender, *A Nation Among Nations: America's Place in World History* (New York: Hill and Wang, 2005), p. 124.
2. CWAL 4: 426.
3. George F. Hoar, *Autobiography of Seventy Years* (London: Bickers, 1904), Vol. I, p. 212, quoted in Peter J. Parish, *The North and the Nation in the Era of the American Civil War: Collected Essays of Peter J. Parish*, ed. Adam I. P. Smith and Susan-Mary Grant (New York: Fordham University Press, 2003), p. 150.

1   SLAVERY AND THE AMERICAN REPUBLIC

1. CWAL, 1: 109.
2. Charles Sellers, *The Market Revolution: Jacksonian America, 1815–1846* (New York: Oxford University Press, 1991).
3. CWAL, 1: 5.
4. CWAL, 8: 333.
5. CWAL, 2: 461.
6. Thomas Jefferson to Edward Coles, August 25, 1814, Jefferson Papers, LoC.
7. Thomas Jefferson to John Holmes, April 22, 1820, Jefferson Papers, LoC.
8. Frederick Douglass, "Address on 'Evangelical Flogging,' delivered at Market Hall, Syracuse, N. Y., September 24, 1847," in Jon Butler and Harry Stout, eds, *Religion in American History: A Reader* (New York: Oxford University Press, 1998), p. 425.
9. Eugene Genovese, *The Political Economy of Slavery: Studies in the Economy and Society of the Slave South* (New York: Pantheon, 1965); John Ashworth, *Slavery, Capitalism and Politics in the Antebellum Republic* (Cambridge: Cambridge University Press, 1995); Thomas Bender, ed., *The Antislavery Debate: Capitalism and Abolitionism as a Problem in Historical Interpretation* (Berkeley: University of California Press, 1992).
10. James Huston, *Calculating the Value of the Union: Slavery, Property Rights and the Economic Origins of the Civil War* (Chapel Hill: University of North Carolina Press, 2003).
11. Speech of Alexander H. Stephens, Kenneth M. Stampp, ed., *The Causes of the Civil War* (New York: Simon and Schuster, 1991 edn), p. 153.
12. On changing concepts of race in the nineteenth century British Empire see Catherine Hall, *Civilizing Subjects: Metropole and Colony in the English Imagination, 1830–1867* (Cambridge: Cambridge University Press, 2002).

13. The key works are Steven Hahn, *The Roots of Southern Populism: Yeoman Farmers and the Transformation of the Georgia Upcountry, 1850–1890* (New York: Oxford University Press, 1985) and Stephanie McCurry, *Masters of Small Worlds: Yeoman Households, Gender Relations and the Political Culture of the Antebellum South Carolina Low Country* (New York: Oxford University Press, 1995).

14. William H. Truettner, ed., *The West as America: Reinterpreting Images of the Frontier, 1820–1920* (Washington DC: Smithsonian, 1991), p. 101.

15. Quoted in Leonard Richards, *The Slave Power: The Free North and Southern Domination 1780–1860* (Baton Rouge: Louisiana State University Press, 2000), p. 152.

16. Quoted in Kenneth M. Stampp, *America in 1857: A Nation on the Brink*, (New York: Oxford University Press, 1990), p. 111.

17. Quoted in Huston, *Calculating the Value of the Union*, p. 67.

18. Quoted in Susan-Mary Grant, *North Over South: Northern Nationalism and American Identity in the Antebellum Era* (Lawrence: Kansas University Press, 2000), p. 71.

19. Charles W. Ramsdell, quoted in Michael A. Morrison, *Slavery and the American West: The Eclipse of Manifest Destiny and the Coming of the Civil War* (Chapel Hill: University of North Carolina Press, 1997), p. 12.

20. Robert V. Remini, *Henry Clay: Statesman for the Union* (New York: W. W. Norton, 1991), p. 736.

21. Ulysses S. Grant, *Memoirs and Selected Letters* (New York: Penguin Library of America edition, 1990), pp. 164–165.

22. *North Carolina Standard*, November 13, 1850, quoted in Avery O. Craven, *The Growth of Southern Nationalism, 1848–1861* (Baton Rouge: Louisiana State University Press, 1953), p. 103.

23. *Congressional Globe*, 31st Congress, 2nd Session, Appendix, 322.

24. George S. Hillard to Francis Lieber, June 2, 1854, quoted in Nevins, *Ordeal*, 2: 152–153.

25. Quoted in Larry Gara, *The Liberty Line: The Legend of the Underground Railroad* (Lexington: University Press of Kentucky, 1967), p. 131.

26. Suzanne L. Bunkers, ed., *The Diary of Caroline Seabury, 1854–1863* (Madison: University of Wisconsin Press, 1991), pp. 29, 42–43.

27. Quoted in Sean Wilentz, *The Rise of American Democracy: Jefferson to Lincoln* (New York: Norton, 2005), p. 667.

2 POLITICAL CRISIS AND THE RESORT TO WAR

1. CWAL, 8: 332–333.

2. CWAL, 2: 276.

3. Horace White, "Abraham Lincoln in 1854", *Putnam's Magazine*, March 1909, p. 724, quoted in Joshua Wolf Shenk, *Lincoln's Melancholy: How Depression Challenged a President and Fueled His Greatness* (Boston: Houghton Mifflin, 2005), p. 132.

4. John B. Allen to Charles Sumner, June 5, 1854, Charles Sumner Papers, Houghton Library, Harvard University.

5. Quoted in Mark Voss-Hubbard, *Beyond Party: Cultures of Antipartisanship in Northern Politics before the Civil War* (Baltimore: Johns Hopkins University Press, 2002), p. 5.
6. *Atlantic Monthly*, I (1857): 22–46.
7. CWAL, 3: 146, 179.
8. Ibid.: 315.
9. Ibid.: 550.
10. Vivien Green Fryd, *Art and Empire: The Politics of Ethnicity in the US. Capitol, 1815–1865* (New Haven and London: Yale University Press, 1992).
11. George C. Rable, *The Confederate Republic: A Revolution Against Politics* (Chapel Hill: University of North Carolina Press, 1994), p. 11.
12. M. R. H. Garnett to William H. Trescott, May 3, 1851, in Henry O'Reilly, *Origin and Objects of the Slaveholders' Conspiracy against Democratic Principles* (New York, 1862), 10–11, quoted in Wilentz, *Rise of American Democracy*, p. 645.
13. Quoted in Wilentz, *Rise of American Democracy*, pp. 724–725.
14. George Fitzhugh, *Cannibal's All! Or, Slaves Without Masters* (Richmond, VA: A. Morris, 1857), p. xxi.
15. Quoted in Rable, *Confederate Republic*, p. 17.
16. Bertram Wyatt-Brown, *Southern Honor: Ethics and Behavior in the Old South* (New York: Oxford University Press, 1982); William J. Cooper, *The South and the Politics of Slavery, 1828–1856* (Baton Rouge: Louisiana States University Press, 1978), pp. 69–74.
17. Quoted in Rable, *Confederate Republic*, p. 6.
18. F. B. Sanborn, *The Life and Letters of John Brown* (Boston: Roberts Brothers, 1891), p. 620.
19. James M. McPherson, *Battle Cry of Freedom: The Civil War Era* (New York: Oxford University Press, 1988), pp. 209–211.
20. Quoted in Wilentz, *Rise of American Democracy*, p. 766.
21. New Orleans *Daily Crescent*, November 18, 1860, in Dwight L. Dumond, ed., *Southern Editorials on Secession* (New York: Century Co., 1931), p. 235.
22. Quoted in Morrison, *Slavery and the American West*, p. 257.
23. Raynor to Caleb Cushing, quoted in ibid.
24. Calvin H. Wiley to Governor Z. B. Vance, September 26, 1862, in Christopher M. Watford, ed., *The Civil War in North Carolina: Soldiers' and Civilians' Letters and Diaries, 1861–1865* (Jefferson, NC: McFarland & Co., 2003), p. 71.
25. Letter to Senator Clement Clairborne Clay quoted in Morrison, *Slavery and the American West*, p. 261.
26. *Vicksburg Weekly Sun*, November 19, 5, 1860, in Dumond, *Southern Editorials*, p. 243.
27. Michael p. Johnson, *Towards a Patriarchal Republic: The Secession of Georgia* (Baton Rouge: Louisiana State University Press, 1977).
28. David Brown, *Southern Outcast: Hinton Rowan Helper* (Baton Rouge: Louisiana University Press, 2006).

29. Quoted in Martin Crawford, *Ashe County's Civil War: Community and Society in the Appalachian South* (Charlottesville: University of Virginia Press, 2001), p. 70.
30. Quoted in Wilentz, *Rise of American Democracy*, p. 776.
31. Quoted in Robert W. Johannsen, *Stephen A. Douglas* (New York: Oxford University Press, 1973), p. 832.
32. Victor Davoust to Buchanan, January 1, 1861, James Buchanan Papers, Historical Society of Pennsylvania, Philadelphia.
33. Quoted in Glyndon G. Van Deusen, *William Henry Seward* (New York: Oxford University Press, 1967), p. 246.
34. CWAL, 4: 150.
35. New York, *Courier and Enquirer*, December 1, 1860.
36. Philadelphia, *Public Ledger*, November 21, 1860.
37. CWAL, 5: 527.
38. CWAL, 4: 426
39. Philadelphia, *Press*, December 21, 1860.
40. CWAL, 4: 271.
41. Ibid.: 268–269.
42. Harriet Beecher Stowe, *Abraham Lincoln* (Collection of 1864 election campaign pamphlets, Widener Library, Harvard University).
43. J. Robert Lane, *A Political History of Connecticut During the Civil War* (Washington: Catholic University of America Press, 1941), p. 175.
44. Quotes from Alice Fahs, *The Imagined Civil War: Popular Literature of the North and South, 1861–1865* (Chapel Hill: University of North Carolina Press, 2001), pp. 18–19.
45. Jonathan Worth to Daniel G. Worth, May 15, 1861, in Watford, ed., *The Civil War in North Carolina*, p. 7.
46. Quoted in Wilentz, *Rise of American Democracy*, p. 787.
47. John Keegan, *The Mask of Command* (London: Pimlico, 1999), p. 189.
48. Marcus Cunliffe, *Soldiers and Civilians: The Martial Spirit in America* (London: Eyre and Spotiswode, 1969), p. 5.
49. McPherson, *Battle Cry of Freedom*, p. 344.
50. James B. Fry, "McDowell's Advance to Bull Run," in R. U. Johnson and C. C. Buel, eds, *Battles and Leaders of the Civil War*, vol. 1 (New York: Century Co., 1884–88), pp. 175–205.

3 THE FAILURE OF LIMITED WAR, 1861–1862

1. Richard N. Current, "God and the Strongest Battalions," in David Herbert Donald, ed., *Why the North Won the Civil War* (Baton Rouge: Louisiana State University Press, 1960), p. 22.
2. Quoted in William Barney, *Flawed Victory: A New Perspective on the Civil War* (New York: Praeger, 1975), p. 11.
3. Robert G. Angevine, *The Railroad and the State: War, Politics, and Technology in Nineteenth Century America* (Stanford, CA: Stanford University Press, 2004), p. 131.

4. Jerome Mushkat, ed., *A Citizen-Soldier's Civil War: The Letters of Brevet Major General Alvin C. Voris* (Dekalb: Northern Illinois University Press, 2002), p. 91.
5. Quoted in James M. McPherson, *Ordeal by Fire: The Civil War and Reconstruction* (New York: Knopf, 1982), p. 218.
6. Archer M. Jones, "Military Means, Political Ends: Strategy," in Gabor S. Boritt, ed., *Why the Confederacy Lost* (New York: Oxford University Press, 1992), pp. 45–77; James M. McPherson, "Lincoln and the Strategy of Unconditional Surrender," in Gabor S. Boritt, ed., *Lincoln, the War President: The Gettysburg Lectures* (New York: Oxford University Press, 1992), pp. 35–37.
7. Grady McWhiney and Perry D. Jamieson, *Attack and Die: Civil War Military Tactics and the Southern Heritage* (Tuscaloosa: Alabama University Press, 1982), p. 14.
8. CWAL, 4: 432.
9. McPherson, *Ordeal by Fire*, p. 479.
10. Paddy Griffith, *Battle Tactics of the American Civil War* (Marlborough, Wiltshire: The Crowood Press, 1987), p. 189.
11. CWAL, 4: 332.
12. CWAL, 5: 48–49.
13. Grant to his father, November 1861, quoted in Keegan, *Mask of Command*, p. 231.
14. James M. McPherson, *The Struggle for Equality: Abolitionists and the Negro in the Civil War and Reconstruction* (Princeton, NJ: Princeton University Press, 1964), p. 52; Beecher sermon in David Chesebrough, ed., *"God Ordained This War": Sermons on the Sectional Crisis, 1830–1865* (Columbia, SC: University of South Carolina Press, 1991), p. 84.
15. *Frederick Douglass Monthly*, May 1861.
16. Charles Sumner to Wendell Phillips, August 3, 1861, in Charles Sumner, *The Selected Letters of Charles Sumner*, ed. Beverly Wilson Palmer, 2 vols (Boston: Northeastern University Press, 1990), vol. 2, p. 74.
17. T. Harry Williams, *Lincoln and His Generals* (New York: Knopf, 1952), pp. 45–46.
18. RWAL, 315.
19. Josiah Gorgas, *The Journals of Josiah Gorgas, 1857–1878*, ed. Sarah Woolfolk Wiggins (Tuscaloosa: University of Alabama Press, 1995), pp. 42–43.
20. *Richmond Whig*, June 16, 1862.
21. *New York Times*, March 12, 1862.
22. Senator Charles Sumner reported these remarks in a letter to John A. Andrew, April 27, 1862. RWAL, 434.
23. Benjamin Brown French, *Witness to the Young Republic: A Yankee's Journal, 1828–1870*, ed. Donald B. Cole and John J. McDonough (Hanover, NH: University Press of New England, 1989), p. 388.
24. Sumner, *Selected Letters*, vol. 2, p. 119.
25. John Beauchamp Jones, *A Rebel War Clerk's Diary at the Confederate States Capital*, 2 vols (1866; reprint, Alexandria, VA: Time-Life, 1982), vol. 1, pp. 123–124.

26. Catherine Ann Devereux Edmondston, *"Journal of a Secesh Lady": The Diary of Catherine Ann Devereux Edmondston, 1860–1866*, ed. Beth Gilbert Crabtree and James W. Patton (Raleigh: North Carolina Division of Archives and History, 1979), p. 189.

27. Philip Kearny, *Letters from the Peninsula: The Civil War Letters of General Philip Kearny*, ed. William B. Styple (Kearny, NJ: Belle Grove Publishing, 1988), p. 116.

28. French, *Witness to the Young Republic*, pp. 400–401.

29. Quoted in Bruce Tap, *Over Lincoln's Shoulder: The Committee on the Conduct of the War* (Lawrence: University Press of Kansas, 1998), p. 125.

30. Grace Brown Elmore, *Heritage of Woe: The Civil War Diary of Grace Brown Elmore, 1861–1868*, ed. Marli F. Weiner (Athens: University of Georgia Press, 1997), p. 35.

31. Herman Hattaway and Archer Jones, *How the North Won: A Military History of the Civil War* (Urbana: University of Illinois Press, 1983), pp. 200–201. For similar arguments, see Alan T. Nolan, *Lee Considered: General Robert E. Lee and Civil War History* (Chapel Hill: University of North Carolina Press, 1991); McWhiney and Jamieson, *Attack and Die*.

32. Michael C. C. Adams, *Our Masters the Rebels: A Speculation on Union Military Failure in the East, 1861–1865* (Cambridge, MA: Harvard University Press, 1978), p. 99.

33. Stephen W. Sears, *The Civil War Papers of George B. McClellan: Selected Correspondence* (New York: Da Capo, 1992), p. 477.

34. George B. McClellan to Abraham Lincoln, July 7, 1862, ALP.

35. CWAL, 6: 28–31.

36. Henry M. Turner, quoted in James M. McPherson, *Marching Toward Freedom: Blacks in the Civil War* (New York: Knopf, 1967), p. 21.

37. Ira Berlin *et al.*, *Slaves No More: Three Essays on Emancipation and the Civil War* (Cambridge: Cambridge University Press, 1992), p. 12.

38. Montgomery Blair to Benjamin F. Butler, May 29, 1861, in *Private and Official Correspondence of General Benjamin F. Butler, During the Period of the Civil War*, 2 vols (Norwood, MA: Plimpton Press, 1917), vol. 1, pp. 116–117.

39. General William T. Sherman to General Alexander McDowell McCook, 8 November, 1861, in Brooks D. Simpson and Jean V. Berlin, eds, *Sherman's Civil War: Selected Correspondence of William T. Sherman, 1861–1865* (Chapel Hill: University of North Carolina Press, 1999), p. 246.

40. David W. Blight, ed., *When This Cruel War is Over: The Civil War Letters of Charles Harvey Brewster* (Amherst: University of Massachusetts Press, 1992), pp. 78, 81.

41. Ibid., p. 94.

42. Jennifer Cain Bohrnstedt, ed., *While Father is Away: The Civil War Letters of William H. Bradbury* (Lexington: University Press of Kentucky, 2003), p. 24.

43. Chauncey Herbert Cooke, March 20, 1863, in his *Soldier Boy's Letters to His Father and Mother, 1861–1865* (n.p., 1915), p. 28.

44. Charles Francis Adams to Henry Brooks Adams, April 6, 1862, in Worthington Chauncey Ford, ed., *A Cycle of Adams Letters, 1861–1865* (Boston: Houghton, Mifflin, 1920), pp. 129–130.

45. Blight, *When This Cruel War is Over*, p. 57.
46. Lincoln to Albert G. Hodges, April 4, 1864. CWAL, 7: 281.
47. Quoted in McPherson, *Ordeal by Fire*, p. 519.
48. CWAL, 5: 421.
49. Ibid.: 388.
50. Ibid.: 30.
51. Quoted in Peter N. Carroll and David W. Noble, *The Free and the Unfree: A New History of the United States* (New York: Penguin, 1988), p. 217.
52. Berlin *et al.*, *Slaves No More*.
53. Allen C. Guelzo, *Lincoln's Emancipation Proclamation* (New York: Simon & Schuster, 2004), p. 8.
54. Letter from Frances Ellen Watkins Harper in William Still, ed., *The Underground Rail Road: A Record of Facts, Authentic Narratives, Letters, &c: Narrating the Hardships, Hair-breadth Escapes, and Death Struggles of the Slaves in Their Efforts for Freedom* (Philadelphia: Porter & Coates, 1872), p. 766.
55. Ibid.
56. *Diary of Orville Hickman Browning*, p. 589 [November 28, 1862].
57. CWAL, 5: 422
58. Quoted in Kathleen Burk's forthcoming study of Anglo-American relations.
59. Lord John Russell quoted in Guelzo, *Lincoln's Emancipation Proclamation*, p. 225.
60. Quoted in John M. Taylor, *William Henry Seward: Lincoln's Right Hand Man* (Washington: Brassey's, 1992), p. 204.
61. Quoted in James Ford Rhodes, *History of the Civil War, 1861–1865* (New York: Macmillan, 1917), p. 269.
62. R. J. M. Blackett, *Divided Hearts: Britain and the American Civil War* (Baton Rouge: Louisiana State University Press, 2001).
63. CWAL, 6: 63.
64. General Henry W. Halleck to General Ulysses S. Grant, 31 March 1863, quoted in Stephen E. Ambrose, *Halleck: Lincoln's Chief of Staff* (Baton Rouge: Louisiana State University Press, 1962), p. 119.
65. Mary J. Anderson to James Nesbitt, December 8, 1862, Nesbitt-Raub Papers, US Military History Institute, quoted in Earl J. Hess, *Liberty, Virtue, and Progress: Northerners and Their War for the Union* (New York: New York University Press, 1988), p. 99.
66. CWAL, 6: 409.

4 EMANCIPATION AND HARD WAR, 1862–1864

1. Quoted in Allan Nevins, *The War for the Union* (New York: Scribner, 1959), p. 348.
2. Quoted in Shelby Foote, *The Civil War: A Narrative*, 3 vols (New York: Random House, 1958–1974), *Vol. 2: From Fredericksburg to Meridian*, p. 326
3. *Harper's Weekly*, December 27, 1862, quoted in McPherson, *Ordeal by Fire*, pp. 304–305.

4. Quoted in Shenk, *Lincoln's Melancholy*, p. 186.

5. Mark DeWolfe Howe, ed., *Touched with Fire: Civil War Letters and Diary of Oliver Wendell Holmes, Jr., 1861–1864* (Cambridge, MA: Harvard University Press, 1946), p. 73.

6. There are several alternative interpretations of the origin of the term hooker. One is offered by Edwin Burrows and Mike Wallace in their history of New York City. "The adoption of the term *hooker* as a synonym for prostitute," they write, "may have been inspired by the proliferation of brothels and streetwalkers on the Corlear's Hook waterfront [in New York City]." Edwin G. Burrows and Mike Wallace, *Gotham: A History of New York City to 1898* (New York: Oxford University Press, 1999), p. 804.

7. Quoted in Foote, *Fredericksburg to Meridian*, pp. 233–234.

8. CWAL, 6: 79.

9. Foote, *Fredericksburg to Meridian*, p. 236.

10. Noah Brooks, *Washington in Lincoln's Time* (New York, 1896), pp. 57–58.

11. Jack D. Welsh, *Medical History of Confederate Generals* (Kent, Ohio: Kent State University Press, 1995), p. 113.

12. CWAL, 6: 424.

13. James C. Mohr, *The Cormany Diaries: A Northern Family in the Civil War* (Pittsburgh: University of Pennsylvania Press, 1982), p. 330.

14. William Garret Piston, *Lee's Tarnished Lieutenant: James Longstreet and His Place in Southern History* (Athens, GA: University of Georgia Press, 1987).

15. George Edward Pickett to LaSalle Corbell Pickett, July 3, 1863, in *The Heart of a Soldier: As Revealed in the Intimate Letters of General George Pickett* (New York: Seth Moyle, 1913), pp. 95–96.

16. Ibid.

17. This account of the battle is drawn from McPherson, *Ordeal by Fire*, pp. 324–329.

18. George Edward Pickett to LaSalle Corbell Pickett, July 4, 1863, in *The Heart of a Soldier*, pp. 99–100.

19. William Faulkner, *Intruder in the Dust* (New York: Random House, 1948), p. 194.

20. CWAL, 6: 327–328.

21. Frank Vandiver, ed., *The Civil War Diary of General Josiah Gorgas* (University, AL: Alabama University Press, 1947), p. 55.

22. Jones, *A Rebel War Clerk's Diary*, Vol. II, p. 50.

23. Union officer quoted in Foote, *Fredericksburg to Meridian*, p. 856.

24. Gary Gallagher, *The Confederate War* (Cambridge, MA: Harvard University Press, 1997), pp. 36–44.

25. OR series 1, vol. 44, p. 799.

26. Charles Royster, *The Destructive War: William Tecumshe Sherman, Stonewall Jackson, and the Americans* (New York: Knopf, 1991).

27. Archer Jones, *Civil War Command and Strategy: The Process of Victory and Defeat* (New York: Free Press, 1992), p. 242.

28. Quoted in Joseph T. Glatthaar, *The March to the Sea and Beyond: Sherman's Troops in the Savannah and Carolinas Campaigns* (New York: New York University Press, 1985), pp. 6–7.
29. Glatthaar, *March to the Sea*; Mark Grimsley, *The Hard Hand of War: Union Military Policy Toward Southern Civilians, 1861–1865* (Cambridge: Cambridge University Press, 1995).
30. Grant, *Memoirs*, pp. 164–165.
31. Quoted in Shelby Foote, *The Civil War: A Narrative*, 3 vols (New York: Random House, 1958–1974), *Vol. 3: From Red River to Appomattox*, p. 189.
32. Ibid., p. 190.
33. J. Tracey Power, *Lee's Miserables: Life in the Army of Northern Virginia from the Wilderness to Appomattox* (Chapel Hill: University of North Carolina Press, 1998), p. 288.
34. Blight, *When This Cruel War is Over*, p. 298.
35. Quoted in Foote, *Red River to Appomattox*, p. 294.
36. McPherson, *Ordeal by Fire*, p. 428.
37. McWhiney and Jamieson, *Attack and Die*, p. 191.
38. Mushkat, *A Citizen-Soldier's Civil War*, p. 192.
39. Paddy Griffith, *Battle Tactics of the Civil War* (New Haven: Yale University Press, 1989), p. 132.
40. McPherson, *Ordeal by Fire*, p. 427.
41. Ibid.
42. George Michael Neese, *Three Years in the Confederate Horse Artillery* (New York: Neale Publishing Company, 1911), p. 307.
43. Georgina Gholson Walker, *The Private Journal of Georgina Gholson Walker 1862–1865, with Selections from the Post-War Years, 1865–1876*, ed. Dwight Franklin Henderson (Tuscaloosa, AL: Confederate Publishing Co., 1963), pp. 106–107.
44. Douglas Southall Freeman, *R. E. Lee: A Biography*, 4 vols (New York: Charles Scribner's Sons, 1934–1935); Freeman, *Lee's Lieutenants: A Study in Command*, 3 vols (New York: Charles Scribner's Sons, 1942–1944); Gary Gallagher, "The Army of Northern Virginia in May 1864: A Crisis of High Command," *Civil War History* 36: 2 (June 1990), 101–118.
45. Power, *Lee's Miserables*, p. 298.
46. Quoted in ibid., p. 301.
47. Sherman quoted in McPherson, *Ordeal by Fire*, p. 433.
48. Basil H. Liddell Hart, *Sherman: Soldier, Realist, American* (New York: Dodd, Mead and Co., 1929), p. 371.
49. John A. Stevens, ed., *Sherman vs. Hood* (New York: Loyal Publication Society, pamphlet no. 61, 1864).
50. Quotes from McPherson, *Ordeal by Fire*, p. 460.
51. Mrs Nicholas Ware Eppes, ed., *Through Some Eventful Years: The Civil War Diary of Susan Bradford Eppes* (Macon, GA: J.W. Burke, 1926), pp. 256–257, 270–271.
52. Eliza Francis-Andrews, *The War-Time Journal of a Georgia Girl* (New York: D. Appleton, 1908), pp. 153–155 [entry for April 18, 1865].
53. Quoted in McPherson, *Ordeal by Fire*, p. 462.

5   CITIZEN SOLDIERS

1. Crawford, *Ashe County's Civil War*, pp. 90–91.
2. J. William Harris, *Plain Folk and Gentry in a Slave Society: White Liberty and Black Slavery in Augusta's Hinterlands* (Middletown, CT: Wesleyan University Press, 1985), pp. 152–153.
3. Cunliffe, *Soldiers and Civilians*, p. 11.
4. Williams, *Lincoln and His Generals*, p. 11.
5. Blight, *When This Cruel War is Over*, p. 123.
6. Mushkat, *A Citizen-Soldier's Civil War*, p. 6.
7. Quoted in McPherson, *Marching Toward Freedom*, p. 6.
8. CWAL, 5: 357.
9. McPherson, *Ordeal by Fire*, p. 349.
10. Reid Mitchell, *The Vacant Chair: The Northern Soldier leaves home* (New York: Oxford University Press, 1993), pp. 24–25.
11. James W. Geary, *We Need Men: The Union Draft in the Civil War* (DeKalb, IL: Northern Illinois University Press, 1991).
12. Don H. Doyle, *The Social order of a Frontier Community: Jacksonville, Illinois, 1825–1870* (Urbana: University of Illinois Press, 1983), p. 235; Michael H. Frisch, *Town into City: Springfield, Massachusetts, and the Meaning of Community, 1840–1880* (Cambridge, MA: Harvard University Press, 1972), pp. 59, 65.
13. Emily J. Harris, "Sons and Soldiers: Deerfield, Massachusetts and the Civil War," *Civil War History*, 30 (1984), 166–168.
14. Cyrus G. Pringle, *The Civil War Diary of Cyrus Pringle* (Wallingford, PA: Pendle Hill, 1962).
15. Quoted in Bell I. Wiley, *The Life of Billy Yank* (Indianapolis: Bobbs-Merrill, 1952), p. 344.
16. William C. Davis, *The Cause Lost: Myths and Realities of the Confederacy* (Lawrence: University Press of Kansas, 1996), p. 114.
17. Quoted in Crawford, *Ashe County's Civil War*, p. 95.
18. Emil Rosenblat, ed., *Anti-Rebel: The Civil War Letters of Wilbur Fisk* (Privately printed: Croton-on-Hudson, New York, 1983), p. 102.
19. Armstrong Halleck to Mary Armstrong, May 2, 1865, in Mary M. Bronson Armstrong, ed., *Letters from a Pennsylvania Chaplain at the Siege of Petersburg, 1865* (Privately published: Boston, 1961), p. 33.
20. George R. Agassiz, ed., *Meade's Headquaters, 1863–1865, Letters of Colonel Theodore Lyman* (Boston: Massachusetts Historical Society, 1922), quoted in McPherson, *Ordeal by Fire*, p. 420.
21. Welsh, *Medical History of Confederate Generals*, pp. 63–65; *The Making of a Soldier: Letters of General R. S. Ewell*, pp. 127–130, 137–38; Maurice Shaw, *Stonewall Jackson's Surgeon: Hunter Holmes McGuire* (Lynchburg: H. E. Howard, 1993).
22. Alfred Lewis Castleman, *The Army of the Potomac, Behind the Scenes: A Diary of Unwritten History: From the Organisation of the Army to the Close of the Campaign in Virginia, About the First Day of January, 1863* (Milwaukee, WI: Strickland & Co., 1863), p. 125.

23. Chauncey Herbert Cooke, March 20, 1863, in his *Soldier Boy's Letters to His Father and Mother, 1861–1865* (n.p., 1915), p. 28.
24. Quoted in James M. McPherson, *For Cause and Comrades: Why Men Fought in the Civil War* (New York: Oxford University Press, 1997), p. 169.
25. Quotes from ibid., pp. 169–170.
26. Quoted in Mitchell, *Vacant Chair*, pp. 10–11.
27. Mitchell, *Vacant Chair*, p. 7.
28. Quoted in ibid., p. 15.
29. Mushkat, *A Citizen-Soldier's Civil War*, p. 189.
30. Ibid., p. 65.
31. Blight, *When This Cruel War is Over*, p. 300.
32. Quoted in Gallagher, *Confederate War*, p. 52.
33. Gardiner H. Shattuck, *A Shield and a Hiding Place: The Religious Life of the Civil War Armies* (Macon, GA: Mercer University Press, 1987), p. 96.
34. Gustave Cooke to Eliza Cooke, September 16, 1864, GLC 02570.61.
35. Quoted in McPherson, *For Cause and Comrades*, p. 170.
36. Quoted in E. Lawrence Abel, *Singing the New Nation: How Music Shaped the Confederacy, 1861–1865* (Mechanicsburg, PA: Stackpole Books, 2000), p. 3.
37. Blight, *When This Cruel War is Over*, p. 308.
38. Quoted in Mitchell, *Vacant Chair*, p. 12.
39. Fragment of a hand-written speech by an unknown Union Officer, Gilder Lehrman Collection (GLC 03738).
40. Mitchell, *Vacant Chair*, p. 35.
41. Rosenblat, *Anti-Rebel*, p. 7.
42. Blight, *When This Cruel War is Over*, pp. 123, 293, 190, 217.
43. F. M. Sparks to Richard Yates, April 21, 1863, Yates Family Papers, Illinois State historical Library, Springfield.
44. George C. Lawson to wife, April 29, 1864. George C. Lawson Papers in Robert Shaw Collection, Atlanta Historical Society, quoted in Mitchell, *Vacant Chair*, p. 12.
45. Blight, *When This Cruel War is Over*, p. 199.
46. Quoted in McPherson, *For Cause and Comrades*, p. 173.
47. Ibid.
48. Rosenblat, *Anti-Rebel*, p. 7.
49. Burage Rice Diary, October 9, 1861, New York Historical Society, quoted in Mitchell, *Vacant Chair*, p. 14.
50. Quoted in Mitchell, *Vacant Chair*, p. 14.
51. Joseph Allen Frank, *With Ballot and Bayonet: The Political Socialization of Civil War Soldiers* (Athens: University of Georgia Press, 1998), p. 93.
52. Charles Pearce to Father, 15 March 1863, GLC 0066.115.
53. Leander Stillwell, *The Story of a Common Soldier of Army Life in the Civil War, 1861–1865* (Erie, Kansas: Franklin Hudson Publishing Co., 1920), pp. 229–230.
54. Private Edwin C. Hall of Brookfield. Vermont, Company G, 10th Vermont Infantry, to his father, March 26, 1865. *A War of the People*, p. 296.
55. William C. Davis, *Lincoln's Men: How President Lincoln became Father to an Army and a Nation* (New York: Free Press, 1999), p. 130.
56. Richard J. Carwardine, *Lincoln: A Life of Purpose and Power* (New York: Knopf, 2006), p. 275.

6 THE ORDEAL OF THE CONFEDERATE REPUBLIC

1. Quoted in Anne Sarah Rubin, *A Shattered Nation: The Rise and Fall of the Confederacy, 1861–1868* (Chapel Hill: University of North Carolina Press, 2005), p. 32.
2. Daniel Ruggles to Benjamin F. Butler, July 15, 1862 in *Private and Official Correspondence of Gen. Benjamin F. Butler, During the Period of the Civil War*, 2 vols (Springfield, MA: Plimpton Press, 1917), vol. 1, p. 67.
3. De Bow and Rhett quoted in Wilentz, *Rise of American Democracy*, p. 773.
4. Rable, *Confederate Republic*, p. 4.
5. Quoted in Rubin, *A Shattered Nation*, p. 17.
6. Harry S. Stout, *Upon the Altar of the Nation: A Moral History of the Civil War* (New York: Penguin, 2006), p. 199.
7. Rable, *Confederate Republic*, makes this argument most clearly.
8. Quoted in Rubin, *A Shattered Nation*, p. 17.
9. Marshall L. DeRosa, *The Confederate Constitution of 1861: An Inquiry into American Constitutionalism* (Columbia, MO: University of Missouri Press, 1991).
10. Don E. Fehrenbacher, *Constitutions and Constitutionalism in the Slaveholding South* (Athens: University of Georgia Press, 1989), pp. 59–81; William C. Davis, *"A Government of Our Own": The Making of the Confederacy* (New York: Free Press, 1994).
11. Rubin, *A Shattered Nation*, pp. 21–22.
12. Dunbar Rowland, ed., *Jefferson Davis, Constitutionalist: His Letters, Papers and Speeches*, (Jackson, MS: Mississippi Department of Archives and History, 1923), vol. 5, p. 462.
13. Charles East, ed., *Sarah Morgan: The Civil War Diary of a Southern Woman* (New York: Simon and Schuster, 1991), p. 411 [entry for 23 January 1863].
14. Lee to Davis, 8 August 1863, *OR*, ser I, vol. 51, pt. 3, p. 752.
15. William C. Davis, *Jefferson Davis: The Man and His Hour* (New York: HarperCollins, 1991).
16. Thomas B. Alexander and Richard E. Beringer, *The Anatomy of the Confederate Congress* (Nashville: Vanderbilt University Press, 1972), pp. 43–46; Rable, *Confederate Republic*, pp. 88–110.
17. Douglas B. Ball, *Financial Failure and Confederate Defeat* (Urbana: Illinois University Press, 1991).
18. This is an argument made in a classic work of Confederate history: Charles W. Ramsdell, *Behind the Lines in the Southern Confederacy* (Baton Rouge: Louisiana State University Press, 1944).
19. Hans Nathan, *Dan Emmett and the Rise of Early Negro Minstrelsy* (Norman: University of Oklahoma Press, 1962).
20. Walker, *The Private Journal of Georgina Gholson Walker*, pp. 73–74, quoted in Gallagher, *Confederate War*, pp. 76–77.
21. Daniel Pope to his wife, March 12, 1864, in Mills Lane, ed., *"Dear Mother: Don't grieve about me. If I get killed I'll only be dead": Letters from Georgia Soldiers in the Civil War* (Savannah, GA: Beehive Press, 1977), pp. 282–83, quoted in Gallagher, *Confederate War*, p. 8.

22. Bell Irvin Wiley, ed., *Fourteen Hundred and 91 Days in the Confederate Army: A Journal Kept by W. W. Heartsill, For Four Years, One Month, and One Day, or, Camp Life: Day-by-Day, of the W. P. Lane Rangers, from April 19th 1861, to May 20th 1865.*

23. Crawford, *Ashe County's Civil War*, p. 78.

24. Eppes, *Through Some Eventful Years: The Civil War Diary of Susan Bradford Eppes* (Macon, GA: J. W. Burke, 1926), p. 158. Diary entry for August 12, 1861.

25. Entry for March 2, 1861, *A Diary from Dixie.*

26. Quoted in Rable, *Confederate Republic*, p. 75.

27. Robert E. Bonner, "Flag Culture and the Consolidation of Confederate Nationalism," *Journal of Southern History*, 68 (2002), 293–332.

28. Daniel W. Stowell, *Rebuilding Zion: The Religious Reconstruction of the South, 1863–1877* (New York: Oxford University Press, 1998), p. 4.

29. Lancelot Blackford, quoted in Rubin, *Shattered Nation*, p. 83.

30. Mark A. Weitz, *More Damning Than Slaughter: Desertion in the Confederate Army* (Lincoln: University of Nebraska Press, 2005).

31. Quoted by Rubin, *Shattered Nation*, p. 65.

32. Mary Chesnut, *Mary Chesnut's Civil War*, ed. C. Vann Woodward, (New Haven: Yale University Press, 1981), pp. 577–578 [entry for 3 March 1864.]

33. E. S. Miers, ed., *A Rebel War Clerk's Diary* (New York: Sagamore Press, 1958), 316.

34. Edward Younger, ed., *Inside the Confederate Government: The Diary of Robert Garlick Hill Kean, Head of the Bureau of War* (New York: Oxford University Press, 1957), p. 108 [entry for 4 October, 1863].

35. George C. Rable, *Civil Wars: Women and the Crisis of Southern Nationalism* (Urbana: University of Illinois Press, 1989), pp. 108–110.

36. Peter J. Parish, *The American Civil War* (New York: Holmes and Meier, 1975), p. 305.

37. Isaac Read, quoted in Rubin, *Shattered Nation*, p. 67.

38. Thomas H. Watts to James A. Seddon, 19 January 1864, US War Department, *The War of the Rebellion: Compilation of Official Records of the Union and Confederate Armies*, 130 vols (Washington, DC: Government Printing Office, 1880–1901), ser. 4, vol. 3, p. 37.

39. Quoted in Crawford, *Ashe County's Civil War*, p. 107.

40. Ibid., p. 88.

41. Crawford, *Ashe County's Civil War*, p. 121.

42. Ibid.

43. Quoted in Davis, *The Cause Lost*, p. 115.

44. Quoted in Allen C. Guelzo, *The Crisis of the American Republic: A History of the Civil War and Reconstruction* (New York: St Martin's Press, 1995), p. 285.

45. Rable, *Confederate Republic*, especially pp. 174–194; Marc W. Kruman, *Parties and Politics in North Carolina, 1836–1865* (Baton Rouge: Louisiana State University Press, 1983), pp. 242–245.

46. *Official Correspondence of Governor Joseph E. Brown, 1860–1865* (Atlanta, GA: Byrd State Printer, 1910), p. 568.

47. Wayne K. Durrill, *War of Another Kind: A Southern Community in the Great Rebellion* (New York: Oxford University Press, 1992); James Marten, *Texas Divided: Loyalty and Dissent in the Lone Star State, 1856–1874* (Lexington: University Press of Kentucky, 1990); Phillip Shaw Paludan, *Victims: A True Story of the Civil War* (Knoxville: University of Tennessee Press, 1981).
48. Davis, *The Cause Lost*, p. 120.
49. Zebulon Vance to James A. Seddon, January 5, 1863, in US War Department, *The War of the Rebellion: Compilation of Official Records of the Union and Confederate Armies*, 130 vols (Washington, DC: Government Printing Office, 1880–1901) ser. 1, vol. 18, pp. 821–822, quoted in Crawford, *Ashe County's Civil War*, p. 108.
50. Power, *Lee's Miserables*, p. 302.
51. Quoted in ibid., p. 309.
52. Weitz, *More Damning Than Slaughter*; Lee quoted in Ella Lonn, *Desertion During the Civil War* (New York: Century, 1929), p. 28.
53. Rubin, *Shattered Nation*, p. 50.
54. *Diary of John B. Jones*, II: 236.
55. *The Journal of a Milledgville Girl, 1861–1867*, ed. James C. Bonner (Athens: University of Georgia Press, 1864), p. 63 [entry for November 25, 1864], quoted in Gallagher, *Confederate War*, p. 6.
56. Edmondston, *Journal of a Secesh Lady*, p. 576.
57. Quoted in Rubin, *A Shattered Nation*, p. 18.
58. Speech of Alexander H. Stephens, Kenneth M. Stampp, ed., *The Causes of the Civil War* (New York: 1991 edn), p. 153.
59. Richard L. Troutman, ed., *The Heavens are Weeping: The Diaries of George Richard Browder, 1852–1886* (Grand Rapids, Michigan: Zondervan Publishing House, 1987), p. 194 [Diary entry for January 1, 1865].
60. Quoted in Leon F. Litwack, *Been in the Storm So Long: The Aftermath of Slavery* (New York: Knopf, 1979), p. 144.
61. Peter Kolchin, *American Slavery* (New York: Hill and Wang, 2003), p. 203.
62. Eugene Genovese, *Roll Jordan Roll: The World the Slaves Made* (New York: Pantheon, 1974), pp. 97–100, 106.
63. Unknown woman to Governor Zebulon B. Vance, December 11, 1864, in Watford, ed., *The Civil War in North Carolina*, p. 186. See John Hutchinson, *No Ordinary Lives: A History of Richmond County, N.C., 1750–1900* (Virginia Beach, VA: Dunning Publishing Co., 1998).
64. Howell Purdue and Elizabeth Purdue, *Pat Cleburne, Confederate General: A Definitive Biography* (Hillsboro, TX: Hill College Press, 1973), p. 267.
65. Quotes from McPherson, *For Cause and Comrades*, pp. 170–171.
66. Quotes from Richard E. Berringer, Herman Hattaway, Archer Jones and William N. Still, *Why the South Lost the Civil War* (Athens: Georgia State University Press, 1986), pp. 384–385.
67. Rable, *Confederate Republic*, pp. 287–296; Ervin L. Jordan, *Black Confederates and Afro-Yankees in Civil War Virginia* (Charlottesville: University of Virginia Press, 1995); James L. Roak, *Masters Without Slaves: Southern Planters in the Civil War and Reconstruction* (New York: Norton, 1977), pp. 52–54.

68. William Allan, "Memoranda of Conversations with General Robert E. Lee," in Gary Gallagher, ed., *Lee the Soldier* (Lincoln: University of Nebraska Press, 1996), p. 12.
69. Bruce Levine, *Confederate Emancipation: Southern Plans to Free and Arm Slaves During the Civil War* (New York: Oxford University Press, 2006), p. 154.
70. Gallagher, *Confederate War*, p. 57.

7   THE LAST BEST HOPE OF EARTH: THE WAR FOR THE UNION

1. Mushkat, *A Citizen-Soldier's Civil War*, p. 193.
2. Ibid., p. 231.
3. CWAL, 4: 268.
4. Ibid.: 438
5. *Cincinatti Daily Commercial*, May 6, 1861, in *Northern Editorials on Secession*, ed. Howard Cecil Perkins, 2 vols. (New York: D. Appleton, 1942), vol. 2, pp. 826–827.
6. Chesebrough, *God Ordained This War*, pp. 84–85.
7. Ernest A. McKay, *Civil War and New York City* (Syracuse: Syracuse University Press, 1990), pp. 78–79.
8. Russell quoted in Sven Beckert, *Monied Metropolis: New York City and the Consolidation of the American Bourgeoisie* (Cambridge University Press, 2001), p. 116.
9. Grant, *Memoirs*, p. 153.
10. Mushkat, *A Citizen-Soldier's Civil War*, pp. 19–20.
11. Jeanie Attie, *Patriotic Toil: Northern Women in the American Civil War* (Ithaca, NY: Cornell University Press, 1998), p. 139.
12. Elizabeth Livermore Diaries, New Hampshire Historical Society, entries for March 11, 1862, November 1, 1864, November 7, 1864, November 8, 1864, November 9, 1864.
13. James G. Blaine, *Twenty Years in Congress: From Lincoln to Garfield, With a Review of the Events Which Led to the Political Revolution of 1860*, 2 vols. (Norwich, CT,: Henry Bill, 1884), vol. 1, p. 433.
14. *The New-York Times*, July 7, 1861.
15. "The true Jersey blue," by T. T. Price, M.D. (n.p., [1861]), Civil War Song Sheets, ser. 1, vol. 3, Rare Book and Special Collections Division, Library of Congress; "The Sword and the Red, White and Blue" (New York: H. De Marsan, 1861), American Songs and Ballads, ser. 4, vol. 4, Library of Congress.
16. *Cincinnati Daily Enquirer*, October 11, 1861; Lancaster (Pa.) *Daily Evening Express*, January 17, 1861, in Perkins, ed., *Northern Editorials on Secession*, vol. 2, pp. 1046–1047.
17. Kenneth M. Stampp, *Indiana Politics During the Civil War* (Indianapolis: Indiana Historical Bureau, 1949).
18. Quoted in Wood Gray, *The Hidden Civil War: The Story of the Copperheads in the Middle West* (New York: Viking 1942), p. 115.

19. McPherson, *Ordeal by Fire*, p. 345.
20. *A Rebel War Clerk's Diary*, I: 253.
21. Congressman Richardson (Illinois), speech to the US House of Representatives, *Congressional Globe*, 37 Congress, 2nd Session, p. 2207, quoted in V. Jaques Voegeli, *Free but Not Equal: The Midwest and the Negro during the Civil War* (Chicago: University of Chicago Press, 1967), p. 15.
22. *New York World*, October 23, 1862.
23. Quoted in John Niven, *Salmon P. Chase: A Biography* (New York: Oxford University Press, 1995), p. 345.
24. *Chicago Times*, November 11, 1863, quoted in Silbey, *A Respectable Minority*, p. 75.
25. James Maitland to Joseph Maitland, July 31, 1863, GLC: 323.10 no. 87.
26. James Maitland to Joseph Maitland, May 21, 1863, GLC: 3523.10.
27. Lincoln to Albert G. Hodges, April 4, 1864. CWAL, 7: 281.
28. Frank L. Klement, *The Limits of Dissent: Clement L. Vallandigham and the Civil War* (Lexington, KY: University Press of Kentucky, 1970), pp. 62–63.
29. McPherson, *Ordeal by Fire*, p. 344.
30. Allan Thurman to the Ohio Democratic State convention in 1862, quoted in William F. Zornow, *Lincoln and the Party Divided* (Norman, Oklahoma, 1954), p. 160.
31. *Congressional Globe*, 38th Cong., 1st Sess., January 19, 1864, p. 245. For a discussion of the test oath issue in the senate see Hyman, *Era of the Oath*, pp. 25–32.
32. "Yeaman vs McHenry," *Congressional Serial Set* 1200: 28th Cong, 1st Sess. (1863): House of Representatives Misc. Doc. 36, 15.
33. Troutman, *The Heavens are Weeping*, p. 153 [Diary entry for May 17, 1863].
34. Karl Marx and Freidrich Engels, *The Civil War in the United States*, ed. Richard Enmale (New York: International Publishers, 1937), p. 281.
35. Francis Lieber, *No Party Now But All for Our Country* (New York: Loyal Publication Society, 1863), p. 3.
36. Quoted in George Parsons Lathrop, *History of the Union League of Philadelphia, From its Origin and Foundation to the Year 1882* (Philadelphia: Union League of Philadelphia, 1884), p. 42.
37. Henry Bellows, *Unconditional Loyalty* (New York: A. D. L. Randolph, 1863), p. 6.
38. Thomas Wentworth Higginson, ed., *Harvard Memorial Biographies*, 2 vols (Cambridge, MA: Harvard University Press, 1867), vol. 1, p. v.
39. *Detroit Free Press*, January 8, 1864.
40. CWAL, 7: 21.
41. CWAL, 8: 151.
42. Michael Fellman, "Lincoln and Sherman," in Gabor S. Bortt, ed., *Lincoln's Generals* (New York: Oxford University Press, 1994).
43. Whitelaw Reid to Anna E. Dickinson, April 3, 1864, Anna E. Dickinson Papers, Manuscripts Division, Library of Congress.
44. "Wade-Davis Manifesto," in Harold Hyman, ed., *Radical Republicans and Reconstruction* (Indianapolis: Bobbs-Merrill, 1967), pp. 137–147.
45. CWAL, 7: 243.

46. Greeley to Lincoln, July 7, 1864, ALP; CWAL, 8: 451.
47. Raymond to Lincoln, August 8, 1864, ALP.
48. "Interview with Alexander W. Randall and Joseph T. Mills," August 17, 1864. CWAL, 7: 507.
49. *Worcester Palladium* [date unknown], quoted in *The Campaign for the Union*, November 3, 1864.
50. William Swinton, *The War for the Union: The first, second, third and fourth years of the war* (New York: Loyal Publication Society, 1864), p. 13.
51. Joseph Holt, *Report of the Judge Advocate General on the 'Order of American Knights' or 'Sons of Liberty.' A Western conspiracy in aid of the Southern rebellion* (Washington: Government Printing Office, 1864).
52. M. A. Croft to Simon Cameron, August 31, 1864, Cameron Papers, Library of Congress; *New York Times*, June 18, 1864; *Cincinnati Daily Enquirer*, July 28, 1864; *Chicago Tribune*, September 2, 1864.
53. *Country Before Party: The Voice of the Loyal Democrats* (New York: War Democratic State Committee, 1864).
54. Anon., *The "Only Alternative": A Tract for the Times by a Plain Man* (Philadelphia, 1864).
55. Rev. Roswell D. Hitchcock, *Thanksgiving for Victories: A Discourse* (New York: William E. Whiting, 1864).
56. George R. Crooks, *The Life of Bishop Matthew Simpson of the Methodist Episcopal Church* (New York: Harper, 1891), p. 382.
57. *Chicago Tribune*, September 28, 1864.
58. Michael Vorenberg, *Final Freedom: The Civil War, the Abolition of Slavery and the Thirteenth Amendment* (New York: Cambridge University Press, 2001), pp. 141–176.
59. John Murray Forbes, *Letters and Recollections of John Murray Forbes*, ed. Sarah Forbes Hughes, 2 vols (Boston: Houghton, Mifflin and Co., 1899).
60. Henry C. Bowen to Abraham Lincoln, November 10, 1864, ALP.

8   THE MAGIC WORD, "FREEDOM"

1. Quoted in McPherson, *Ordeal by Fire*, p. 474.
2. Captain Arthur p. Morey of Norwich, Vermont, Company F, 22nd US Colored Troops, to his cousin, April 4, 1865. *A War of the People*, p. 297.
3. R. J. M. Blackett, ed., *Thomas Morris Chester: Black Civil War Correspondent, His Dispatches from the Virginia Front* (New York: Da Capo Press, 1991), p. 297.
4. Grant, *Memoirs*, p. 455.
5. Jefferson Davis to Robert E. Lee, April 9, 1865, in *Jefferson Davis: Private Letters, 1823–1889*, ed. Hudson Strode (New York: Harcourt Brace, 1966), p. 151.
6. Grant, *Memoirs*, p. 460.
7. Francis-Andrews, *War-Time Journal*, pp. 153–155 [entry for April 18, 1865].

8. Eppes, *Through Some Eventful Years: The Civil War Diary of Susan Bradford Eppes* (Macon, GA: J. W. Burke, 1926), p. 270 [entry for April 10, 1865].
9. Francis-Andrews, *War-Time Journal*, pp. 219–220.
10. Letter from Anonymous Confederate Solder (Jim to sister Lizzy), April 13, 1865 in Spencer Glasgow Welch, *A Confederate Surgeon's Letters to His Wife* (District of Columbia: Neale Publishing Company, 1911), p. 121.
11. Judith White Brockenbrough McGuire, *Diary of a Southern Refugee, During the War* (Richmond, VA: J. W. Randolph & English, 1889), p. 347.
12. Clifford Dowdey and Louis H. Manarin, eds, *The Wartime Papers of R. E. Lee* (Boston: Little, Brown, 1961), pp. 934–935.
13. Geoffrey C. Ward, *The Civil War: An Illustrated History* (New York: Knopf, 1990), p. 272.
14. Paul W. Gates, *Agriculture and the Civil War* (New York: Knopf, 1965).
15. Charles S. Wainwright, *A Diary of Battle: The Personal Journals of Colonel Charles S. Wainwright, 1861–1865*, ed. Allan Nevins (New York: Harcourt, Brace & World, 1962), pp. 520–521.
16. Quoted in Hattaway and Jones, *How the North Won*, p. 18.
17. Gary Gallagher, " 'Upon Their Success Hang Momentous Interests': Generals," in Gabor S. Boritt, ed., *Why the Confederacy Lost* (New York: Oxford University Press, 1992), p. 104.
18. Jefferson Davis, *The Rise and Fall of Confederate Government*, 2 vols (New York: Appleton, 1881), vol. 1, p. 518.
19. Eric McKitrick, "Party Politics and the Union and Confederate War Efforts," in William Nisbet Chambers and Walter Dean Burnham, eds, *The American Party Systems: Stages of Political Development* (New York: Oxford University Press, 1967), pp. 117–151.
20. Drew Gilpin Faust, *Mothers of Invention: Women of the Slaveholding South in the American Civil War* (Chapel Hill: University of North Carolina Press, 1996).
21. Irene Bell, Annie Samuels, and others to James A. Seddon, December 2, 1864, quoted in Gallagher, *Confederate War*, p. 77.
22. Mushkat, *A Citizen-Soldier's Civil War*, p. 180.
23. Francis-Andrews, *War-Time Journal*, p. 13 [entry for April 18, 1865].
24. Berringer, Hattaway, Jones and Still, *Why the South Lost the Civil War*, pp. 439–440, 425–426.
25. Charles G. Sellers, "The Travail of Slavery," in Sellers, ed., *The Southerner as American* (Chapel Hill: University of North Carolina Press, 1960), p. 40.
26. Troutman, *The Heavens are Weeping*, p. 179 [Diary entry for June 8, 1864].
27. Bell I. Wiley, *The Road to Appomattox* (Memphis: Memphis State College Press, 1956), pp. 104–105.
28. Kenneth M. Stampp, "The Southern Road to Appomattox," in Kenneth M. Stampp, ed., *The Imperiled Union: Essays on the Background of the Civil War* (New York: Oxford University Press, 1980), pp. 260, 264–267.
29. Lee to his wife, April 19, 1863, in Dowdy and Manarin, eds, *Wartime Papers*, p. 438.
30. Hattaway and Jones, *How the North Won*, p. 692.
31. Mushkat, *A Citizen-Soldier's Civil War*, p. 188.

32. "Reconstruction", *Atlantic Monthly*, April 1865, p. 544.
33. Ibid.
34. CWAL, 8: 333.
35. Ibid.: 332–333.
36. Sarah E. Andrews to James A. Andrews, April 16, 1865, in Sarah Andrews, *Postmarked Hudson: The Letters of Sarah Andrews to Her Brother, James A. Andrews, 1864–1865. With a Geneology of the Andrews Family*, ed. Harry Willis Miller (Hudson WI: Star-Observer Printer, 1955), p. 54.
37. Ann Eliza Smith of St Albans to her husband, Governor J. Gregory Smith, April 1, 1865, Smith Family Papers, University of Vermont, *A War of the People*, p. 301.
38. Catherine E. Parker of Burlington to her family, April 27, 1865, in Jeffrey D. Marshall, ed., *A War of the People: Vermont Civil War Letters* (Hanover, NH: University Press of New England, 1999), p. 305.
39. Mushkat, *A Citizen-Soldier's Civil War*, p. 265.
40. *The Radical Republicans and Reconstruction, 1861–1870*, ed. Harold Hyman (Indianapolis: University of Indiana Press, 1967), pp. 480, 483.
41. David W. Blight, *Race and Reunion: The Civil War in American Memory* (Cambridge, MA: Harvard University Press, 2001), p. 384; Jim Weeks, *Gettysburg: Memory, Market and an American Shrine* (Princetin, NJ: Princeton University Press, 2003).
42. Quoted in Hess, *Liberty, Virtue and Progress*, p. 29.
43. Edward L. Ayers, "Worrying about the Civil War," in Karen Halttunen and Lewis Perry, eds, *Moral Problems in American Life: New Perspectives on Cultural History* (Ithaca, NY: Cornell University Press, 1998).

Guide to Further Reading

GENERAL HISTORIES AND HISTORIOGRAPHIES OF THE CIVIL WAR ERA

The two outstanding one-volume histories of the war years (both considerably longer than the present study) are Peter J. Parish, *The American Civil War* (New York: Holmes and Meier, 1975) and James M. McPherson, *Battle Cry of Freedom: The American Civil War Era* (New York: Oxford University Press, 1988). Two multivolume epics are essential reading for the serious Civil War scholar: Shelby Foote's, *The Civil War* (3 vols, 1958–1974), the ultimate battlefield narrative; and Allan Nevins's *Ordeal of the Union* (4 vols, New York: Scribner, 1959–1971). A useful collection of historiographical essays is James M. McPherson and William J. Cooper, eds, *Writing the Civil War: The Quest to Understand* (Columbia, SC: University of South Carolina Press, 1998). Still the most readable account of the turbulent years between the Mexican war and secession is David Potter's *The Impending Crisis, 1848–1861* (New York: Harper & Row, 1976). See also Bruce Levine, *Half Slave and Half Free: The Roots of the Civil War* (New York: Hill & Wang, 1992). To date there is no full-length study which compares the Civil War to other nationalist movements in the mid-nineteenth century, but Chapter 3 of Thomas Bender's *A Nation Among Nations: America's Place in World History* (New York: Hill & Wang, 2006) charts the way for such a book.

SLAVERY AND THE ANTEBELLUM SOUTH

In a series of groundbreaking books, David Brion Davis has analyzed the complex relationship between slavery and the ideologies of the Enlightenment and post-Enlightenment Atlantic world. See especially Davis, *The Problem of Slavery in the Age of Revolution, 1770–1823* (New York: Oxford University Press, 1998). On the interrelationship between slavery and the evolution of democracy, see Edmund Morgan, *American Slavery, American Freedom: The Ordeal of Colonial Virginia* (New York: W. W. Norton, 1975); and Sean Wilentz, *The Rise of American Democracy: Jefferson to Lincoln* (New York: W. W. Norton, 2005). The issue of the relationship between southern slavery and market capitalism has provoked heated debate, best sampled in Thomas Bender, ed., *The Antislavery Debate: Capitalism and Abolitionism as a Problem in Historical Interpretation* (Berkeley: University of California Press, 1992).

249

There has also been much debate over the related issue of the nature of the political culture created by slaveholders. The major landmarks in the discussion are Eugene Genovese, *The Political Economy of Slavery: Studies in the Economy and Society of the Slave South* (New York: Pantheon, 1965); Bertram Wyatt-Brown, *Southern Honor: Ethics and Behavior in the Old South* (Baton Rouge: Louisiana State University Press, 1982); Kenneth S. Greenberg, *Masters and Statesmen: The Political Culture of American Slavery* (Baltimore: Johns Hopkins University Press, 1985); Robert E. Shalhope, "Race, Class, Slavery and the Antebellum Southern Mind," *Journal of Southern History* 37:4 (1971), 557–574; and James Oakes, *The Ruling Race: A History of American Slaveholders* (New York: Knopf, 1982).

For an overview of southern antebellum politics, see William W. Freehling, *The Road to Disunion: vol. 1, Secessionists at Bay* (New York: Oxford University Press, 1990); and William J. Cooper, *Liberty and Slavery: Southern Politics to 1860* (New York: Knopf, 1982). The best state studies are William A. Link, *Roots of Secession: Slavery and Politics in Antebellum Virginia* (Chapel Hill: University of North Carolina Press, 2003); Marc W. Kruman, *Parties and politics in North Carolina 1836–1865* (Baton Rouge: Louisiana State University Press, 1983); J. Mills Thornton III, *Politics and Power in a Slave Society: Alabama, 1800–1860* (Baton Rouge: Louisiana University Press, 1978); and Lacy K. Ford, Jr., *Origins of Southern Radicalism: The South Carolina Upcountry, 1800–1860* (New York: Oxford University Press, 1988). On the idea of southern separatism, see John McCardell, *The Idea of a Southern Nation: Southern Nationalists and Southern Nationalism, 1830–1860* (New York: W. W. Norton, 1979). Critical insights into the strains in antebellum southern society are provided in David Brown, *Southern Outcast: Hinton Rowan Helper and the Impending Crisis of the South* (Baton Rouge: Louisiana State University Press, 2006).

For the best way into the fraught and fascinating debate about the nature of the American "martial tradition" and whether the South was more habituated to violence than the North, see R. Don Higginbotham, "The Martial Spirit in the Antebellum South: Further Speculations in a National Context," *Journal of Southern History* 58:1 (1992), 3–26. The debate about whether the South had become a distinctively different society and had in some sense departed from the American mainstream is at least implicit in many of the works cited so far but is explicit in James M. McPherson, "Antebellum Southern Exceptionalism: A new look at an old question," *Civil War History* 50:4 (2004), 418–433; and Edward Pessen, "How different from each other were the antebellum North and South?" *American Historical Review* 85:5 (1980), 1119–1149.

THE POLITICAL CRISIS OF THE 1850s

The principal focus of debate over the causes of the war concerns the nature and timing of the political crisis of the 1850s. Eric Foner's *Free Soil, Free Labor, Free Men: The Ideology of the Republican Party Before the Civil War*

(New York: Oxford University Press, 1970) is the reference point around which much subsequent scholarship has focused. Foner argued that its commitment to free labor distinguished northern society from the South, and that the unique ability of the new Republican Party to embody this sectional ideology explains that party's sudden emergence. Other historians, notably Michael Holt in *The Political Crisis of the 1850s* (New York: Wiley, 1978), have argued that the ideological conflict over slavery was only one of many factors acting to disrupt the Second Party System. William E. Gienapp's *The Origins of the Republican Party, 1852–1856* (New York: Oxford University Press, 1987), broadly agrees with Holt's analysis on many points but also develops the idea that what mobilized Republican voters was not slavery *per se* but the threat that the "Slave Power" appeared to pose to northern white liberty and republican institutions. A longer perspective on northern anxiety about the political consequences of slavery is provided by Leonard L. Richards, *The Slave Power: The Free North and Southern Domination* (Baton Rouge: Louisiana State University Press, 2000). Susan-Mary Grant explores the emergence of a distinctively sectional version of American nationalism in the North in *North over South: Northern Nationalism and American Identity in the Antebellum Era* (Lawrence: University Press of Kansas, 2001).

Important state studies of the rise of the Republican party include Dale E. Baum, *The Civil War Party System: The Case of Massachusetts* (Chapel Hill: University of North Carolina Press, 1984); Stephen L. Hansen, *The Making of the Third Party System: Voters and Parties in Illinois, 1850–1876* (1980); and Robert Cook, *Baptism of Fire: The Republican Party in Iowa, 1838–1878* (Ames: Iowa State University Press, 1994), which deftly blends a Foner-esque study of ideology with a sensitive account of the rapidly changing political context. On Nativism, see Tyler Anbinder, *Nativism and Slavery: Northern Know Nothings and the politics of the 1850s* (New York: Oxford University Press, 1992), and Mark Voss-Hubbard, *Beyond Party: Cultures of Antipartisanship before the Civil War* (Baltimore: Johns Hopkins University Press, 2002). The standard biography of Stephen A. Douglas is Robert W. Johannsen, *Stephen A. Douglas* (New York: Oxford University Press, 1973). For a less sympathetic perspective, see Graham A. Peck's perceptive article, "Was Stephen A. Douglas Antislavery?" in the *Journal of the Abraham Lincoln Association* 26 (2005), 1–21.

The role of religion in antebellum American politics is best approached through Richard J. Carwardine's *Evangelicals and Politics in Antebellum America* (New Haven: Yale University Press, 1993). Many insights into the complexities of antislavery politics can be gleaned from David H. Donald's *Charles Sumner and the Coming of the Civil War* (New York: Knopf, 1974). To understand why the slavery extension issue became so intractable, see Michael A. Morrison, *Slavery and the American West: The Eclipse of Manifest Destiny and the Coming of the Civil War* (Chapel Hill: University of North Carolina Press, 1997). On the fight over the extension of slavery into Kansas, see Nicole Etcheson, *Bleeding Kansas: Contested Liberty in the Civil War Era* (Lawrence: University Press of Kansas, 2004). On Lincoln's perception of the emerging crisis in the 1850s, see Don E. Fehrenbacher, *Prelude to Greatness: Lincoln in the 1850s* (Stanford: University of Stanford Press, 1962); and Harry Jaffa,

Crisis of the House Divided: An Interpretation of the Issues in the Lincoln–Douglas Debates (Chicago: University of Chicago Press, 1959). The standard work on the court case that revolutionized American politics is Don E. Fehrenbacher, *The Dred Scott Case: Its Significance in American Law and Politics* (New York: Oxford University Press, 1978).

State-level studies of secession include Steven Channing, *Crisis of Fear: The Secession of South Carolina* (New York: Simon and Schuster, 1970); William L. Barney, *The Secessionist Impulse: Alabama and Mississippi in 1860* (Princeton, NJ: Princeton University Press, 1974); and Michael P. Johnson, *Towards a Patriarchal Republic: the Secession of Georgia* (Baton Rouge: Louisiana State University Press, 1977). Charles B. Dew's *Apostles of Disunion: Southern Secession Commissioners and the Causes of the Civil War* (Charlottes-ville: University Press of Virginia, 2001) sheds important light on the polit-ical maneuvering that preceded secession, while Daniel W. Crofts' *Reluctant Confederates: Upper South Unionists in the Secession Crisis* (Chapel Hill: University of North Carolina Press, 1989) is a masterful exploration of the opposition to the fire-eaters in the Upper South and their links with Washington politicians including Seward. The standard works on the Sumter crisis are David M. Potter, *Lincoln and His Party in the Secession Crisis* (New Haven: Yale University Press, 1942); and Kenneth Stampp, *And the War Came: The North and the Secession Crisis, 1860–1861* (Baton Rouge: Louisiana State University Press, 1950).

MILITARY HISTORY

Perhaps the most engaging short military history of the war is T. Harry Williams, *Lincoln and His Generals* (New York: Knopf, 1952). An accessible recent work is Brian Holden Reid, *The American Civil War and the Wars of the Industrial Revolution* (London: Cassell, 1999). Herman Hattaway and Archer Jones provide a standard overview in *How the North Won: A Military History of the Civil War* (Urbana: University of Illinois Press, 1983). A stimulating book that places the Civil War in a long military tradition is Paddy Griffith, *Battle Tactics of the Civil War* (New Haven: Yale University Press, 1989). For the argument that the Civil War was a "total war", see Daniel E. Sutherland, *The Emergence of Total War* (Forth Worth, TX: Ryan Place Publishers, 1996). The term "total war" is useful in the sense that it captures the centrality of war to everything that happened in the South, and, to a lesser extent, to describe the Union army's developing realization that they needed to wage war on southern society as a whole. But the term carries baggage. Coined to describe the mobilization of industrial societies in the twentieth century, it can be a distraction when applied to mid-nineteenth-century America, which is why I avoided it in this book. For an extended discussion of this theme, see Mark E. Neely, "Was the Civil War a Total War?" *Civil War History 37* (1991), 5–28. Increasingly historians are turning their attention to the often brutal irregular warfare that does not fit neatly into the conventional presentation of battles and campaigns. See Michael Fellman, *Inside War: The Guerrilla Conflict in Missouri During the American Civil War* (New York: Oxford University Press, 1990); Daniel E. Sutherland, ed., *Guerillas, Unionists and Violence on the Confederate Home Front* (Fayetteville: University of Arkansas Press, 1999); and Noel C. Fisher, *War at Every Door: Partisan Politics and Guerilla Violence in East Tennessee, 1860–1869* (Chapel Hill: University of North Carolina Press, 1997).

For generally positive assessments of Confederate strategy, see Thomas L. Connelly & Archer Jones, *The Politics of Command: Factions and Ideas in Confederate Strategy* (Kent, OH: Kent State University Press, 1998), Richard M. McMurry, *Two Great Rebel Armies: An Essay in Confederate Military History* (Chapel Hill: University of North Carolina Press, 1989), Joseph L. Harsh, *Confederate Tide Rising: Robert E. Lee and the Making of Southern Strategy, 1861–1862* (Kent, OH: Kent State University Press, 1998); Harsh, *Taken at the Flood: Robert E. Lee and Confederate Strategy in the Maryland Campaign of 1862* (Kent, OH: Kent State University Press, 1999); and Gary W. Gallagher, *The Confederate War* (Cambridge, MA.: Harvard University Press, 1997). Michael C. C. Adams, *Our Masters the Rebels: A Speculation on Union Military Failure in the East, 1861–1865* (Cambridge, MA: Harvard University Press, 1978), argues that McClellan's failures in 1862 profoundly demoralized the Army of the Potomac. Works which claim that Confederate strategy was ultimately counterproductive include Alan T. Nolan, *Lee Considered: General Robert E. Lee and Civil War History* (Chapel Hill: University of North Carolina Press, 1991); and Grady McWhiney and Perry D. Jamieson, *Attack and Die: Civil War Military Tactics and the Southern Heritage* (University: University of Alabama Press, 1982). There are vast libraries of books on particular battles and campaigns. Some of the best recent works, which go beyond the concerns of traditional military history, include George C. Rable, *Fredericksburg! Fredericksburg!* (Chapel Hill: University of North Carolina Press, 2002); Gary W. Gallagher, ed. *Three Days at Gettysburg: Essays on Confederate and Union Leadership* (Kent, OH: Kent State University Press, 1999); Stephen W. Sears, *Landscape Turned Red: The Battle of Antietam* (New Haven: Ticknor and Fields, 1983); James M. McPherson, *Crossroads of Freedom: Antietam* (New York: Oxford University Press, 2002); and a series of fine books, all edited by Gary W. Gallagher and published by the University of North Carolina Press, including *Chancellorsville: The Battle and its Aftermath* (1996), *The Spotsylvania Campaign* (1998), *The Antietam Campaign* (1999), *The Richmond Campaign of 1862: The Peninsular and the Seven Days* (2000), and *The Shenandoah Valley Campaign of 1864* (2006).

The best book on the evolution of Union strategy is Mark Grimsley, *The Hard Hand of War: Union Military Policy Toward Southern Civilians, 1861–1865* (New York: Cambridge University Press, 1995). Grimsley makes clear that however devastating the impact of Union occupation of the South, it was driven by a clear political logic, and that the northern war effort always aimed at Reconstruction of the Union rather than the wholesale devastation of the South. Still worth reading is an older study: Basil H. Liddell Hart, *Sherman: Soldier, Realist, American* (New York: Dodd, Mead and Co., 1929). See also Charles Royster, *The Destructive War: William Tecumseh Sherman, Stonewall Jackson, and the Americans* (New York: Knopf, 1991). On the place of railroads in military operations, see John E. Clark, *Railroads in the Civil War: The Impact of Management on Victory and Defeat* (Baton Rouge: Louisiana State University Press, 2001). On intelligence gathering, see William B. Feis, *Grant's Secret Service: The Intelligence War from Belmont to Appomattox* (Lincoln: University of Nebraska Press, 2002).

There is a substantial literature on the diplomacy of the Civil War, especially on British relations with both sides. See, David P. Crook, *The North, the South and the Powers* (New York: Wiley, 1974); Charles M. Hubbard, *The Burden of Confederate Diplomacy* (Knoxville: University of Tennessee Press, 1998); and Howard M. Jones, *Union in Peril: The Crisis over British Intervention in the Civil War* (Chapel Hill: University of North Carolina Press, 1992). Jay Sexton's *Debtor Diplomacy: Finance and American Foreign Relations in the Civil War Era, 1837–1873* (Oxford: Oxford University Press, 2005) shows how British financiers had a stake in the contest. On British reactions to the war, see Richard Blackett, *Divided Hearts: Britain and the American Civil War* (Baton Rouge: Louisiana State University Press, 2000).

SOLDIERS

For a long time the standard accounts of the lives and motivations of Civil War soldiers were Bell I. Wiley's, *The Life of Johnny Reb: The Common Soldier of the Confederacy* (Indiana: Bobbs-Merrill, 1943) and *The Life of Billy Yank: The Common Soldier of the Union* (Indiana: Bobbs-Merrill, 1952). Wiley claimed that ideological motivations were largely irrelevant to Civil War soldiers, but this view has been challenged by James M. McPherson's, *For Cause and Comrades: Why Men Fought in the Civil War* (New York: Oxford University Press, 1997), which stresses ideological motivation. Joseph Allan Frank, *With Ballot and Bayonet: The Political Socialization of Amer-ican Civil War Soldiers* (Athens GA: University Press, 1998), stresses the role of a small cadre of politically aware soldiers in influencing the views of the rest.

A major trend in Civil War historiography in the last twenty years has been to break down the artificial separation of military and social history. See Reid Mitchell, *Civil War Soldiers: Their Expectations and their Experiences* (New York: Viking, 1988); Earl J. Hess, *The Union Soldier in Battle: Enduring the Ordeal of Combat* (Lawrence: University Press of Kansas, 1997); Gerald F. Linderman, *Embattled Courage: The Experience of Combat in the American Civil War*, (New York: Free Press, 1987); Reid Mitchell, *The Vacant Chair: The Northern Soldier Leaves Home*, (New York: Oxford University Press, 1993); James I. Robertson, *Soldiers, Blue and Gray*, (Columbia SC: University of South Carolina Press, 1988); Joseph T. Glatthaar, *The March to the Sea and Beyond: Sherman's Troops in the Savannah and Carolinas Campaigns*, (New York: New York University Press, 1985); J. Tracy Power, *Lee's Miserables: Life in the Army of Northern Virginia from the Wilderness to Appomattox* (Chapel Hill: University of North Carolina Press, 1998); and Drew Gilpin Faust

"Christian soldiers: The Meaning of Revivalism in the Confederate Army", *Journal of Southern History* 53 (1987), 63–90. There are many fine regimental histories, but one that stands out for the quality of the writing and the intrinsic fascination of the subject is Richard F. Miller, *Harvard's Civil War: A History of the Twentieth Massachusetts Volunteer Infantry* (Hanover, NH: University Press of New England, 2005).

On the experience of black soldiers, see Joseph T. Glatthaar *Forged in Battle: The Civil War Alliance of Black Soldiers and White Officers* (New York: Free Press, 1990); John David Smith, ed., *Black soldiers in Blue: African American troops in the Civil War era* (Chapel Hill: University of North Carolina Press, 2002); James G. Hollandsworth, *The Louisiana Native Guards: The Black Military Experience during the Civil War* (Baton Rouge: Louisiana State University Press, 1995); Noah Andre Trudeau, *Like Men of War: Black Troops in the Civil War, 1862–1865* (New York: Little, Brown, 1999); and Margaret Creighton, *The Colors of Courage: Gettysburg's Forgotten History: Immigrants, Women, and African Americans in the Civil War's Defining Battle* (New York: Basic Books, 2005).

On the stomach-churning but unavoidable subject of medical care and the staggering high death toll from disease, see Stewart Brooks, *Civil War Medicine* (Springfield, Ill: C. C. Thomas, 1966); Jack D. Welsh, *Two Confederate Hospitals and their Patients: Atlanta to Opelika* (Macon, GA.: Mercer University Press, 2005); Ira M. Rutkow, *Bleeding Blue and Gray: Civil War Surgery and the Evolution of American Medicine* (New York: Random House, 2005); and two extraordinary encyclopedias of woe by Jack D. Welsh: *Medical Histories of Union Generals* (Kent, OH: Kent State University Press, 1996) and *Medical Histories of Confederate Generals* (Kent, OH: Kent State University Press, 1995).

THE CONFEDERACY

Much recent historiography on the Confederacy has focused on tensions within southern society. See, for example, Drew Gilpin Faust, *Mothers of Invention: Women of the Slaveholding South in the American Civil War* (Chapel Hill: University of North Carolina Press, 1996); Paul Escott, *After Secession: Jefferson Davis and the Failure of Confederate nationalism* (Baton Rouge: Louisiana State University Press, 1978); Stephen V. Ash, *When the Yankees Came: Conflict and Chaos in the Occupied South, 1861–1865* (Chapel Hill: University of North Carolina Press, 1995); and Richard E. Beringer *et al.*, *Why the South Lost the Civil War* (Athens: University of Georgia Press, 1986). On Southern Unionists, see John C. Inscoe and Robert C. Kenzer, eds, *Enemies of the Country: New Perspectives on Unionists in the Civil War South* (Athens: University of Georgia Press, 2001); Richard N. Current, *Lincoln's Loyalists: Union Soldiers From the Confederacy* (Boston: Northeastern University Press, 1992); and William H. Freehling, *The South versus the South: How Anti-Confederate Southerners Shaped the Course of the Civil War* (New York: Oxford University Press, 2001).

Gary Gallagher, *The Confederate War* (Cambridge, MA: Harvard University Press, 1997), makes a powerful case for the resilience and unity of southern society in the face of great pressure. Moving beyond the debate about the unity or otherwise of the white South, Anne Sarah Rubin's *A Shattered Nation: The Rise and Fall of the Confederacy, 1861–1868* (Chapel Hill: University of North Carolina Press, 2005), stresses the strength and coherence of Confederate identity, while also exploring the tensions and ambiguities created by the intersection of religion and the southern cause. There is a thoughtful appraisal of "internal" and "external" explanations of Confederate defeat in James McPherson's essay "Why Did the Confederacy Lose?" in McPherson, *Drawn With the Sword: Reflections on the American Civil War* (New York: Oxford University Press, 1996). A useful collection of essays on this theme is Gabor Boritt, ed., *Why the Confederacy Lost* (New York: Oxford University Press, 1992).

There are a multitude of excellent local and state studies of the Confederate wartime experience. Among the best are William Blair, *Virginia's Private War: Feeding Body and Soul in the Confederacy, 1861–1865* (New York: Oxford University Press, 1998); Martin Crawford, *Ashe Country's Civil War: Community and Society in the Appalachian South* (Charlottesville: University of Virginia Press, 2001); Edward L. Ayers, *In the Presence of Mine Enemies: The Civil War in the Heart of America, 1859–1863* (New York: Norton, 2003); Clayton E. Jewett, *Texas in the Confederacy: An Experiment in Nation Building* (Columbia: University of Missouri Press, 2002); Daniel E. Sutherland, *Seasons of War: The Ordeal of a Confederate Community, 1861–1865* (New York: Free Press, 1995); and David Williams, *Rich Man's War: Class, Caste and Community in the Lower Chattahoochee Valley* (Athens, GA: University of Georgia Press, 1998).

On Confederate politics, see George C. Rable, *The Confederate Republic: A Revolution Against Politics* (Chapel Hill: University of North Carolina Press, 1994), which explores antipartisanship and its implications; Douglas F. Ball, *Financial Failure and Confederate Defeat* (Urbana: University of Illinois Press, 1991), which blames incompetence in the Richmond treasury for much that went wrong; and Larry E. Nelson, *Bullets, Ballots and Rhetoric Confederate Policy for the United States Presidential Contest of 1864* (University, AL: University of Alabama Press, 1980), which reminds us that Confederates themselves believed that their best chance of victory was if Lincoln was defeated. The best biography of Jefferson Davis is William C. Davis, *Jefferson Davis: The Man and His Hour* (New York: HarperCollins, 1991).

On wartime slavery and emancipation, see James L. Roark, *Masters Without Slaves: Southern Planters in the Civil War and Reconstruction* (New York: Norton, 1977); Lynda J. Morgan, *Emancipation in Virginia's Tobacco Belt, 1850–1870* (Athens: University of Georgia Press, 1992); Clarence L. Mohr, *On the Threshold of Freedom: Master and Slaves in Civil War Georgia* (Athens: University of Georgia Press, 1986); Winthrop D. Jordan, *Tumult and Silence at Second Creek: An Inquiry into a Civil War Slave Conspiracy* (Baton Rouge: Louisiana State University Press, 1993); John Cimprich, *Slavery's End in Tennessee, 1861–1865* (University, AL: University of Alabama Press, 1985); Noralee Frankel, *Freedom's Women: Black Women and Families in Civil War Era Mississippi* (Bloomington, IN: Indiana University Press, 1999); and Willie

Lee Rose, *Rehearsal for Reconstruction: The Port Royal Experiment* (Indianapolis: Bobbs-Merrill, 1964).

THE WARTIME NORTH

The northern home front experience is surveyed in Phillip Shaw Paludan, *"A People's Contest": The Union and the Civil War, 1861–1865* (New York: Harper & Row, 1988); J. Matthew Gallman, *The North Fights the Civil War: the Home front* (Chicago: I. R. Dee, 1994); Paul A. Cimbala and Randall Miller, eds, *An Uncommon Time: The Civil War and the Northern Home Front* (New York: Fordham University Press, 2002); and Jean Cashin, ed., *The War Was You and Me: Civilians in the American Civil War* (Princeton, NJ: Princeton University Press, 2003).

Earl J. Hess, *Liberty, Virtue and Progress: Northerners and their War for the Union* (New York: New York University Press, 1988); Randall C. Jimerson, *The Private Civil War: Popular Thought during the Sectional Conflict* (Baton Rouge: Louisiana University Press, 1988); Anne C. Rose, *Victorian America and the Civil War* (Cambridge: Cambridge University Press, 1992); and George Fredrickson, *The Inner Civil War: Northern Intellectuals and the Crisis of the Union* (New York: Harper & Row, 1965), all explore the intellectual, religious and cultural context in which northerners understood their wartime experiences. A nuanced study of the evolution of the northern public's attitudes to the escalation of the war is Silvana R. Siddali, *From Property to Person: Slavery and the Confiscation Acts, 1861–1862* (Baton Rouge: Louisiana State University Press, 2005). Melinda Lawson, *Patriot Fires: Forging a New American Nationalism in the Civil War North* (Lawrence: University Press of Kansas, 2002), is an excellent study of the impact of the war on national identity, and see also Garry Wills, *Lincoln at Gettysburg: the Words that Re-made America* (New York: Simon & Schuster, 1992). It is impossible to enter into the world of Civil War Americans without an appreciation of the power of evangelical religion in shaping their world view. On this subject, see James H. Moorhead, *American Apocalypse: Yankee Protestants and the Civil War, 1860–1869* (New Haven: Yale University Press, 1978); and Mark A. Noll, *The Civil War as a Theological Crisis* (Chapel Hill: University of North Carolina Press, 2006).

Women's wartime experiences are best approached through Catherine Clinton & Nina Silber, eds, *Divided Houses: Gender and the Civil War* (New York: Oxford University Press, 1992); and Jeanie Attie, *Patriotic Toil: Northern Women and the American Civil War* (Ithaca, NY: Cornell University Press, 1998). James Marten, *The Children's Civil War* (Chapel Hill: University of North Carolina Press, 1998) explores the experiences of children in the Union and the Confederacy.

Studies of the impact of the Civil War in big northern cities are Mary P. Ryan, *Civic Wars: Democracy and Public Life in the American City during the Nineteenth Century* (Berkeley: University of California Press, 1997); Thomas H. O'Connor, *Civil War Boston: Home Front and Battlefield* (Boston: Northeastern University Press, 1997); J. Matthew Gallman, *Mastering Wartime: A*

Social History of Philadelphia during the Civil War (Cambridge & New York: Cambridge University Press, 1990); Ernest A. McKay, *The Civil War and New York City* (Syracuse, NY: Ithaca University Press, 1990). The experience of small towns and rural areas are explored by Michael Frisch, *Town into City: Springfield, Massachusetts, and the Meaning of Community, 1840–1880* (Cambridge MA: Harvard University Press, 1972); Don Harrison Doyle, *The Social Order of a Frontier Community: Jacksonville, Illinois, 1825–1870*, (Urbana, IL: University of Illinois Press, 1978); and John Mack Faragher, *Sugar Creek: Life on the Illinois Prairie*, (New Haven, CT: Yale University Press, 1986).

Northern enlistment and recruiting patterns are discussed in William J. Rohrbaugh, "Who Fought for the North in the Civil War? Concord, Massachusetts, Enlistments," *Journal of American History 73* (1986), 695–701; and the impact of the draft in James W. Geary, *We Need Men: The Union Draft in the Civil War* (Dekalb, IL: Northern Illinois University Press, 1991). Antiwar dissent and unrest is the focus of Grace Palladino, *Another Civil War: Labor, Capital and the State in the Anthracite Regions of Pennsylvania* (Urbana IL: University of Illinois Press, 1990); and Iver Bernstein, *The New York City Draft Riots: Their Significance for American Society and Politics in the Age of the Civil War* (New York: Oxford University Press, 1990). Mark E. Neely, Jr, *The Fate of Liberty: Abraham Lincoln and Civil Liberties* (New York: Oxford University Press, 1991) is an important book that explores the Lincoln administration's treatment of dissenters. On northern racial attitudes and the politics of emancipation, see, Michael Vorenberg, *Final Freedom: The Civil War, the Thirteenth Amendment and the Abolition of Slavery* (Cambridge: Cambridge University Press, 2001); David W. Blight, *Frederick Douglass' Civil War: Keeping Faith in Jubilee* (Baton Rouge: Louisiana State University Press, 1989). On copperheads, see Frank L. Klement, *Dark Lanterns: Secret Political Societies, Conspiracies and Treason Trials in the Civil War* (Baton Rouge: Louisiana State University Press, 1984).

There is a vast literature on Lincoln. The best recent biographies are Richard J. Carwardine, *Lincoln: A Life of Purpose and Power* (New York: Knopf, 2006); and Allen C. Guelzo, *Abraham Lincoln: Redeemer President* (Grand Rapids, MI: Eerdmans, 1999). Also valuable is Phillip S. Paludan, *The Presidency of Abraham Lincoln* (Lawrence: University Press of Kansas, 1994). The radical changes to economic, fiscal and domestic policy introduced by the Republicans are explored in Heather Cox Richardson, *The Greatest Nation of the Earth: Republican Economic Policy in the Civil War* (Cambridge, MA: Harvard University Press, 1997); and Allan G. Bogue, *The Congressman's Civil War* (Cambridge: Cambridge University Press, 1989). Richard Franklin Bensel's *Yankee Leviathan: the origins of central state authority in America, 1859–1877* (Cambridge: Cambridge University Press, 1990), argues that the war greatly expanded the state capacity of the federal government.

On northern party politics, see Joel H. Silbey, *A Respectable Minority: the Democratic Party in the Civil War Era* (New York: W. W. Norton, 1977); Michael F. Holt, "Abraham Lincoln and the Politics of Union" in John L. Thomas, ed., *Abraham Lincoln and the American Political Tradition*, (Amherst:

University of Massachusetts Press, 1986); James A. Rawley, *The Politics of Union: Northern Politics During the Civil War* (Hinsdale, Ill.: Dryden Press, 1974); Mark E. Neely, *Jr, The Union Divided: Party Conflict in the Civil War North* (Cambridge, MA: Harvard University Press, 2002); and Adam I. P. Smith, *No Party Now: Politics in the Civil War North* (New York: Oxford University Press, 2006). On congressional relations with the White House, see Bruce Tap, *Over Lincoln's Shoulder: The Committee on the Conduct of the War* (Lawrence: University Press of Kansas, 1998); and Robert Cook's forthcoming study of William Pitt Fessenden. A solid biography of a critical figure in wartime politics is John M. Taylor, *William Henry Seward: Lincoln's Right-hand* (New York: HarperCollins, 1991).

LEGACY OF THE WAR

There is a vast literature on Reconstruction and its aftermath which I will not attempt to summarize here beyond noting the two books that are essential reading for this complex subject: Eric Foner, *Reconstruction: America's Unfinished Revolution* (New York: Harper & Row, 1988); and Heather Cox Richardson's forthcoming survey of the United States, 1865–1901, to be published by Yale University Press.

On the memory of the war, see David Blight, *Race and Reunion: The Civil War in American Memory* (Cambridge, MA: Harvard University Press, 2001); Carol Reardon, *Pickett's Charge in History and Memory* (Chapel Hill: University of North Carolina Press, 1997); David R. Goldfield, *Still Fighting the Civil War: The American South and Southern History* (Baton Rouge: Louisiana State University Press, 2002); Gary W. Gallagher and Alan T. Nolan, eds., *The Myth of the Lost Cause and Civil War History* (Bloomington: Indiana University Press, 2000); Nina Silber, *The Romance of Reunion: Northerners and the South, 1865–1900* (Chapel Hill: University of North Carolina Press, 1993); Jim Weeks, *Gettysburg: Memory, Market and an American Shrine,* (Princeton, NJ: Princeton University Press, 2003); Jim Cullen, *The Civil War in Popular Culture: A Reusable Past* (Washington: Smithsonian Institution Press, 1998); Tony Horwitz, *Confederates in the Attic: Dispatches from the Unfinished Civil War* (New York: Pantheon, 1998); and Edward L. Ayers, "Worrying about the Civil War," in Karen Halttunen and Lewis Perry, eds, *Moral Problems in American Life: New Perspectives on Cultural History* (Ithaca, NY: Cornell University Press, 1998).

Chronology of Key Events

Note: Major battles are highlighted in bold

1820	Missouri Compromise prohibits future expansion of slavery into US territories north of the 36′30° line of latitude.
1833	Slavery abolished in British Empire
	Formation of American Anti-Slavery Society
1844	Democrat James K. Polk narrowly wins presidential election
1846–1847	Mexican War brings vast new territories into the United States; David Wilmot introduces a proviso which would ban slavery from new territories, sparking political crisis over slavery expansion
1848	Formation of Free Soil Party
	Whig Zachary Taylor elected President
1850	Taylor dies and is succeeded by Millard Fillmore
	Compromise measures passed by Congress to settle status of slavery in Mexican cession
1852	Democrat Franklin Pierce elected President
1854	Kansas Nebraska Act rescinds the Missouri Compromise and reopens slavery controversy
1856	Charles Sumner attacked in Senate
	Kansas in state of civil war
	Democrat James Buchanan elected President
1857	*Dred Scott* decision
1858	Lincoln–Douglas debates in Illinois
1859	John Brown's raid on Harpers Ferry
1860	*Nov 6* Lincoln elected President
	Dec 20 South Carolina legislature votes for secession
1861	*Jan 9–Feb 1* Secession of Mississippi, Florida, Alabama, Georgia, Louisiana and Texas
	Mar 4 Lincoln inaugurated
	Mar 11 Montgomery Convention approves Confederate constitution
	Apr 12–13 Bombardment and surrender of Fort Sumter
	Apr 17–May 20 Secession of Virginia, Arkansas, Tennessee and North Carolina
	May 13 British government declares neutrality
	May 20 Kentucky declares neutrality
	Jul 21 **Confederate victory at Bull Run**
	Sept 3–6 End of Kentucky's "neutrality"
	Nov–Dec Trent crisis

1862 *Feb 6–25* **Union capture of Forts Henry and Donelson** on Tennessee River

  Mar 6 Lincoln proposes gradual emancipation to Congress

  Mar 7–8 **Union victory at Battle of Pea Ridge**

  Mar 8–9 ***Virginia*** v ***Monitor*** **in Hampton Roads**

  Mar 17–Apr 2 McClellan moves Army of the Potomac to James River for Peninsular Campaign

  Apr 6–7 **Grant turns near-defeat into victory at Shiloh**

  Apr 16 Confederate Congress passes Conscription Act

  Apr 24–25 New Orleans occupied by Union

  May 8–9 **Jackson's Shenandoah Valley Campaign**

  Jun 1 Lee takes command of Army of Northern Virginia

  Jun 26–Jul 2 **Lee drives McClellan back from Richmond in Seven Days battles**

  Jul 11 Halleck appointed general-in-chief of Union armies

  Jul 22 Lincoln reads draft of Emancipation Proclamation to cabinet

  Aug 27 Bragg leads Confederate invasion of Kentucky

  Aug 29–30 **Confederate victory at Second Bull Run**

  Sept 4 Lee invades Maryland

  Sept 17 **Battle of Antietam**, followed by Lee's withdrawal into Virginia

  Sept 22 Preliminary Emancipation Proclamation issued

  Oct–Nov Republicans lose seats in Congressional midterm elections

  Dec 13 **Union defeat at Battle of Fredericksburg**

  Dec 31–Jan 1 **Battle of Stones River followed by Bragg's withdrawal**

1863 *Jan 1* Emancipation Proclamation issued

  Mar 3 Conscription Act passed by US Congress

  Apr 2 Bread riot in Richmond

  Apr 24 Confederate Congress imposes sweeping new taxes

  Apr 30–May 6 **Lee routs Hooker's Army of the Potomac at Chancellorsville**

  May 10 Death of "Stonewall" Jackson

  Jun 3 Lee invades North

  Jul 1–3 **Union victory at Gettysburg** followed by Lee's withdrawal

  Jul 4 **Vicksburg falls to Grant** after long campaign

  Jul 13–16 New York City draft riots

  Nov 19 Lincoln delivers Gettysburg Address

  Nov 24–25 **Union victory at Chattanooga** opens way for Union invasion of Georgia

1864 *Feb* Confederate Congress passes series of tough new laws on tax, impressments and suspension of habeas corpus

  Mar 9 Grant becomes General-in-Chief of all Union armies

  Apr 12 Massacre of black Union troops at Fort Pillow

  May 5–6 **Battle of the Wilderness**

  May 8–21 **Battles at Spotsylvania Court House**

  Jun 1–3 **Battle of Cold Harbor**

Jun 7 Lincoln renominated by Baltimore Convention of the National Union Party

Jun 15–18 Attacks on Petersburg, beginning of siege

Jul 11 Confederate raid led by Jubal E. Early threatens Washington

Jul 30 Battle of the Crater

Aug 5 Union victory at Mobile Bay

Aug 5 Wade–Davis Manifesto

Sept 2 Sherman captures Atlanta after long campaign through Georgia

Oct 19 Union vivtory at Cedar Creek ends Confederate threat in Shenandoah Valley

Nov 8 Lincoln reelected President

Nov 15 Sherman begins march to the sea

Dec 21 Savannah falls to Sherman

1865   *Jan 31* US Congress passes Thirteenth Amendment abolishing slavery

Feb 17 Confederates evacuate Charleston

Mar 4 Lincoln's second inauguration

Mar 13 Confederate Congress authorises recruitment of slaves into army

Apr 2 Fall of Petersburg

Apr 3 Fall of Richmond

Apr 9 Lee surrenders to Grant at Appomattox Court House

Apr 14 Lincoln shot by John Wilkes Booth, dies next morning

Apr 26 General Johnston surrenders in North Carolina

May 10 Jefferson Davis captured in Georgia

May 26 Surrender of General Kirby Smith in west brings war formally to an end

Index

263